DATE DUE

#47-0108 Peel Off Pressure Sensitive

GETTING FROM
HERE TO THERE

Also by W. W. Rostow

Essays on the British Economy in the
Nineteenth Century, 1948

The Growth and Fluctuation of the British Economy,
1790–1850 (*With A. D. Gayer and A. J. Schwartz*),
1953; *Second Edition* 1975

The Process of Economic Growth, 1952; *Second Edition* 1960

The Stages of Economic Growth, 1960; *Second Edition* 1971

The United States in the World Arena, 1960

Politics and the Stages of Growth, 1971

The Diffusion of Power, 1972

How It All Began, 1975

The World Economy: History and Prospect, 1978

GETTING FROM HERE TO THERE

W. W. Rostow

McGraw-Hill Book Company

NEW YORK   ST. LOUIS   SAN FRANCISCO
DÜSSELDORF   MEXICO   TORONTO

Book design by Ingrid Beckman.

1 2 3 4 5 6 7 8 9 0 F G R F G R 7 8 3 2 1 0 9 8

Library of Congress Cataloging in Publication Data

Rostow, Walt Whitman,
Getting from here to there.
Includes index.
1. Economic history—1945–   2. United States—
Economic conditions—1971–   I. Title.
HC59.R653   330.9'04   77-25836
ISBN 0-07-053898-0

American Philosophical Society and John D. Durand, for material from
John D. Durand, "The Modern Expansion of World Population," *Proceedings
of the American Philosophical Society,* Vol. 111, No. 3 (June 22, 1967).

Lloyds Bank Review, for material from F. W. Paish, "Inflation, Personal
Incomes and Taxation," *Lloyds Bank Review,* No. 116 (April 1975).

TO ELSPETH

CONTENTS

LIST OF TABLES AND CHARTS

CHARTS

PREFACE

THIS IS a book about economic survival over the next quarter-century. Although it stands on its own, it is part of a larger effort. In 1972, I decided it was time to put together what I thought I had learned from some forty years of studying and teaching economic history. The first result was *How It All Began* (McGraw-Hill, 1975). It seeks to explain the origins of the industrial revolution of the eighteenth century, which launched the world into two centuries of modern economic growth. The book was designed as an introductory chapter to a larger work, but took on a life of its own and became a separate volume. The story of modern economic growth itself, from the eighteenth century down to 1977, is told in *The World Economy: History and Prospect* (University of Texas Press, 1978).

As I wrote these two books, I realized that the perspective on the present state of the world economy—and our own—generated by this historical exercise was quite different from the perspectives that informed the views of both conventional liberal and conventional conservative economists.

It was also clear that my perspective led to a good many prescriptions for policy. To have included detailed policy matters in works devoted primarily to economic history would have distorted their structure and balance. I decided, therefore, to write this final piece of what turned out, somewhat to my surprise, to be a trilogy.

The reference to the Kondratieff cycle throughout this book is fully explained in Chapter 2. N. D. Kondratieff was a Russian economist who, writing in the 1920's, discerned two and a half cycles in prices, interest rates, and money wages reaching back to the late eighteenth century. Although he produced no coherent theory to explain these cycles, his assertion that capitalism oscillated around a stable trend was judged a counter-Marxist heresy; and he died in a Siberian prison camp. As part of my work as an economic historian, I have, since the 1940's, studied and written about the long cycles (or trend periods) Kondratieff identified. I developed a theory explaining them, centered primarily on the causes and consequences of periods of relatively high and relatively low prices of foodstuffs and raw materials. The unfolding of events in the world economy since 1972 has fitted roughly the pattern of four previous periods when the relative prices of basic commodities suddenly rose and then oscillated at a high level for a generation. I found the notion of the fifth Kondratieff upswing was a useful shorthand device with which to shake my colleagues out of the conventional neo-Keynesian framework which, consciously or unconsciously, controlled their view of the economic phenomena around them, and to intrude a somewhat different view of where we are, what we face, and what needs to be done.

This book is written for the interested general reader rather than the professional economist. But in Chapter 3 it does contain a frontal assault on neo-Keynesian theory. The fact is, as Paul Samuelson acknowledged in an amiable public discussion we had in Austin in April 1977: "We live in the post-Keynesian age." That is not quite good enough: if we agree that the neo-Keynesian framework will no longer suffice, we require an alternative. Without elaborating here its formal theoretical underpinnings, which can be found in *The Process of Economic Growth* (Clarendon Press, 2d ed., 1960), the present book does supply an alternative and puts it to the test of prescription on a wide range of urgent problems.

The issues with which this book deals suffuse the world economy as a whole and concern its future. I have tried to indicate the global roots and ramifications of the population, food, energy, and other problems which have altered the contours of the world economy and its agenda. On the other hand, the detailed analysis and prescriptions are mainly addressed to the American scene. This approach not only rendered the writing of the book more manageable, but it also reflected an important fact. Although the economic, as well as military and political capacities, of the United States is evidently dilute in a world of diffused power, we remain a critical margin. Our capacity to solve the energy problem, maintain a large agricultural surplus, return our economy to sustained high growth rates, generate higher levels of productivity, and master inflation will not only determine our own future but also influence greatly the ability of other nations to transit in reasonable order the fifth Kondratieff upswing.

I have tried here to keep the mechanics of scholarly writing to the minimum. There are relatively few footnotes, statistical tables, or charts. The reader who wishes to pursue further the summary historical passages in this book will find them fully elaborated and documented in *The World Economy: History and Prospect*.

A good many people helped mobilize data, shared their perceptions of particular problems, or criticized drafts. I wish to thank the following for that kind of collegial assistance: W. O. Baker, Harvey Brooks, William Brown, McGeorge Bundy, John Cremeans, Charles Hitch, David Kendrick, John W.

Kendrick, Bruce MacLaury, Hans Mark, Leon Martel, Paul Olum, Gerard Piel, Nathan Rosenberg, Eugene Rostow, Stephen Spurr, John Wheeler, and Jeff Wolff. With respect to energy, I learned much from William Fisher and my other colleagues associated with the Council on Energy Resources at The University of Texas at Austin.

The book—and I—owe much to the painstaking reading and editing by Lois Nivens and Elspeth Rostow, who found the time to do this while carrying other heavy responsibilities.

Virginia Fay typed and retyped the various drafts briskly and with good cheer.

W. W. ROSTOW

October 15, 1977
Austin, Texas

1

The Significance of
the Next Quarter-Century

A N important turning point occurred in the world economy and, indeed, in industrial civilization during the first half of the 1970's. A pattern of economic and social progress which had persisted for almost a quarter-century was broken. Politicians, economists, and citizens found themselves in a somewhat new and uncomfortable world. Familiar modes of thought and action were challenged as they no longer seemed to grip the course of events. Expectations of the future became uncertain when they were not somber, except among the oil exporters who suddenly saw the possibility of vastly accelerated economic and social progress, as well as unaccustomed influence on the world scene.

For two hundred years the concept of endless economic progress had become embedded in the mind of Western man, gradually spreading out over most of Latin America, Africa, the Middle East, and Asia. This conviction had been deeply shaken by events between 1914 and 1945 but reasserted itself after the Second World War. Suddenly, in the 1970's, the

1

inevitability, even the legitimacy, of economic growth was questioned. The shock was universal, but particularly severe in the United States. The peoples of Europe and Japan, with longer historical memories and lesser natural resources, had assumed that a dependence on imports was inevitable and that there were limits on the use of resources which had to be respected. They were somewhat more used to husbanding their resources at the margin. But Americans, from the beginning, had been surrounded by ample land, raw materials, and sources of energy. In the early 1970's, they were brusquely made aware that they, like others, had become vitally dependent on imports. Even more striking, they confronted for the first time as a nation the fact that air and water, as well as gas and oil, are finite commodities. Historian David Potter, writing a generation earlier, described Americans as "a people of plenty." To some it looked as if the land of abundance depicted by Potter had suddenly, once and for all, run short.

The experience of the 1950's and 1960's was a poor preparation for this shock. After the Second World War and reconstruction, world production and trade had expanded at rates never before known in history. That expansion was remarkably regular in North America, Western Europe, and Japan. A style of life hitherto associated with North America spread across the Atlantic and Pacific: the mass use of the private automobile; the substitution of durable consumers goods for increasingly scarce servants; the proliferation of supermarkets and all the other paraphernalia of suburban life. By standards of the past, business cycles were mild, unemployment was low. Modern fiscal and monetary policy appeared to have guaranteed not only that the stagnation which had occurred in Europe between the wars would not recur, nor would there be another Great Depression like that after 1929, but also that the pre-1914 rhythm of business cycles had been permanently modulated. Governments and a considerable part of the electorate in the advanced industrialized nations came to assume that material affluence was assured. A margin of the affluent young in these fortunate countries, placing a low value on the things they took for granted, explicitly turned their backs on material progress and sought instead to find and act on new canons for the good life. In a less dramatic way, the citizens of the northern industrial countries as a whole and their political representatives also came to place a higher value on nonmaterial goals: they allocated increasing proportions of income for higher education, medical care, the protection of the environment, and the improvement of the lot of the less advantaged, at home and abroad.

Progress in the 1950's and 1960's was not confined to the affluent North. In Latin America, Africa, the Middle East, and Asia average growth rates in income per head were sustained at a much higher level than had obtained in the now industrialized nations at equivalent stages of modernization. In the nineteenth century, for example, the United States averaged an annual rate of increase in income per capita of about 1.6%; the developing regions as a whole averaged over two percent in the 1960's. Progress in the developing regions was, of course, uneven and erratic. And even when a particular developing nation moved forward rapidly, the life of many of its people was marked by large-scale malnutrition, unemployment, and other human burdens characteristic of the early stages of economic and social modernization. These problems were exacerbated in our time by excessive rates of population increase. As of 1970, there were no grounds for complacency as one viewed the developing regions. But progress in the 1950's and 1960's provided enough success stories to make it possible to believe that if the economic and social momentum of those decades could be sustained, the developing nations too would, in time, find their way to some meaningful level of mass affluence.

Looking back from the late 1970's, there were ample warnings that the foundations for this majestic global expansion were infirm. In the United States the 1962 publication of Rachel Carson's *Silent Spring* is a useful benchmark. Symbolic of its impact was Miss Carson's appearance at Robert Kennedy's Hickory Hill Seminar in the autumn of that year in order to explain to a substantial group of high public officials (including the Soviet Ambassador) her concern about the impact on nature and man of industrial society. Public pressure to contain air and water pollution built up during the 1960's, and was reflected in new legislation. The cumulative effort was climaxed in the United States by the creation in 1970 of the Environmental Protection Agency; on the world scene, by the Stockholm Conference of 1972 on the Human Environment, sponsored by the United Nations.

There was a somewhat similar build-up of anxiety about the rate of population increase in the developing continents. India and certain other nations had evolved modest programs of family planning by the early 1960's, recognizing in public policy the costs and dangers of excessively high birth rates. With caution and against some congressional resistance, American aid programs began to provide limited assistance, short of birth control devices, in support of such programs. By 1964 American agricultural experts and foreign policy planners, projecting the existing rates of population increase and food production, were predicting severe shortages in the second half of the 1970's, shortages which might well be beyond the capacity of the food-surplus nations to manage.

The successive Indian crop failures caused by monsoons in 1965–67 dramatized for all the potential catastrophe that might lie ahead. An extraordinary international effort was required to mobilize the grain imports necessary to feed perhaps a hundred million people endangered in India in those two years. By January 1967 President Johnson could say: "The time for rhetoric has clearly passed. . . . The developed nations must all assist other nations to avoid starvation in the short run and move rapidly towards the ability to feed themselves. Every member of the world community now bears a direct responsibility to help bring our most basic human account into balance." The fact was that the world's reserves of grain, including those which could be harvested from arable land held idle in the United States, were rapidly declining as a proportion of world grain consumption. The introduction of new wheat and rice strains of high productivity bought a little time; but governments in a good many developing nations raised the priority of family planning and agricultural development in the wake of the Indian famines.

No such traumatic event underlined in the 1960's an equally significant process, the rapidly contracting American energy base. Energy consumption began regularly to outstrip the rate of growth in production, and the United States shifted into increased reliance on oil imports: About 7% of U.S. energy consumption was imported in 1960; 14% in 1972, on the eve of the quadrupling of the oil price. Meanwhile, the proved reserves of oil in the U.S. declined regularly during the 1960's except for the discovery of the North Slope deposits in Alaska. New reserves were not only progressively harder to find, they were more expensive to establish and exploit. In 1970, an absolute decline in American oil production began, which continued relentlessly down to 1977.

A parallel process was taking place with respect to natural gas. Encouraged by arbitrarily low prices set by the government in interstate commerce in the 1950's, the proportion of natural gas in American energy consumption had risen from 20% in 1950 to 32% in 1960. The proportion continued to rise, reaching 36.5% a decade later. But in 1968 proved reserves of natural gas had begun to decline. Production peaked out in 1972 and declined steadily down to 1977. Evidently the U.S. could not continue to rely on this convenient, clean, and cheap domestic fuel. Coal, America's most abundant form of energy, had been set aside in these two decades in favor of oil and gas. Coal tended to pollute the environment and had to be mined under difficult and sometimes dangerous conditions. In 1950 it had supplied 38% of America's energy requirements; in 1970, 19%.

The underlying change in the American energy base was ominous for a particular reason. The expansion of the American economy in the 1950's and 1960's had been facilitated because the cost of energy declined relative to the general price level. Between 1951 and 1971 the relative price for refined petroleum products fell 17%; for electricity, 43%. These price trends encouraged the abundant use of energy in industry, transport, and homes. To a lesser extent this was also true in Western Europe and Japan. In fact, the extraordinary growth of the advanced industrial economies had been assisted in the 1950's by a general decline in the relative prices of food and raw materials as well as energy. This decline not only meant that essential materials could be acquired rather cheaply, it also helped contain inflationary pressures. During the 1960's this relative price decline began to bottom out; but food and raw materials were relatively much cheaper in 1972 than they had been at their peak in 1951.

These developments, affecting the supply of air, water, food, and energy, were noted and discussed by experts; and, to a degree, there was some answering response in public policy. But they were not phenomena to which the most influential economists paid much attention. The economists and the politicians whom they advised focused primarily on the level of effective demand in the various advanced industrial countries and on the prospects for next year's growth, level of employment, balance of payments, and rate of inflation. The conventional, neo-Keynesian economists had, it is true, their disagreements. Should one, for example, rely more on manipulating the money supply or on manipulating government budgets to control effective demand? Should one accept a higher level of unemployment in order to damp inflation, or risk a higher rate of inflation while enjoying the advantages of somewhat lower unemployment? These were important questions. They had been argued for a generation and more in graduate seminars, books, and learned journals. They easily found their way into debates among politicians. Indeed, the second question—the appropriate trade-off between unemployment and inflation—lay at the heart of the debate between the two major political parties as late as the American presidential campaign of 1976. But, explicitly or implicitly, the neo-Keynesian economists assumed meat and wheat and oil and gas, and all the other basic commodities, would, somehow, look after themselves through the normal workings of a more or less competitive price system, if only the level of effective demand were right. The problem of pollution was recognized; and textbooks expanded their treatment of what the profession had long called "external diseconomies"* to deal with problems of pollution. But, as children of the 1930's, the conventional economists maintained their primary loyalty to the task of defeating unemployment. They found this increasingly difficult to do in the world which had emerged by the mid-1970's.

In public policy the turning point in the world economy is evidently associated with the quadrupling of the price of oil by OPEC in the autumn of 1973. In the world of ideas, the turning point came earlier with the publication of a small book called *The Limits to Growth*. It was sponsored by the Club of Rome, an international association of businessmen and others concerned with the future of humanity. In 1970 the Club of Rome took the imaginative step of throwing its resources behind a computerized study of global economic growth and its limits. The study flowed from techniques of systems analysis developed at the Massachusetts Institute of Technology by Jay Forrester. Directed by Dennis Meadows, working with a small team of associates, *The Limits to Growth* reached an apoca-

---

* "External diseconomies" are costs imposed on others by the otherwise normal economic activities of individuals or business firms.

lyptic conclusion: "If the present growth trends in world population, industrialization, pollution, food production, and resource depletion continue unchanged, the limits to growth on this planet will be reached sometime within the next one hundred years. The most probable result will be a rather sudden and uncontrollable decline in both population and industrial capacity."[1] The Meadows team arrived at this result by putting into its computer a set of equations which related four critical variables: population, food availability, industrial raw material requirements, and pollution. The model treated the world as a single economic unit and predicted the future by projecting forward past rates of change in these variables and by assuming certain connecting links among them.

The Meadows group experimented with various versions of its model; but in all cases it found, soon or late, that a crisis in industrial civilization occurred. Crisis was brought on either by the pollution of the environment, stemming from universal and expanding industrialization, or by diminishing returns in agriculture and the extraction of raw materials.* The operation of diminishing returns would require the diversion of an increasing proportion of the world's resources to feed an expanding global population and to supply industry with raw materials. In *The Limits to Growth* models, the diversion is on such a scale as to reduce drastically the investment resources available for other needs.

Thus, redoubtably pessimistic, Meadows urged the earliest possible achievement of a stable equilibrium state in the world economy. Industrial plant and population were to be maintained at constant levels, as were food and industrial production per capita, while pollution would be safely contained. This outcome would require both the acceptance by the more

* Diminishing returns is the concept used by economists to describe a situation where the addition of equal increments of a variable factor (say, labor) to a fixed factor (say, land) yields successively smaller increments in output.

advantaged nations of radical income redistribution within the world community and the acceptance by all of a standard of living less dependent on industrial output than was the affluence which had emerged in North America, Western Europe, and Japan.

In short, *The Limits to Growth* preached the doctrine that the world community should quickly abandon the concept of progress and the pursuit of affluence as they had come historically to be defined; radically alter the social values of modern life, as they had emerged; and make all the adjustments required to achieve soon and maintain an egalitarian steady state on a global basis.

Published after a decade of increasing anxiety about problems of pollution, and the evidently gathering tension between population and food supply, *The Limits to Growth* had a dramatic impact on the minds of many of its readers. That effect was powerfully amplified by the world food crisis which emerged at the close of 1972 and then by the quadrupling of the oil price a year later. These events seemed, in some way, to confirm *The Limits to Growth* analysis, although that analysis had not predicted nor did it depend upon such a prompt increase in the relative prices of food and energy.

The Meadows study has been examined carefully by scholars in many parts of the world and subjected to the acute criticism appropriate to so fundamental a theme. In my view *The Limits to Growth* has the virtue of dramatizing effectively a real set of problems. Moreover, its emphasis on the interconnections among population, food, energy, raw materials, and pollution is salutary in a world where we train our intellectuals and bureaucrats as specialists. But it suffers from five serious weaknesses.

First, the calculations are global. In fact, of course, the world economy consists of national or closely interconnected regional units. There are, for example, the intimate ties among the Western European economies as well as those between the United States and Canada. Japan is closely linked to North America, Europe, Australia, and the developing nations of Southeast Asia. By and large it is not unrealistic to conceive of what might be called an OECD economy.* On the other hand, China is virtually self-sufficient; the U.S.S.R. and most of Eastern Europe are closely linked, with modest but expanding ties to the OECD world. The developing nations, however, are at quite different stages of growth, with limited ties to each other and generally close but widely varying relations to the OECD world. Among them, India, like China, is an economy so large, and its external links so limited, that its destiny must be considered in primarily national terms despite the critical marginal role of external assistance and foreign trade.

There are, of course, forces operating more or less pervasively in the world economy; e.g., the price of grain and oil and, perhaps, certain types of pollution. But an analysis set up in global terms is highly abstract and its conclusions potentially misleading. Acute limits-to-growth crises can occur—indeed, are occurring—in some parts of the world while others go forward. Bangladesh, for example, and parts of Africa are caught in what might be called a low-level growth trap: the pressure of population on food supply and, in some African cases, the small size of their internal markets renders difficult the movement into sustained modern growth. The nature of the current situation and tasks in the world economy can thus be obscured by focusing on the possibility of a relatively distant global crisis.

Second, the factual basis for the Meadows model is exceedingly weak. Only the population calculations are reasonably satisfactory, but even here we still have a good deal to learn, for example, about the possibilities of bringing birth rates

---

* The OECD is the Organisation for Economic Cooperation and Development, located in Paris. Its membership includes the noncommunist countries of Europe, Japan, North America, Australia, and New Zealand. Yugoslavia is an associate member.

down more rapidly than in the past. The data on pollution, which plays a critical role in causing catastrophe in *The Limits to Growth* models, are fragmentary. From the incomplete evidence now available, the containment, or even rollback, of air and water pollution is an expensive but economically manageable task.

Third, the handling of technological and resource constraints in *The Limits to Growth* exercises is misleading. The authors usually relax these constraints by assuming a once-and-for-all expansion in, say, acreage, productivity, or resource availabilities. In fact, productivity changes, the bringing in of additional resources, or the creation of new resources are an incremental process whose limits we cannot predict. This problem is compounded in *The Limits to Growth* by acceptance of one of the oldest propositions in economics, one that reaches back to Adam Smith's *The Wealth of Nations*: the assumption of a high rate of technological progress in industry coupled with diminishing returns in agriculture and raw materials. I have already noted that in certain of Meadows' computer runs, the assumption of diminishing returns to agriculture and raw material acquisition helps cause the system's downturn by requiring more and more investment in order to maintain a given flow of food and mineral supplies, thus starving the flow of investment in other necessary directions. The assumption of diminishing returns in agriculture has not proved true over the sweep of the past two centuries, although, as we shall see in Chapter 2, there were periods when diminishing returns did force up the price of agricultural products.

A fourth weakness of *The Limits to Growth* is the lack of the economic mechanism which, historically, has helped validate the proposition that necessity is the mother of invention. No price system operates in these computerized world models, no increasing incentives to invent or discover, to constrain consumption of scarce items, or to find substitutes. The relative price mechanism has been, for two centuries and more, a powerful engine for setting in motion compensatory action in the face of resource constraints.

Finally, there is no evidence that the Meadows prescription is politically, socially, and psychologically viable. On the contrary, the thrust of the less advantaged for affluence, within societies and among nations, is one of the most powerful forces operating on the world scene. As a black colleague of mine once said, the disadvantaged of this world both within the United States and elsewhere sense that they are "about to buy tickets for the show"; they are quite unmoved by the affluent emerging from the theater and pronouncing the show bad; they are determined to find out for themselves.

Among the critics of *The Limits to Growth* is a spectrum of relative optimists about the prospects for the world economy over the next century.* All recognize the reality of present and prospective problems of population pressure, food and energy supply, as well as certain environmental dangers. All recognize that trees do not grow to the sky, and that sometime in the future not only population but income per capita must level off. But they hold that man's technological performance over the past two centuries, plus present scientific capacity and future prospects, all justify faith that we can find or create the new resources and can generate the methods of conservation and of pollution control necessary for growth to continue. Although anticipating many vicissitudes and setbacks, they foresee in a century or two the achievement of a plateau of more or less universal affluence as a possible and statistically more likely outcome for industrial civilization than either a great convulsive global crisis and decline or an early and pur-

* See, for example, H. S. D. Cole (ed.), *Thinking About the Future*, London: Chatto and Windus for Sussex University Press, 1973; Wilfred Beckerman, *In Defence of Economic Growth*, London: Jonathan Cape, 1974; Herman Kahn et al., *The Next 200 Years*, New York: William Morrow, 1976.

poseful adoption of a no-growth, income redistribution strategy.

Despite its technical character, there is an ideological strand running through the debate about *The Limits to Growth*. Meadows and his colleagues appeared at times to embrace the arguments of those who believe that for aesthetic and moral reasons the pursuit of economic growth should cease. One cannot help feeling that in commending an egalitarian state, less dependent upon industrial progress, *The Limits to Growth* is commending an outcome which its authors believe to be good as well as necessary. The critics of this doctrine would not only affirm the potential creativity of science and technology in facing the problems that lie ahead, but they, too, take an ideological position. They would argue that modern economic progress has been the basis for a vast improvement in the quality of human life as well as in its material amenities: longer lives for children, homes with more space and privacy, better education for all, a widened range of opportunities to travel and, in the broadest sense, to fulfill the potentialities with which individual human beings are born.

Formal debate about *The Limits to Growth* has, in the past few years, lost its cutting edge. Meadows and his colleagues, in later work, have reacted constructively to the lively debate they inspired. They now acknowledge that, if the concept of continuous incremental improvement in technology is introduced, and if their somewhat fragile assumptions about the scale of pollution are belied, industrial civilization could proceed toward universal levels of affluence without encountering an apocalyptic crisis.

In the end, this debate takes its place with four predecessors. Each occurred at times of pressure on food and raw material supplies and relatively high or rising prices for basic products. Each was, as Chapter 2 indicates, the product of a Kondratieff upswing.

The first debate was triggered by Thomas Malthus' pessimism about the consequences of Britain's population increase in the 1790's, and David Ricardo's pessimism about the productivity prospects in agriculture. Both views, generated by population–food tension during the French Revolutionary and Napoleonic Wars, were ultimately rooted in the notion of diminishing returns to investment in agriculture.

The second debate concerned the future of Britain's coal supply, an issue raised with some force by W. S. Jevons in the 1860's. Jevons projected forward the then current rate of increase in consumption (3.5%), emerged with impossible levels of British coal requirements, and, like Meadows, concluded "our motion must be reduced to rest." A more general subject of debate at this time might have been the question of the population–food balance, in the wake of the Irish famine of 1845–7 and Europe's food supply problems of the early 1850's; but the potentialities of the American Middle West and the railroads were palpably available to provide Europe with more grain.

The third occasion for concern arose out of the relative rise of foodstuff and raw material prices in the pre-1914 generation and the consequently unfavorable shift in the British terms of trade.* In 1912 the young John Maynard Keynes, looking at relative British export and import prices, re-evoked the classic specter: "There is now again a steady tendency for a given unit of manufactured product to purchase year by year a diminished quantity of raw product. The comparative advantage in trade is moving sharply against industrial countries." This

---

* The terms of trade, conventionally measured, is the ratio of a country's export prices to its import prices. A "favorable" movement is one in which export prices rise more or fall less than import prices, and a given volume of exports provides a greater volume of imports. An "unfavorable" movement is obverse. But an "unfavorable" movement may reflect a relatively high rate of increase of productivity in export industries and can, therefore, be a positive rather than negative factor in a nation's growth. Because of productivity increase, a given amount of labor and capital may earn a larger volume of imports despite the relative decline in export prices.

was the anxious view of the position of the industrial nations Keynes took to the Versailles Peace Conference. It strongly shaped his gloomy view of the Treaty in his *Economic Consequences of the Peace*, published in 1919. But just as the wheat price tumbled after the Napoleonic Wars and the coal price after 1873 (with oil and electricity emerging on the horizon), the British terms of trade turned favorable after 1920 to an embarrassing degree. British import prices became relatively so cheap that Britain's overseas customers could no longer afford to buy British exports at the previous rate. Idle capacity emerged in Britain's export industries and those related to them; for example, ship-building. Keynes quickly turned to the problem of chronic unemployment.

The fourth period of anxiety of this kind came after the Second World War, when food and raw material prices continued to rise relative to industrial products, as they had since the mid-1930's. This process stimulated the massive report in 1952 by the President's Materials Policy Commission, chaired by William S. Paley. The Commission was luckier than the line of pessimists running from Malthus to Keynes of 1919. Relative prices broke favorably for the industrial nations in 1951 as agriculture revived and the modern productivity revolution in agriculture took hold in the United States and elsewhere. The Commission's final report (*Resources for Freedom*), written in the altered price setting, took the temperate view that resources should be viewed in terms of the cost of acquisition rather than in terms of absolute depletion, and that the unfolding of technology was a powerful force in fending off classical diminishing returns. In the wake of the Paley Commission a permanent Washington-based but privately financed institution to monitor food, raw material, and energy problems was created—Resources for the Future. It continues to do authoritative studies in this field.

Thus, on four occasions in the past serious analysts of the world economy became anxious about the capacity of food or raw material production to sustain population or industrial growth. Behind their anxiety were projections of geometric increases in demand set off against absolutely limited or arithmetically expanding supplies, shadowed by diminishing returns. On all four occasions, their projections were belied by the emergence of new supplies or the development of new technologies. As this book argues, this tale of recurrent but unjustified pessimism is no cause for complacency now. But the sequence I shall trace out briefly in Chapter 2 does raise the question of how useful long-run projections of current situations and trends really are.

I believe they are of some use. After all, most public policy is made in response to incoming cables or other immediate pressure on the political process. As Jean Monnet has recently written: "Men only accept change in the face of necessity; and they see that necessity only when confronted by crisis." It is rare for governments to act with even a five- or ten-year horizon in view. Nevertheless, the attempt to predict or even to speculate systematically about the world fifty or seventy-five years from now is not an empty intellectual exercise. Given the rates of population increase in the past, and the large numbers of young people in our populations, it will be a long time before most developing nations can achieve a constant population even if birth rates fall very rapidly. If unmanageable levels of population in the next century are to be avoided, the governments and peoples of the developing continents must bring about a decline in birth rates from the present forward. The time lag is also long in creating, rendering efficient, and diffusing some of the wholly new technologies in energy and other fields that will urgently be required by the end of the century. Above all, attitudes must change before measures even the optimists regard as necessary (e.g., resource conservation) can be effectively carried out in democratic societies. Here the lag can be long, indeed.

There is another more human reason for taking the long run seriously—say, the middle of the next century. It is not all that far away. Children now born in the advanced parts of the world have a good statistical chance of living until 2050. When we talk of what may transpire between now and then, we are talking about what will or will not be achieved in the span of a single lifetime, the kind of world our children and grandchildren will experience. We owe them a bit of farsightedness.

In short, there are good reasons to look ahead a half-century and more, to identify palpably dangerous problems, and to begin now to mitigate or solve them if we can.

But the excessive refinement of long-range projections is a risky business. No matter how much the data base and the equations of interaction are improved by mobilizing additional historical or contemporary evidence, errors compound as the computer hums into the future. The potentialities for a great crisis in the industrial civilization built since the eighteenth century are clear enough. The challenges of feeding the populations scheduled to be born, of providing the energy and raw materials for the industrial structures scheduled to emerge are real. The tasks of maintaining a viable environment of air and water will certainly be expensive and can be ignored only at considerable risk. In confronting those challenges, it is evident that significant changes in policy and ways of doing things will be required both within national societies and among them. Long-run projections, pessimistic and optimistic, have helped create an intellectual consensus that such tasks must be faced if industrial civilization is to survive. That has been an important contribution. In both science and public policy the correct identification of the problem is a considerable part of its solution.

But the critical question is not: Are the pessimists or the optimists correct? Evidently, tragic or successful outcomes are conceivable. The critical question is: How do we get from here to there? What needs doing now is the creation of policies that will maximize the chance that the optimists' vision of the twenty-first century comes to pass.

It is, I believe, the next quarter-century that will prove critical. By the year 2000, with wisdom and some luck, we as a human race may have succeeded at these critical tasks:

—The governments and peoples in the developing world will have brought gross annual birth rates down from their present explosive level, at or close to 40 per 1000, to 20 or fewer.

—We will have greatly increased the level and productivity of agriculture, notably in the developing regions, so that the expanded populations can be decently fed and gross Malthusian crises avoided in the most vulnerable parts of the world.

—We will have solved the scientific and technical problems in creating a new economic energy source, based on renewable or essentially infinite sources.

—We will have faced and begun to overcome by expanded production, substitution, economy, and recycling, a growing list of raw material shortages.

—We will have proved we know how to control air, water, and other forms of pollution and have the will to allocate the resources necessary for its control.

—We will have radically restructured our patterns of investment, including the scale and directions of research and development, to accomplish the above results and to provide the technologies in agriculture, energy, and raw materials required in the century ahead.

—We will have learned how to reconcile high and steady rates of growth with price stability.

—Within the human community, the developing nations, taken as a whole, will have doubled their present income per capita. They will be approaching levels of per capita income normally associated with rapidly declining rates of population increase. They will have acquired another quarter-century's experience of modernization as well as competence in a much widened range of technologies. They will be much more capable of adjusting to changing circumstance and solving their problems in the century beyond.

If the human community succeeds at these tasks, and does not destroy its somewhat fragile civilization in nuclear war, the next century could see movement towards a more or less universal affluence. No doubt affluence will be defined and shaped in new ways we cannot now predict. No doubt differences in income level will persist among countries and within them. No doubt new, difficult, and contentious problems will arise as older problems are subdued. But the greatest challenge to industrial civilization since it began to take shape two centuries ago is upon us now and in the generation ahead. As nearly as we can perceive through the mists of the future, with imperfect data and imperfect understanding, the hardest part of the transition is that on which we are now embarked. It is in the next quarter-century that we must turn some rather difficult corners, in technology, public policy, and attitudes of mind, if we are ultimately to succeed without great human suffering.

The balance of this book explores the implications of that proposition.

2

The Next Quarter-Century Seen as the Fifth Kondratieff Upswing

B EFORE considering the specific lines of policy which might permit the world community to transit with reasonable success the next quarter-century, it is worth exploring an intellectual framework which, I believe, can provide a certain order and perspective to the task as a whole.

Over the past several years I have often suggested that the world economy is in the early phase of a fifth Kondratieff upswing.* Despite this effort, few are asking: Who was Kondratieff and what is a Kondratieff cycle? The answer is, nonetheless, that N. D. Kondratieff was a Russian economist. Writing in the 1920's, he suggested that capitalist economies were subject to long cycles, some 40–50 years in length. His views were published in the United States in summary in the mid-1930's. They generated considerable professional discussion and debate, but dropped from view in the great boom after the Second World War. Most contemporary economists

* See, for example, "Caught by Kondratieff," *Wall Street Journal,* March 8, 1977.

20

vaguely remember having run across his name and ideas in graduate school but have forgotten precisely what it was he said.

Looking back from the mid-1920's, Kondratieff saw two and one-half cycles in various statistical series covering prices, wages, interest rates, and other data expressed in monetary terms. And he found these cycles in a number of countries including Great Britain, the United States, and France. Their troughs came about 1790, in the late 1840's, and the mid-1890's; their peaks about 1815, 1873, and 1920. He sought but failed to find persuasive evidence of concurrent cycles in production indexes.

Kondratieff did not attempt directly to provide a theory of the long cycle, beyond the assertion that prices and production oscillated in a rhythm of 40–50 years about an equilibrium path. But he counter-attacked his many critics. Critics in the West asserted that the phenomena he was examining reflected special historical occasions: changes in technology, wars and revolutions, the bringing of new countries into the world economy, and fluctuations in gold production. His counter-attack asserted that none of these phenomena could be properly regarded as independent of the workings of the world capitalist system. He implied that a coherent explanation must exist; but, in his own phrase, he never developed "an appropriate theory of long waves."

In addition to his pragmatic critics of the West, Kondratieff faced severe criticism from orthodox Marxists within the Soviet Union. The notion that capitalism unfolded in a series of long cycles around some sort of stable long-term equilibrium position ran counter to Marxist dogma. That dogma asserted that capitalism was subject to progressively more severe crises until it disintegrated and gave way to socialism and then communism. For whatever reasons, Kondratieff died, according to Solzhenitsyn's *Gulag Archipelago,* in one of Stalin's prison camps.

There have been various efforts to explain the long irregular cycles that Kondratieff first effectively dramatized. They are worth trying to explain because they have, in a rough-and-ready way, continued to unfold in the period after Kondratieff first wrote about them. There was a trough in the mid-1930's; a peak about 1951; and a trough again in 1972 on the eve of the explosive rise of grain and then oil prices.

My explanation for Kondratieff cycles would focus on the relative prices of food and raw materials on the one hand, industrial products on the other.[1] Other forces were, evidently, at work; but, at their core, I believe that what we observe in these cycles are periods of relative shortage and relative abundance of food and raw materials. Changes in relative prices underlie the shifts in income distribution, the directions of investment, trends in interest rates, real wages, and the overall price level which are the hallmarks of a Kondratieff cycle.

If oscillations in relative prices are the heart of the matter, why were these cycles so long compared, for example, to conventional business cycles which averaged, say, nine years? The answer seems to lie in the fact that the opening up of new sources of food and raw materials required substantial periods of time—much more time than it takes to build a new factory or house. The lags involved in responding to a relative rise in food or raw material prices, and the fact that the response often required the development of whole new regions, led to an overshooting of world requirements and a period of surplus. A relative fall in the prices of food and raw materials then followed. This trend persisted, gradually slowing down, until expanding world requirements caught up with the excess capacity and stocks generated in a Kondratieff upswing.

In the Kondratieff upswings, the world economy exhibited certain characteristics familiar to all of us since the close of 1972: accelerated general inflation, high interest rates, pressure on the real wages of urban labor and on those on fixed incomes, combined with relative prosperity for the producers of food and raw materials. During downswings (excepting that

from 1951 to 1972) the general price level tended to fall, interest rates were rather low, and real wages were lifted by the fall
in living costs. But farmers and producers of raw materials felt
the pressure of the relative decline in their prices. This was,
for example, the position of American farmers in the 1920's or
Latin American exporters of food and raw materials in the
1950's. In the exceptional case of 1951–72 the relative prices
of energy, raw materials, and food tended to decline, notably
during the 1950's, but in the generally inflationary environment of that period (considered in Chapter 11) the absolute fall
of basic commodity prices in the 1950's was limited and there
was a slow rising tendency in the 1960's.

It cannot be emphasized too strongly that these cycles did
not unfold smoothly in history. For one thing, their shape was
distorted by the occurrence of wars, which played a large but
never exclusive role in certain of the Kondratieff upswings. In
addition, the upswings were marked by a sharp initial rise in
relative prices. These explosive intervals generally lasted two
or three years. The most recent example of such a sudden shift
in the price environment occurred between 1972 and 1974.
After the price explosion, both recently and earlier, there followed not a continuing steady rise in relative prices, but
erratic fluctuations usually with a gently rising trend. Downswings were also irregular. There was usually a sharp downward break as the overshooting in supply had its immediate
effect in the form of a rapid relative decline in food and raw
material prices. That happened, for example, in the years after
the Kondratieff peak in 1951. Then came a bottoming out of
the decline in relative prices, a growing tension between demand and supply, marked by a running down of stocks and
reserves. This process set the stage for the next upswing.

In the course of these roughly cyclical movements there
were exceptional periods when the trends temporarily reversed. One came in the 1830's, when food and raw material
prices (notably cotton and wheat) sharply rose for several
years during the first Kondratieff downswing. Another oc-

curred during the second Kondratieff downswing in the late 1880's, when large flows of capital were directed to building the Argentine railroads and opening the fertile pampas. Despite the falling trend of wheat prices, this enterprise was correctly judged to be profitable, given the productivity of the land and rapidly declining transport costs on land and sea. In the 1840's and the 1890's the characteristics of a Kondratieff downswing reasserted themselves.

The contours of these long cycles were affected also by the technological developments occurring in each period within the world economy. Since the late eighteenth century the habit of invention and technological innovation has been built into the world economy and has recurred unceasingly. Technological development is the work of many hands and minds building, indirectly, on the insights of science and, directly, on the impulse to perform the immediate task better and cheaper. A great deal of technological change takes place by small steps. But there has also been a sequence of massive innovations which have radically reshaped the structure of industrial economies. The first round of great inventions, which began to be effectively absorbed into the British economy in the 1780's, included the new cotton textile machinery, methods for producing iron of good quality with coke, and the improved steam engine that James Watt contrived. To these should be added the powerful contribution of Eli Whitney's cotton gin across the Atlantic. The second round was, quite simply, the railroad with all its consequences for agriculture and industry as well as for the cost of transport itself. It reshaped the Atlantic world between 1830 and 1890, as well as many regions beyond. The third, coming in the last quarter of the nineteenth century, centered on the cheap production of steel. The fourth, which has dominated the twentieth century, embraced the internal combustion engine, a whole new range of chemicals, electricity, and then electronics—the latter still unfolding in ways we cannot wholly predict.

The rhythm of the great technological innovations did not conform systematically to the rhythm of relative prices for basic commodities; but the rise and fall of the great innovations did leave their marks on relative price movements. The story of the Kondratieff cycles must be told, then, by weaving together the impulses imparted to the world economy by periods of relative scarcity or overabundance of food and raw materials with the saga of technological change.

I shall now summarize as briefly as possible the sequence of Kondratieff upswings and downswings from 1790 to 1977.

1790–1815. The French Revolutionary and Napoleonic Wars (1793–1815) came after almost a half-century of gathering pressure of rising population on the British and European food supply. Britain, a food surplus country early in the eighteenth century, gradually became a more or less regular importer of grain from Eastern Europe. The war broke out a decade after the British industrial revolution had begun in earnest, centered on the expansion of factory-made cotton textiles, the new methods of iron-making, and Watt's steam engine. There was, in the 1790's, a sharp rise in relative prices of agricultural products and raw materials. The claims of war on resources, and the necessity for expanding agriculture in Britain, damped the pace at which the major leading sector, cotton textiles, would otherwise have expanded.* On the other hand, war conditions may have somewhat accelerated

* A leading sector is a segment of the economy whose disproportionately rapid expansion, in its direct and indirect consequences, helps explain phases of overall rapid growth in the economy. In most cases leading sectors represent the diffusion of a new technology or, at least, a technology not previously absorbed by a particular economy. The sequence of progressively more sophisticated leading sectors is the basis for *The Stages of Economic Growth* (Cambridge University Press, 2d ed., 1971). In a given business expansion, however, the leading sector can be one which does not necessarily incorporate new technology; for example, a postwar housing boom or the kind of rapid expansion the United States might experience in the late 1970's and 1980's due to enlarged investment in energy production and conservation.

the expansion of the modern British iron industry. In the United States, war in Europe provided the new nation with an initial phase of high prosperity, based on the prices of its food and raw material exports. This interval of almost OPEC-like American prosperity not only eased the political problems of the new nation, but it also foreshadowed the dynamic process by which new nations and regions were to be drawn into the network of world trade by rising global requirements for food and raw materials. After 1807, Jefferson's Embargo on foreign trade and the War of 1812 forced the United States to substitute its own manufactures for imports, which helped prepare the way for the post-1815 New England movement into modern industrialization. Some areas on the continent experienced similar forward movement in cotton textiles; but the British industrial lead as of 1793 had increased by 1815. Overall, the years down to 1815 were, for Britain and continental Europe, a period of relatively high food prices, which pressed down on the real wages of the urban worker.

1815–1848. Here we have a classic Kondratieff downswing. With the coming of peace and normal access to Eastern European grain, agricultural and raw material prices broke sharply downward. The postwar abundance of grain and, after 1818, of cotton set a framework of relatively cheap foodstuffs and raw materials for the next decade. Cotton textile manufacture, the coming of the steamship on the rivers, and the diffusion of the steam engine to industry could proceed rapidly in this environment because basic commodities were relatively cheap. The 1830's broke the pattern temporarily. The pace of cotton industry expansion in the 1820's, in the United States and Western Europe as well as in Britain, yielded a price explosion in 1833–35. This made profitable the diversion of large U.S. and British capital flows to expand acreage in the American South; and the West, too, absorbed substantial capital for transport development to make its agricultural products more marketable in the East. The great boom of the 1830's overshot world market needs at existing prices. Prices and interest rates resumed their post-1815 trends in the 1840's, a period of rapid railroad and industrial expansion on both sides of the Atlantic: in the American Northeast and Britain, Belgium, Germany, and France. This period experienced no significant diversions or distortions due to wars. But in the 1840's (notably, but not exclusively, in Ireland) there were signs that Europe's food–population balance was going awry. The potato crisis of 1845–47 yielded a population push from land pressed too hard into European cities and across the Atlantic, leaving its mark to this day on populations as widely dispersed as New England, the upper Middle West, and central Texas.

1848–1873. The trends reverse sharply in this second Kondratieff upswing. As was the case for a few years after the Indian food crisis, one hundred and twenty years later, the situation temporarily eased after the Irish potato famine. But the precarious balance in the Atlantic world between food and population increase yielded a sharp rise in grain prices in 1852–54. Capital flowed lavishly from London and the American Northeast to open up the Middle West with a railway network. Cotton, after a decade's slack, also moved up in price, and acreage was opened up to the west as far as Texas. Urban real wages on both sides of the Atlantic came under severe pressure. The new leading sector—railroads—converged with food and raw material requirements, providing the means for bringing new acreage into production.

These agricultural demands for capital did not, however, prevent Western Europe from also moving forward rapidly with the railroads and the expansion of heavy industry down to 1873. The American Civil War, however, set back the United States and imposed transient constraints on the world's cotton supply, despite expanded cotton production in Brazil, Egypt, and India.

The course of prices, interest rates, terms of trade, income distribution, and flows of capital in the world economy is distorted in this period by a series of minor wars and, for the first time, by the attractions of gold mining. The falling trend in prices since 1815 made gold a more attractive commodity because the price of gold was fixed in dollars and other currencies on the gold standard. Its real value, therefore, rose as the price level fell. A given amount of gold, commanding a fixed number of dollars, could purchase more goods and services. The incentive to find and mine gold increased; and around midcentury prospectors struck it rich in California and Australia. The trans-Mississippi railroad extension after 1865 again drew (as in the 1850's) large flows of capital from London and the eastern American states. This process yielded in time enormous increases in grain exports, further cheapened by falling shipping rates. There was a transient energy crisis in the early 1870's, as the demand for British coal, at home and abroad, exceeded current mining capacity. An explosive rise in coal prices occurred; but accessible mines were quickly expanded. The framework was set for the second Kondratieff downswing, which was marked by strong downward trends in the prices of grain, coal, cotton, and most other raw materials.

1873–1896. In an interval of relative peace and abundance of foodstuffs and raw materials, as after 1815, the leading industrial sectors were driven forward in an uninhibited way. By the 1870's, railways had peaked out as a leading sector in most of the more industrialized countries. But they held up through the 1880's in the United States, where feeder lines and double-tracking were required to fill out and exploit the potentialities of the transcontinental railway structure earlier completed. Out of the railway's need for long-lasting rails had come, in the 1870's, cheap steel: the most powerful leading sector of the second Kondratieff downswing. Steel was soon being used for building and bridge construction, machine tools, ships, and more efficient steam engines. Meanwhile, electricity and new forms of chemicals began to move from laboratories to an early phase of application in the economy. But the railroad was not quite finished. In Canada and Australia, India, Argentina, and Russia it was beginning to transform the agricultural sectors—and not a moment too soon. For the limits of the American frontier were formally reached in the 1890's; and the pull of the American agricultural and industrial economy in the post-Civil War period generated increases in population and urbanization which were about to limit the United States' grain export capacity.

From the early 1870's to the mid-1890's (as between 1815 and 1850) the trends in the world economy for prices and interest rates were down; real wage movements and income distribution favored the urban worker in industrial societies. As in the 1830's, there was a break in the continuity of these trends. The Argentine boom of the late 1880's drew large amounts of capital from abroad and stimulated the world economy in ways which triggered a brief inflationary interval. But in the first half of the 1890's the post-1873 trend phenomena, notably falling prices and interest rates, reasserted themselves. Then came a reversal much like that of the early 1850's.

1896–1920. In this third Kondratieff upswing relative shortages of foodstuffs and raw materials again emerged in an environment of small wars, enlarged military outlays, and then a great war. We are back in a period bearing a family resemblance to that of 1850–73, including increased gold mining, notably in South Africa and Alaska. Large flows of capital to redress the balance in the world economy went this time not to the United States but to Australia, Argentina, Canada, and Russia. All except Argentina experienced rapid industrial as well as agricultural expansion. Urban real wages in the older industrialized countries (e.g., Britain, U.S., Germany) came under pressure, and profits did relatively well. The decline or deceleration of urban real wages contributed to the expansion of trade unions, to the rise of the British Labour party and the German Social Democratic party, and to pressure on demo-

cratic governments in the Atlantic world generally to allocate
more resources to welfare purposes. In the United States, the
forces generated by the third Kondratieff upswing helped
strengthen the Progressive movement, as those feeling the
constraint on real wages, imposed by the rising cost of living,
turned to politics for redress.

The effects of the diversion of resources to agriculture (and
to wider purposes in agricultural nations), to gold mining, to
increased arms outlays, and to war were heightened by a tran-
sitional phase in the leading sectors of the more advanced
industrial nations of the Atlantic world. The railroads were
now an old and, at best, slowly expanding sector in these
countries. Steel and all its related subsectors were still expanding; but expansion was at declining rates and, more important, with much diminished increases in productivity. As
in the 1970's, there was in these pre-1914 years a general tendency for the rate of increase in productivity to slow down.
Electricity, certain new chemicals, and the internal combustion engine were moving forward rapidly, but not at a rate
sufficient to compensate for the decline in momentum and
productivity of the older leading sectors. The net result of this
tension between various diversionary capital and military outlays and the leading sector transition was not uniform among
the major industrial nations. It was most marked in Britain,
where the Boer War was quite expensive; and it was followed
by hitherto unprecedented levels of capital exports. It was a
clear but less marked phenomenon in Germany and the United
States, where the momentum of steel and all related to it,
while decelerating, was sustained better than in Britain. In
France, whose progress in the three preceding decades was
relatively slow, there was some acceleration as the coming of
electricity helped compensate for the lack of a Ruhr and the
loss of Alsace–Lorraine in 1870.

In Europe, the First World War, on balance, accentuated
and distorted the pattern of this trend period; that is, the char-

acter of the military conflict created artificially high requirements for steel and other heavy-industry products of the aging
leading sectors, while also inducing a further expansion of
agriculture in non-European areas which proved unprofitable
after 1920. The United States and Canada shared, of course,
in this transient agricultural expansion; but it was during the
First World War that the United States moved solidly into the
age of the mass automobile, with Canada in line astern, providing a strong leading sector for the prosperity of the 1920's.

1920–1933. In 1920, the prices of agricultural products and
raw materials broke sharply downward, in both absolute and
relative terms. This movement, favorable to industrial societies and regions, lifted the real income of urban families,
but reduced the incomes and purchasing power of those dependent on the production and sale of food and raw materials.
Stocks of these commodities built up in the 1920's and over-
whelmed the markets when general depression struck the
world economy in 1929. Excepting the United States, where
the new leading sectors of high mass-consumption (motor
vehicles and electric-powered durable consumers goods) carried the economy forward at a rate consistent with high levels
of employment, the more advanced industrial nations of Europe did not fully recover in the 1920's. France from 1925–29
did best, aided by a currency devaluation which strengthened
its relative export and tourist positions. But, in general, the
weakness of Europe's traditional pre-1914 export markets and
a level of income per capita that was lower than in the United
States converged to produce a situation where the new leading
sectors of high mass-consumption did not move forward
rapidly enough to bring the major economies back to sustained
full employment. Then came the Great Depression, with catastrophic consequences in both industrial and basic commodity
sectors.

There are, of course, many unique features to the interwar
period but, as compared to its predecessors (1815–48 and

1873–96), its central characteristic is that relatively cheap prices for basic commodities did not, in themselves, encourage a sufficiently accelerated diffusion of the new leading sectors to avoid a retardation of overall growth in the most advanced economies.

1933–1951. Here, again, we are in a time of relatively rising prices of basic commodities and the distortions of war. Recovery after 1932–33 occurred against a background of reduced output of basic commodities which, at last, began to yield a reduction of the large stocks which had overhung the markets in the 1920's and early 1930's. From about 1936 rearmament accelerated. The war reduced agricultural production in most of Europe and increased it in overseas areas, as had happened a quarter of a century earlier. Relative shortages persisted, however, down to 1951, affected by the slower pace of European agricultural than industrial recovery and by the Korean War. Then, as in 1920, prices broke downward, relatively as well as absolutely.

1951–1972. This time the outcome for the world economy was quite different from that between the wars. The leading sectors of high mass-consumption moved forward rapidly in North America, Western Europe, and Japan, strengthened by cheap energy, food, and raw materials. There was another difference: despite weakened prices for basic commodities, especially in the 1950's, Asia, the Middle East, Africa, and Latin America also moved forward in earlier stages of growth. Their capacity to do so, in what might otherwise have been adverse circumstances, was assisted by the extraordinary and sustained boom in the advanced industrial nations which provided strong markets for their exports; and by the provision of a substantial official flow of capital for development purposes, on concessional terms, in addition to considerable flows of private capital. For the first time in history, a large number of the nations of Latin America, Africa, the Middle East, and

Asia sought systematically to modernize their economic and social life through development plans of increasing, if uneven, sophistication and effectiveness.

In the United States from the late 1950's, the automobile and durable consumers goods sectors (embracing also the movement to suburbia, massive road-building, etc.) began to lose their momentum. They were superseded as a basis for growth by a rapid expansion of private and public outlays for education, health, and travel. These service sectors also expanded in Western Europe and Japan where the automobile–durable consumers goods revolution continued swiftly down through the 1960's, but at a decelerating pace towards the end of the decade.

As the 1960's wore on, it was also evident, beneath the surface, that the rapid global expansion in food and energy requirements was altering the balance which had existed since the downward price turn in 1951. As noted in Chapter 1, one region after another moved into a grain deficit position or enlarged its imports: Latin America, Eastern Europe and the Soviet Union, Africa, and Asia. The United States, Canada, Argentina, and Australia were left virtually alone as food-surplus nations. Grain reserves as a proportion of annual global consumption fell away. A food crisis in India from 1965 to 1967 was a significant warning of what was to come. Similarly, the pace of energy consumption in the United States converged with a reduction of American gas and oil reserves to require a rapid increase in United States oil imports. In 1972 the food situation came to crisis; in 1973, OPEC (Organization of Petroleum Exporting Countries), perceiving its monopolistic leverage in a world where the United States was no longer a potential energy exporter, moved to exploit that leverage by a fourfold increase in prices. In a sense, the second Kondratieff downswing was ended by the United States reaching the end of its agricultural frontier, given existing agricultural prices and technologies; the fourth Kondratieff downswing was ended by the United States reaching the end of its gas and oil frontier, given existing energy prices and technologies.

1972–1977. The Price Revolution of 1972–77, like its four predecessor Kondratieff upswings, altered the terms of trade, income distribution, and the rate of inflation in familiar ways. Its effects on the balance of payments position of the industrial world also set in motion a severe recession, bringing to an end the great post-1945 boom. It struck directly at the leading sectors: the automobile, durable consumers goods, and a new range of chemicals (e.g., plastics and synthetic textiles). All were energy-intensive. The recession also struck at tax revenues on which the continued expansion of key public services depended. In the United States, its impact was particularly severe in the northern industrial states. In the developing world, the direct impact was most severe among the poorest nations; but virtually all, except the oil monopolists, were hit by the stagnation of the advanced industrial world, as well as by the higher costs of oil imports. A recovery began in 1975–76, but the prospects were for lower growth rates in the OECD world (and higher unemployment) than in the Kondratieff downswing of the 1950's and 1960's; and this probability diminished also the prospects for the developing nations which did not command oil surpluses.

What are the implications for public policy of this irregular cyclical sequence covering almost two centuries? The first is, I believe, that when the world economy confronts a rise in relative prices of basic commodities, the correct response is to change the directions of investment. Specifically, increased resources have to be allocated to increase the supply or to economize the use of those commodities where the pace of demand has outstripped supply from existing sources. In the past, this diversion of investment resources to bring the world economy back into balance was also, in part, the foundation for relatively full employment during the first four Kondratieff upswings. Historically, the principal commodities affected by these cycles were grain and cotton. In our time, the list has extended to energy production and conservation, the supply of clean air and water, the supply of water itself, and, quite probably, to the supply of a wide range of raw materials. Moreover, unlike the situation in the pre-1914 world, there are no major new physical frontiers whose development might solve our resource problems. To be sure, a few frontiers remain: Alaska, the North Sea, and, perhaps, the South China Sea for oil; the sea beds for minerals. But there are no vast open territories to bring into the world economy to redress the balance of a spreading industrialization. The great frontier will, therefore, be in new technologies which will permit us both to expand and conserve the flow of resources required to sustain an expanding global, increasingly industrial civilization.

A second policy implication emerges, one which also differentiates the present from the longer past. When relative price movements in the past signalled a period of shortage, it was primarily private capital that responded to the profit possibilities which had emerged; and the response was generally quite prompt. Governments did play a role, but it was mainly supportive; for example, by permitting or encouraging the building of railroads and, in some cases, assisting in their finance. But the funds to permit the compensatory expansion of agricultural production flowed out of the private capital markets, notably from London, Paris, and the eastern United States.

The fourth Kondratieff upswing, running from the mid-1930's to 1951, was also somewhat different from its predecessors. The agricultural expansion which began in that period was based on a productivity revolution involving not merely the further diffusion of agricultural machinery but also the more intensive use of fertilizers and pesticides, as well as new seed strains. Governments, notably the American government, played a part in generating and diffusing some of the new technologies; but, as in the pre-1914 world, innovations were carried out in North America and Western Europe mainly by the private sector. The post-1945 exploitation of the Middle East oil reserves, essential for the growth of Western Europe and Japan, ranks in energy with the opening of the Middle West in agriculture a century earlier. As before, the bulk of the required capital was mobilized from private sources.

A fundamental theme of this book emerges from this historical review: The compensatory investments now required to bring the world economy back towards balance will, in the fifth Kondratieff upswing, require a larger and more conscious government role than was necessary in the past. In part, this need stems from the nature of the sectors involved; for example, the containment of air and water pollution, a task that inevitably comes to rest heavily on government regulation and government action. A further reason for the augmented role of the public sector is the extent to which policy towards energy, agriculture, and raw materials has, for good or ill, become inextricably caught up in the political processes of many countries. This does not mean that the price system cannot play a substantial part in stimulating the flow of investment in the right directions. In fact, some of the most important forms of government action will consist of measures to permit the price system accurately to reflect the underlying scarcities and thus encourage private acts of investment, conservation, and the generation of new technologies. But, in the end, a range of positive government actions will be required on a scale never before necessary to deal with the relative scarcities of a Kondratieff upswing. In an important sense, if the world economy is to thrive, governments will have to think and act their way through the fifth Kondratieff upswing.

The question then arises: Will the fifth Kondratieff upswing give way in time to a downswing? Or does the world economy confront an indefinitely protracted period of relatively expensive energy, food, and raw materials? This is a question which cannot be answered dogmatically. My guess is that a sharp downward break in relative prices of basic commodities awaits the breakthrough to some new, cheap, hopefully infinite and nonpolluting, source of energy. At the moment, as noted in Chapter 5, the two most promising candidates are fusion power and a method for concentrating solar energy which we have not yet discovered. The breeder reactor is another possibility. The reason for focusing in this context on the possibility of such a breakthrough in energy is that agriculture has become, and is likely to remain, an energy-intensive activity, dependent as it is on farm machinery and the pumping of irrigation water, as well as on fertilizers and pesticides. Moreover, the acquisition of raw materials and their processing are also energy-intensive activities. The cost of energy is a critical factor in converting sea water into fresh water and for pumping water over long distances to supply arid agricultural areas. Until a major breakthrough occurs in the cost and supply of energy, a convergence of powerful forces at work in the world economy is likely to keep the prices of basic commodities oscillating in a high range. These forces include: the rate of population increase in relation to food supplies; the pressure of expanding industrial production on raw material supplies; the high cost of energy itself from conventional resources and technologies; and the inescapable cost of preserving an adequate supply of clean water and air. This does not mean that the rich nations must stagnate and the poorer nations cease to grow. It does mean that growth and the expansion of welfare for human beings will take place in a somewhat more austere setting, in which difficult choices will be required; and some old-fashioned virtues, like hard work and creative ingenuity, might enjoy an unexpectedly renewed high priority in our societies.

3

The Bankruptcy of Neo-Keynesian Economics*

THOSE who bear policy responsibilities in the world economy confront the tasks of the fifth Kondratieff upswing with an awkward intellectual heritage. That heritage is the body of theory, analytic technique, and operating experience which developed out of the germinal ideas associated with John Maynard Keynes.

Although the title of this chapter is seriously meant, I should say immediately that the development of neo-Keynesian economics represents one of the major achievements of the social sciences in their long history. Surely, the lessons we have learned about how to control the overall level of effective demand through public policy must not be lost. But bank-

---

* I use the phrase neo-Keynesian economics for two reasons. First, the initial Keynesian propositions have been clarified and greatly refined since the 1930's. Second, as noted in Chapter 1 (pp. 14–15), Keynes was exceedingly sensitive to the relative price movements of food and raw materials. It is most unlikely that he would have remained, like most neo-Keynesians of our time, frozen to theoretical models and policy positions rendered irrelevant by the course of events since the latter months of 1972.

ruptcy is not a state where assets have been reduced to zero. It is a state where assets do not match liabilities. I believe the concepts and tools of neo-Keynesian economics are grossly inadequate to deal with the problems imposed on the world economy by the coming of the fifth Kondratieff upswing.

To understand why this is so one must go back to the historical setting within which Keynes (and others) developed new theories, and then observe the changing context in which they were applied down to the present.

What moved certain British, Scandinavian, and American economists to begin to think in new ways was the high chronic unemployment of Europe in the 1920's as well as the almost universally catastrophic unemployment levels of the early 1930's. Between 1921 and 1929, for example, when the United States experienced an average of 4% unemployment, in a setting of prosperity, unemployment averaged 12% in Britain, 14% in Sweden. By 1932, unemployment was over 22% in all three countries. These hard and painful facts clashed with the doctrines of both business cycle theory and the classical economic theory of the labor market. Economists recognized, of course, that the process of modern growth since the 1780's had been marked by more or less regular fluctuations in output and employment. But periods of severe unemployment, however painful, gave way in a few years at most to resumed expansion. This time unemployment proved to be chronic. The self-correcting mechanism was not working. In the classical theory of the labor market, a decline in the demand for labor should have led to a decline in money wage rates sufficient to make it profitable to employ the full labor force. What Keynes came to perceive was that, for better or worse, money wages, in a time of depressed demand, did not decline to the degree classical theory required. Wages proved sticky for two reasons: first, the unions were sufficiently powerful to frustrate the classical remedy of lowered money wages; second, democratic governments were too weak to impose large wage reductions or they judged that the cost of such a policy to the tranquillity of the society as a whole was excessive. Thus, the labor market was not cleared as classical theory suggested. If one assumed sticky money wages, chronic severe unemployment became a theoretical possibility as well as palpable reality. In addition, Keynes dramatized the effect of reduced money wages on the overall level of effective demand. One had to look elsewhere than to a radical fall in money wages to bring about full employment. Keynes perceived that the answer lay in government action that would directly increase the level of effective demand and the demand for labor at existing money-wage rates.

Keynes' insight was heightened by a momentous debate in Britain that came to a climax in 1925.[1] The question was: Should Britain go back to the gold standard at the prewar relationship between the pound and gold? Or, should the gold content of the pound be set lower, to make Britain's exports cheaper and more competitive? The psychological case for asserting continuity with the pre-1914 past was strong in many minds. It was a way of affirming that, despite the human and economic ravages of the First World War, Great Britain was determined to remain the financial and commercial center of the world economy. But, if Britain was to compete in export markets already weakened by the low prices of basic commodities of the third Kondratieff downswing and the increased economic stature of the United States and Japan, it would have to bring about considerably lower money-wage rates. Keynes argued that Britain should devalue the pound about 10% relative to its prewar level rather than confront the need to force money wages down. He lost the argument; and Churchill, then Chancellor of the Exchequer, reluctantly accepted the advice of the majority who felt that only "a moderate sacrifice" in lower wages would be required to maintain Britain's share of world trade. The mine owners duly demanded lower wages and longer hours in the coal mining industry where heavy unemployment existed. The issue built up to the general strike of 1926. The strike failed, leaving traumatic memories which still shadow British political life. But wage rates were not lowered to the extent required to reconcile Britain's balance of payments position with reduced unemployment. Down to 1931 Britain had to protect the revalued pound with high interest rates and over 10% unemployment. Its share of world markets fell from 13% to 11% between 1924 and 1929.

The story is not merely an important event in modern economic, political, and intellectual history; it also illustrates what I mean by bankruptcy. The debate over the appropriate value for the pound in 1925 did not involve the acceptance or rejection of the whole received body of international trade and monetary theory of the time. It involved a question of policy in which the key issue was the feasibility and wisdom of bringing about in British society a decline in money wages which would permit Britain to maintain or increase its share of world exports. The received body of doctrine assumed the requisite wage reduction was feasible and wise policy. It proved neither feasible nor wise. The equivalent question now is whether it is realistic and wise to assume, as the neo-Keynesians do, that the necessary scale and pattern of investment will emerge in the United States and the world economy if we simply stimulate effective demand in now-conventional ways. As the morality tale of Britain in 1925–31 illustrates, a 10% error in a matter of this kind can make the difference between a society's viability and major debilitating crisis. It is the sort of error the United States of 1977 appears in danger of making with respect to energy policy, as I will argue in Chapter 5.

Returning to Keynes, he moved on from the debates of 1925 to formulate in the 1930's a revision of the theory of employment in which the inflexibility of money wages was more or less accepted as a fact of life. The level of employment became a function of the level of effective demand which could be influenced by the fiscal and monetary policies of government. Keynes' ultimate prescription, of direct stimulus to effective demand and consumers' income, made sense for two reasons which he did not explicitly set forth. Western Europe had come to a stage in development in which the diffusion of the automobile and durable consumers goods and the expansion to the suburbs was a natural foundation for rapid growth and full employment. Indeed, that pattern of expansion was taking place in Britain and Western Europe of the 1920's, and with it the expansion of a whole range of metal-working, chemical, and electrical industries required for its support. In Britain, for example, the regions of the country caught up in these expanding sectors were quite prosperous. But their prosperity was not sufficient to draw and employ fully the labor from the older sectors dependent on the expansion of foreign trade; for example, cotton textiles, coal, and shipbuilding. The interwar problem for Western Europe was, then, that the pace of this pattern of expansion was not rapid enough to generate the high level of employment that the United States enjoyed in the 1920's, sparked by the same group of leading sectors. The momentum of such sectors depended on a rising level of consumers' income. It was, therefore, appropriate to generate at this time a theory of employment that focused on the level and rate of expansion of consumers' demand.

The second factor which made a Keynesian focus on effective demand relevant was that the period from 1920 down to the mid-1930's was, as noted in Chapter 2, one of relatively cheap food and raw materials. In Western Europe a concern for this problem (except among hard-pressed farmers on the European continent) mainly focused on the weakness of the demand for European exports from overseas agricultural- and raw material-producing areas where relatively low prices had slowed their rates of growth. After 1920 the Keynesians tended to assume that, somehow, relatively cheap food and raw materials were normal; and one could focus on the immediate problem of increasing employment without concerning oneself with where the raw materials and food would come from in the long run to support higher rates of growth. The problem was considered only in the special context of British exports: a lower exchange rate would permit Britain to export more of its products to its somewhat impoverished suppliers of cheap basic commodities.

There is, indeed, no formal place in neo-Keynesian analysis for wheat or meat or oil. One deals with the components of aggregate effective demand: private consumption, private investment, net government expenditures, and the net stimulus to effective demand derived from transactions abroad. If a Keynesian is pressed about the supply of key commodities, his response is likely to be that, so long as a high level of effective demand is sustained, the movements of relative prices will direct investment in the right directions and yield the appropriate flows of the inputs necessary to sustain an industrial society.[2]

The great boom in the OECD world of the fourth Kondratieff downswing, 1951 to 1972, took place in an environment which encouraged neo-Keynesians in the kind of thought generated in the third (1920–33). Once again the prices of food and raw materials were relatively cheap. Moreover, the diffusion of the automobile and durable consumers goods and the movement of populations to the suburbs were tasks the private sectors of industrial societies were well designed to carry out. So long as fiscal and monetary policy maintained a high enough level of effective demand, the process of growth could unfold with relatively little government intervention. All that was needed were roads, schools, hospitals, sewerage, and electric supplies for the suburbs.

There was another important dimension to the great expansion of the OECD economies during the 1950's and 1960's; that is, increased public and private outlays on education, health services, travel, and welfare. Through their political representatives, the citizens of democracies were prepared to see a significant part of the increase in their real income allocated to improve the quality and security of their own lives and to assist the less advantaged within their societies. This was also the period when the OECD world came to allocate regularly a part of its public resources to assist the less developed nations. Some, including myself, believed at the time that those allocations were less than they should have been; but in historical perspective, the emergence of foreign aid as a regular feature of the world economy was a new development. It was rooted in a creditable sense of community responsibility on an international level, as well as in hard-headed national interests within nations enjoying a hitherto unknown pace and regularity of growth in real income per capita.

As the 1960's moved towards their close, the pace of the automobile and durable consumers goods revolution was slowing down in Western Europe, as it had earlier in the United States. There was even some deceleration in Japan, whose post-1955 expansion was at a rate unique in modern economic history. The proportion of most populations enjoying such amenities was not as high as in the United States, but it was nonetheless impressive. As for the automobile, the geography of Western Europe and Japan, their higher prices for gasoline, and better developed systems of public transport made it likely that they would level off with lower automobile densities than those which had been reached in more spacious North America. The nations of Western Europe and Japan, like the United States, had also been approaching in differing degree natural limits on the allocations of public resources to education and health services. But down to the end of 1972 the advanced industrial nations could proceed in reasonable order with comfortable neo-Keynesian policies which progressively enlarged their social services as well as their material standards of living.

The sharp rise in grain prices, beginning at the end of 1972, and then the quadrupling of oil prices by OPEC, struck at the sectoral pillars of growth in the OECD world in multiple ways. The rise in energy prices caused increased consumer outlays for energy (despite some economies) and reduced outlays for other goods and services. This effect was compounded by policies of fiscal and monetary restraint. They were initially imposed because the balance of payments position of the OECD countries deteriorated rapidly as they had to pay for high-priced oil. They could buy less from each other. Sales to oil producers rose, of course, but not enough to compensate for decreased sales in other markets. Within the advanced industrial economies there was a sharp decline in outlays for houses, automobiles, and durable consumers goods, which quickly reduced investment levels. The consequent recession was intensified by increased caution both among businessmen and consumers. Overall, the OECD suffered declines in total output in 1974–75 about twice the level that can be directly attributed to the rise in oil prices.

The rate of inflation after 1972 was also greater than the rise in food and energy prices can directly explain. As the cost of living rose, labor unions sought to protect the real wages of workers by demanding large increases in money wages. It was this rise in money wages, coming on top of the explosive increase in the prices of basic commodities, which brought on the extraordinary onslaught of double-digit inflation in the OECD world in 1974–75, explored in Chapter 11. It also heightened the impulse, already strong due to inescapable balance of payments pressures, to impose policies of fiscal and monetary restraint.

The rise in the price of oil, in any case, would have reduced the real income of the OECD countries. The inflationary sequence just described, and the reaction to it, made that reduction more acute. The recession of 1974–75 was the worst setback in the world economy since the end of the Second World

War. It arose from a sequence of events which did not lend itself well to either Keynesian analysis or Keynesian prescription.

Against this background of price and real income movements, the second pillar of the great postwar boom (increased public and private outlays for certain services) was also weakened. Travel was constrained, for example, as were public outlays for education and other welfare services. As noted earlier, the latter may have been approaching a natural phase of deceleration after two decades of disproportionate expansion. But, in addition, as private real incomes stagnated or declined, a political revolt against increased public outlays at the old rate swept the OECD world. With real incomes either declining or at best increasing at slower rates than in the past, majorities in many democratic countries voted to retain the marginal amount of income rather than to pay it in taxes to continue the expansion of social services. Without the built-in income stabilizers of the past forty years—a direct product of the Keynesian Revolution—an acute world depression might well have been set in motion.

The impact of all this was not uniform within the OECD world. The hardest hit were the less industrialized countries of southern Europe from Portugal to Turkey. They had been enjoying extremely high rates of growth, aided by a remarkable international flow of labor from south to north. This flow not only relieved population pressure in some of these countries, but it earned foreign exchange as the workers remitted part of their income back home. It also upgraded a part of their labor force as the migrant workers quickly learned industrial skills in the factories of Western Europe. The slowdown in Western Europe since 1974 cut back on the demand for the products of southern Europe and for the labor they could supply. Italy, the most advanced of the southern European nations, was particularly hard hit because of its relative lack of indigenous energy resources and the fact that little excess

OPEC earnings flowed back to its capital markets. Extraordinary concerted financial aid from other members of the OECD was required to permit Italy to continue to import the energy and raw materials required to sustain its economy.

Britain also was hard hit, for somewhat different reasons. Its productivity and growth had lagged behind the rest of Europe, once immediate postwar reconstruction was completed. The reasons for this lag are complex and not fully understood. Three elements certainly contributed: an insistence by the electorate on large increases in public services; the existence of substantial idle capacity in certain older industries (for example, textiles and shipbuilding) which became progressively less competitive in world markets; and the nationalization of a number of industries within which even.large increases in public investment failed to generate increases in productivity which would have kept Britain abreast of developments on the European continent and in Japan. In a very real sense, the British electorate insisted on a quality of life which British investment patterns, productivity, and industrial structure were increasingly incapable of sustaining. Behind all this was the lack of a sufficient sense of common national purpose to overcome unresolved, deeply rooted social schisms in British society.

Germany and Japan, on the other hand, which had managed to maintain a good balance between the competitiveness of their industries and public demands for income and services, weathered the shock of the Price Revolution tolerably well. In the German case, however, its lower growth rate had a decelerating impact on southern Europe, whose workers could no longer remain employed in Germany in such large numbers. In the Japanese case, the halving of its growth rate (from an average of, say, 9% in the 1960's to 4.7% for 1974–76) similarly damped export earnings and growth among its Asian suppliers.

The French position was neither as acute as that of Britain

and Italy nor as sturdy as that of Germany and Japan. But a halving of its growth trend as compared to the 1960's, a doubling of its unemployment rate, and phases of acute and then slowly decelerating inflation produced a phase, at least, of social and political tension.

The position of the United States differed from that of Western Europe and Japan in two respects. First, the large American export surplus of food helped in 1973–74 to cushion its balance of payments in the face of increased outlays for oil. The United States also commanded large potential energy resources. Although these were little exploited down to 1977, for reasons considered in Chapter 5, parts of the United States, notably those containing agricultural and energy resources, were cushioned by the relative price movements of the first phase of the fifth Kondratieff upswing. And the continued vitality of these resource-rich regions eased, to a degree, the depressing impact elsewhere of the rise in relative prices of basic commodities—a process explored in Chapter 10. By the indifferent standards of our times, the American performance with respect to inflation was moderately restrained. The average inflation rate for the major OECD countries in 1973 was 7.4%; 1974, 13.6%; 1975, 10.2%. Comparable figures for the United States were: 5.6%, 11.4%, and 8.0%.

The OECD Secretariat has, looking back from 1977, constructed a "Discomfort Index" by adding for each year the average unemployment and inflation rates of the seven major OECD economies. Between 1959 and 1967 the index ranged between 5 and 6%. Between 1968 and 1972 it moved up into a range of 6–9%. For the years 1973 to 1976 the figures were: 10.9%, 17.1%, 16.5%, 13.4%. The prospects for 1977 were not for a great subsidence of "discomfort."

The countries of Latin America, Africa, the Middle East and Asia, which were not oil producers, were hit even harder than the major oil importers of the West and Japan. Since their growth remains extremely sensitive to their capacity to import, the rise in the oil price forced them to allocate an increased proportion of their foreign exchange to maintain energy imports. Some (for example, Mexico and Brazil) were able to sustain their growth rates tolerably well by borrowing from abroad to finance a continued flow of imports. To a degree, many were helped by expanded lending from the World Bank, the International Monetary Fund, the OPEC nations, and some of the advanced industrial countries. But funds from these official sources were insufficient to sustain the prior rate of expansion of imports; and a number of the more advanced countries within the developing world turned to private banks for assistance, building up large, precarious, short-term debts.

More seriously depressed were the very poorest of the developing nations. They included about a billion human beings mainly located in South Asia and Africa. Although some special international efforts were made to assist them, they did not have access to private lending on a large scale. Their relatively low growth rates of the 1960's gave way to virtual stagnation in income per capita.

A good many of the developing countries were affected in 1974–75 by the impact of the recession in the OECD world on their foreign exchange earnings. The impact was double: the industrialized countries bought less, and their recession led to a sharp decline in raw material prices. Meanwhile the oil price remained high; food prices fluctuated with the harvests, but in a high range; and the prices of manufactured imports were affected by the inflationary process going forward in the OECD world. With some exceptions, including a resurgence of the Indian economy, growth in the non-OPEC developing nations slowed down.

As the subsidence of the "Discomfort Index" cited above suggests, the horizon brightened somewhat for the OECD economies in 1975–76. Recovery from the pit of the 1975 recession was general and the inflation rate, while still high, declined. Recovery lost some momentum in the second half of

1976, regathered some strength in the first half of 1977, led by expansion in the United States. As 1977 proceeded, however, there were signs of another slowdown in Western Europe and Japan, while the United States, with increasing balance of payments problems, wavered uncertainly. The prospects ahead, under existing policies, were, then, distinctly mediocre. In the 1960's, the OECD nations averaged annual average growth of over 5%. Predictions down to 1985 suggest a fall to 4% at best, with Japan falling from 11% to 6%; OECD Europe from over 5% to 3–4%; North America, perhaps, returning to its previous 4–5% growth path. Predictions of this sort depend, of course, on assumptions about policies which have not yet been determined. What is clear is that the OECD revival of 1975–77 lacks the inner momentum that marked the 1950's and 1960's. The technical reason is that the rebound from the recession of 1974–75 has not been followed by a subsequent large expansion of private long-term investment. This is true not only in the United States, but also in Japan, Germany, France, Great Britain, and Italy. In the 1950's and 1960's, the strong underlying tendency for real income to expand led, during business revivals, to increased private expenditures which, in turn, induced expansion in investment to enlarge industrial plant. Now the expansion of real income is not sufficient to set that process in motion. Idle industrial capacity exists in most of the major industrial economies of the OECD world, of which the universally depressed steel industry is a dramatic symbol.

This frustration of a pattern of growth which had persisted for a quarter-century has happened because the former sectoral bases for growth (the diffusion of the automobile, etc. and the expansion of certain services) have been weakened by the passage of time and the multiple effects of high energy prices. One can, of course, conceive of some increased level of consumers' income, induced by extravagantly lowered taxes, extravagantly unbalanced government budgets, a rapid increase in the money supply that would permit automobile production and use, expanded sales of energy-intensive durable consumers goods, and a general overriding of high energy prices. But retribution would certainly come in three forms: an accelerated increase in oil imports and severe balance of payments difficulties; accelerated inflation; and currencies gravely weakened on international exchanges. We know instinctively that such an extravagant neo-Keynesian policy makes neither economic nor political sense. Therefore, the proposed remedies in the United States, Germany, and Japan —containing the three strongest economies of the OECD—are relatively modest and incapable of generating the high, stable growth rates familiar in the 1960's. Without such rapid and sustained growth in the United States, Germany and Japan, the prospects for Britain and Italy, southern Europe, and the non-OPEC developing nations are not promising.

In confronting this situation, a useful insight flows from viewing the world economy as in the early phase of the fifth Kondratieff upswing. The surest and most stable route back to full employment is through an expansion of investment in the directions required to re-establish balance in the American and the world economies. Effective demand needs to be increased directly by investments in basic resources on the supply side of the equation, not by waiting until a rise in effective demand induces investment in industries related to enlarged consumers outlays. It will be necessary to achieve in the world economy the equivalent of the opening up of the American West in the third quarter of the nineteenth century or the opening up of the resources of Canada, Argentina, Australia, and the Ukraine in the two decades before the First World War. This time, once again, an accelerated expansion of agricultural production is involved, notably in the developing regions. But the list of basic commodities requiring enlarged investment is longer than in the other four Kondratieff upswings: energy and energy conservation; pollution control;

water supply; raw materials supply and conservation; and research and development in many areas.

The detailed case for seeking a return to full employment through investments which would also restore balance in the U.S. and in the world economy as a whole is developed in detail in the chapters that follow. The simple point to be made here is that it is, as in the 1930's, again a time to change the habits of mind among economists, public servants, and politicians. It will no longer suffice to focus obsessively on the indiscriminate expansion of effective demand. It was all very well for Keynes to propose, in the midst of the depression of the 1930's, that it would be good enough to put men to work with public funds, financed by an unbalanced budget, digging holes in the ground and then refilling them. Unemployment at that time was extremely high, the supplies of food and raw materials were ample if not excessive. But the world of the 1970's and 1980's cannot afford to waste manpower in such ways. The structural problems of the world economy require that every man and woman available in the working forces of the advanced industrial economies be put to work on high-priority tasks. Nor can any nation afford to waste capital. Citizens in the OECD world will be living, for a protracted period, in an era of relatively expensive food, energy, and raw materials; paying more real resources for these basic commodities, including among them two raw materials long taken for granted as virtually inexhaustible gifts of God: air and water. If developed societies are to continue to enjoy high and rising levels of life, the social services now expected, and a continued movement toward equity, they will have to employ resources productively and efficiently.

One of Keynes' most famous observations of the 1930's is now also one of the most corrosive: "In the long run we are all dead." That observation has a technical meaning for economists. The "long period" relates in economic theory to changes on the supply side: the expansion of industrial plant and the availability of natural resources; the generation of new technologies; the expansion and training of the working force. In the 1930's one could argue that these long-period factors in the economic life of advanced industrial nations could be set aside in the pursuit of full employment. Keynes' successors translated that judgment into the view that the long-period factors would look after themselves if only the level of effective demand were high enough and sustained. They assumed the price system and private profit incentives would induce the pattern of investment necessary to assure structural balance. But the fact is that the long-period supply factors Keynes counseled us to ignore press in on us every day of our lives. It is time to say of neo-Keynesian theory what John H. Williams once wrote about the classical theory of international trade: "Classical theory assumes as fixed, for purposes of reasoning, the very things which . . . should be the chief objects of study. . . ."[3] It is the essence of the argument of this book that the appropriate adjustment of long-period factors can no longer be assumed to be automatic. Just as the Keynesian revolution was based on the empirical perception that money wages would no longer decline sufficiently in the face of a reduced demand for labor to yield prompt full employment, the changes in thought and policy which this book commends are rooted in the empirical perception that the changed patterns of investment which are now required both for full employment and structural balance will not take place without the conscious intervention of public policy. We shall have to think and act on problems of supply as sedulously as the Keynesian revolution taught us to to think and act on problems of demand.

4

Population and Food: Will Malthus at Last Be Proved Right?

T HIS chapter begins to explore a strategy which would deal simultaneously with the tasks of resuming a high and stable rate of growth and moving the world economy from its present distortions towards a dynamic equilibrium. The first and overriding problem is that of bringing, in Lyndon Johnson's phrase, "our most basic human account into balance"; that is, a balance between the demand for food and its supply.

The point of departure is the question of population, its present rate of growth and prospects. In fact, the demand for food is not a simple function of the size of the world's population. In the 1960's, for example, world population increased at an annual rate of about 2%; world food production at about 3%. This was not enough, as widespread malnutrition and increased reliance on grain imports in the developing regions attest. At low levels of income people tend to spend a high proportion of their total resources on food. In fact, as their income expands they may initially spend more on food. But as income continues to expand, the proportion spent on food declines, that on textiles, housing, and other goods and services rises. But when people achieve relatively high rates of income their diet shifts towards proteins; that is, meat, poultry, eggs, milk. Meat, especially, is extremely expensive in terms of grain. It takes, perhaps, four pounds of grain to produce a pound of beef. The demand for food is, therefore, a function of income and tastes, as well as of population. But, clearly, the rate of population increase is fundamental.

Sometime between 1970 and 1975 it is likely that the rate of increase of the world's population peaked out and fell below the 2% rate of growth of the 1960's. It remains in 1977 extremely high by historical standards; say, 1.96%. Nevertheless, the peaking out was an important event in human affairs. As Table 1 shows there was a quadrupling in the rate of world population increase in the course of the twentieth century: from about 0.5% per annum to 2.0%. That acceleration produced the astonishing curve in Chart 1. It suggests immediately the grandiose nature of man's performance since 1750 and his magnificent (or, perhaps, tragic) arrogance in programming, as it were, for a 6 billion-plus population level by the year 2000. One is led automatically to ask: how many human beings can a finite planet support? When and how will that frightening, almost vertical curve level off? And how can the extra two billion men, women, and children already programmed be fed?

Another way to look at these figures is to ask what the world's population would be in 1977 if its rate of growth had stayed roughly where it was during the nineteenth century. The answer is that there would now be roughly 2.4 billion human beings on the planet rather than more than 4 billion. There would be 2.7 billion people in the world in the year 2000 rather than the 6 billion or so now likely.

This acceleration in population growth came about because modern medical and public health techniques effected a radical decline in death rates while birth rates in Latin America,

Chart 1. Long-Range Trend of World Population Growth

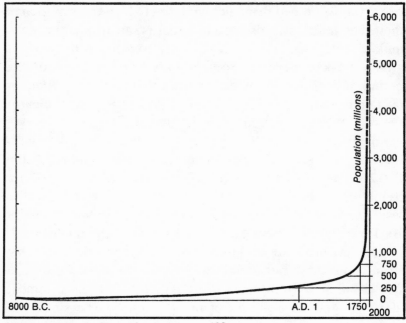

SOURCE: John D. Durand, *op. cit.*, p. 139.

Table 1. Approximate World Population
Growth Rates, 1750–1970
(*Annual percentage rate of increase*)

1750–1800	0.4%
1800–1850	0.5
1850–1900	0.5
1900–1920	0.6
1920–1930	1.1
1930–1940	1.0
1940–1950	1.0
1950–1960	1.8
1960–1970	2.0

SOURCE: John D. Durand, "The Modern Expansion of World Population," *Proceedings of the American Philosophical Society,* 1967, Vol. 3, No. 3, p. 137; and U.N. data for 1950–60, 1960–70.

Africa, the Middle East, and Asia remained high or declined more slowly. It proved easier to cut down infant mortality and reduce deaths from infectious diseases than to convince husbands and wives in the poorer parts of the world that it was in their interest to have fewer children. The death rate in India, for example, in the early 1970's was about 17 per 1,000 each year. That rate was only achieved in Britain and the United States at the turn of the twentieth century when income per capita was, perhaps, ten times that in India of the early 1970's.

The most striking aspect of the global population picture is the difference between the advanced industrial countries and the developing regions of Latin America, Africa, the Middle East and Asia. In North America, Europe, the Soviet Union, and Japan, birth rates now average about 17 per 1,000; death rates, 10 or a little less. Population continues to increase, but an end to that increase is in sight. In a few countries (East and West Germany, Luxembourg, and Austria) population increase has come to a halt. In the other advanced industrial regions population will continue to increase for some time. Because of past growth the population contains a good many more young people who will have children than would be the case had population been stable for, say, the past fifty years. The reason that we can look forward to population stagnation or decline in these advanced industrial countries is because the net reproduction rate is now at or below one.*

The historical course of population movements does not justify dogmatism about the future. There was, for example, the post-1945 baby boom which, quite unexpectedly, con-

---

* The net reproduction rate measures the number of daughters who would be born to a group of girl babies by the end of their childbearing period, assuming that current rates and patterns of fertility and mortality remain fixed. A net reproduction rate of 1 implies that in the long term population will move to stability. As of the early 1970's the net reproduction rate in most of the advanced industrial countries was at or below 1.

tinued down through the 1950's in many of the more advanced industrial societies. Birth rates may rise again; but population pressure is unlikely to be acute in these advanced industrial societies over the foreseeable future.

How did these societies come to a point where their birth rates are under 20 per 1,000 and their net reproduction rates are 1 or less? They passed through what students of population call the demographic transition. The demographic transition describes and measures the typical pattern of death rates and birth rates that accompany the modernization of a society: the rise of real income per capita, increased urbanization, access to medical facilities, expanded education, and other social as well as economic factors that bear on health and on the decisions husbands and wives make about family size. The data available on presently advanced industrial societies in the period before they entered modern economic growth are not good. It is probable, however, that in late eighteenth-century Europe birth rates may have been as high as 40 per 1,000 as they now are in some of the developing nations. By the end of the third quarter of the nineteenth century, in the more advanced parts of Western Europe, they were in the range of 30–35 per 1,000. In the early part of the twentieth century they fell below 30. In the depressed circumstances between the First and Second World Wars they went still lower, falling below 20. They surged after the Second World War, but since about 1960 they have declined again.

Meanwhile, death rates, which persisted during the nineteenth century around 20–25, began to decline rapidly in the twentieth century with the application of medical discoveries that greatly reduced the infectious diseases and infant mortality. Death rates fell below 20 toward the end of the nineteenth or early in the twentieth century; and they fell below 10 after the Second World War with the coming of antibiotics. This sequence of birth and death rates led to increasing and then decreasing rates of population growth, with constant or declining populations in sight.

The demographic pattern has a different shape in the present developing parts of the world because, as noted, it has proved possible to bring down death rates much more rapidly than in the nineteenth century; while, in most cases, birth rates tended to follow a path related to the level and pace of economic and social modernization. Chart 2, relating income per capita to birth and death rates for some 100 countries in the period 1950–70, shows the result. At relatively low levels of income the gap between birth and death rates yields population rates of increase of over 2% a year in the contemporary world. Between 1800 and 1900 the population of Europe (excluding Russia) increased at only 0.7% a year.

Chart 2. The Demographic Transition: A Cross-sectional View (1950–1970)

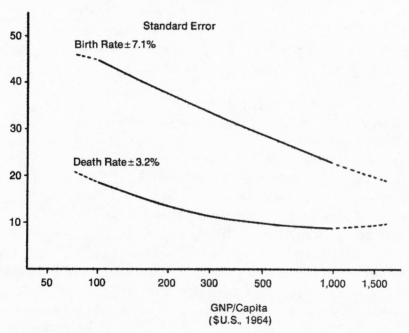

SOURCE: H. B. Chenery and M. Syrquin (assisted by Hazel Elkington), *Patterns of Development, 1950–1970,* Washington, D.C.: World Bank by Oxford University Press, 1975, p. 57.

Nevertheless, the demographic transition is now operating in the countries of Latin America, Africa, the Middle East, and Asia; that is, birth rates are beginning to decline as economic and social progress proceeds. The central question posed for the governments and peoples of those countries is whether they are willing and able to bring birth rates down more rapidly than Chart 2 would suggest. Can the gap between the curves in Chart 2 be narrowed by lowering the birth rates associated with a given real income per capita? Or, must we await the workings of economic and social progress to do the job?

Stripped of a good deal of passionate rhetoric, the issue of inducing an accelerated decline in birth rates was central to debate at the World Population Conference held in Bucharest in August 1974. By and large, representatives of the developing countries argued that the appropriate way to accelerate the decline in birth rates in their regions was to increase the pace of economic and social progress. They, therefore, used the occasion to demand increased development assistance and other economic concessions from the more advanced industrial countries.

In making their case, representatives of the developing nations had a good deal of historical and contemporary evidence on their side. Population experts argue about what particular factors, associated with social and economic progress, yield the decline in birth rates to be observed as income in per capita increases. When people decide to have fewer children, none of us is quite sure whether it is because it becomes clear that infant mortality is declining and more children will survive in a family of a given size; or because a child in the city can contribute less to a family's income than a child on the farm; or because educated parents understand better than uneducated the case for smaller families. Experts are not sure precisely which elements in economic and social progress, or what combination of elements, cause declining birth rates. But the broad association is well established.

The spokesmen of the more developed nations at Bucharest did not, of course, deny the connection between declining birth rates and the pace of economic and social progress. What they argued, in effect, was for purposeful public policies in the developing world that would bring the birth rate down more rapidly than if governments merely relied on the powerful but somewhat obscure dynamics of social and economic progress. In some cases one could even argue that economic and social progress itself might be indefinitely frustrated unless such special efforts to reduce the birth rate were made. But, even where increases in income per capita could be envisaged despite rapid rates of population increase, representatives of the developed countries could argue that, so long as very high rates of population growth persisted, there would be heavy unemployment and partial unemployment, extremely uneven income distribution, and that high proportions of the population would live with inadequate diets, education, housing, and health services.

There were other views than these presented at the Bucharest meeting. Some countries argued that, in their circumstances, rapid rates of population increase were necessary and that adequate agricultural resources existed to feed the added millions; for example, Argentina. The Soviet Union took the orthodox Marxist view that there was no population problem, only the problem of the iniquities of capitalism. In the end, the degree of agreement at Bucharest was limited, obscurely formulated, but real. The agreed Plan of Action called for family-planning policies which would take "into account universal solidarity in order to improve the quality of life of the peoples of the world." On the other hand, national sovereignty with respect to population policy was strongly reasserted. The hopeful fact is that an increasing number of sovereign nations in Latin America, Africa, the Middle East, and Asia have, indeed, decided that their national interests demand a positive effort to bring down birth rates more rapidly than Chart 2 suggests was typical of the period 1950–70.

The number of developing countries with family planning programs increased from four in 1960 to fifty-three in 1974. The proportion of developing nations with such programs is lowest in Africa (19%), around 50% in Latin America and Asia. Among these, there have been significant success stories. Costa Rica, for example, brought its birth rate down from 50 to 34 in the decade 1960–70; El Salvador from 50 to 40. In Asia, the South Korean birth rate declined from 43 in 1960 to 29 in 1971. On Taiwan the decline was from 39 to 28, in Singapore from 39 to 23, and in Hong Kong from 36 to 19. The latter two striking cases occurred, of course, among urban populations enjoying particularly rapid improvements in economic and social welfare.

Most important of all, both China and India, the two most populous nations in the world, are now seriously committed to programs of family planning; and they are making some progress. The birth rate of India may have fallen from 39 in 1972 to under 35 in 1977. Experts disagree about the results in China of the effort to reduce birth rates. Some would argue that the results have been modest, and that average birth rates are at about the same level as India. They have on their side the casual remark of a Chinese official that, in the early 1970's, the Chinese population was still increasing at about 2% per year. At the other extreme there are experts who believe the Chinese birth rate may now have been reduced to as low as 19 per 1,000, not significantly higher than in Japan, Europe, and North America. There are others whose views fall in between. The reason for this unresolved debate is, simply, that the Chinese have not published any recent official overall estimates of birth and death rates; and, it is possible, that, lacking a recent census, the authorities in Peking do not themselves know the exact state of affairs. What is clear is that after vacillating on this matter for the first twenty years or so of Communist rule, the Chinese government launched a sustained and sophisticated program to bring down birth rates.

The program includes political and social pressure to induce late marriages; the availability of medical services, including abortion, in the villages as well as in the cities; the widespread availability of all manner of modern birth control devices; and programs of public education designed to underline the private as well as the public advantages of smaller families.

In sum, nations in the contemporary developing world have demonstrated that it is possible to bring down birth rates at something like 1 per 1,000 per annum. Those countries with birth rates of 40 per 1,000 could be under 20 within twenty years. The capacity of governments to achieve, in fact, some such rates of decline in birth rates, assuming their wish to do so, is by no means uniform. For example, the requisite administrative effort may be beyond the resources of some of the smaller African nations. The degree of cultural and social resistance in the various nations appears to vary in ways we do not wholly understand. Mexico, for example, has had a birth rate over 40, South Korea, under 30, although in 1971 Mexico's average income per capita was twice as great.

The point to be made here, however, is that the first of the great tasks of the next quarter-century cited in Chapter 1 appears to be not beyond the demonstrated capacity of peoples and governments; namely, to bring average birth rates in the developing continents under 20 per 1,000 by the close of the present century.

This task, more than any other, falls squarely on the shoulders of the leaders of the developing countries. Only they can effectively make the case for smaller families to their peoples; only they can organize the human and economic arguments, the administrative arrangements, and the resources which must reach the men and women in the villages as well as in the cities. Nevertheless, the advanced industrial world can help. It can help with policies of aid and trade which would permit local peoples and governments to generate the environment of economic and social progress which makes easier the bringing about of an accelerated decline of birth rates. Scientists in the industrialized world, along with those in the developing countries, could help by creating methods of birth control which are cheaper, longer lasting, and psychologically easier to accept.

An accelerated decline of birth rates could significantly ease the problem of food supply in the next quarter-century. The margin of easement may be between the need to feed a global population of 6.5 billion in the year 2000 rather than, say, 5.8 billion. That margin of about 10% could make a good deal of difference in terms of human hunger and the extent of malnutrition. Moreover, an effective effort in the next quarter-century to bring down the birth rate will enormously ease the task of economic and social progress in the following half-century. If population increased at 2% from the year 2000 to 2050, from a base of 6.5 billion, it would be over 17 billion at midcentury. A 1% rate of increase on a base of 5.8 billion would yield less than 10 billion. The difference is over 80%. Thus, if a rapid movement to affluence in the developing world is going to occur during the next century, it is essential that birth rates within the developing continents be brought down in the next quarter-century at something like the pace of 1 per 1,000 per year. This does not seem to be an impossible task.

The next question, however, is whether the world commands the capacity to feed an extra 2 billion human beings over the next quarter-century, and to do so under circumstances where perhaps 90% of the increase will take place in Latin America, Africa, the Middle East, and Asia. All four of these regions now run food deficits. There is no realistic possibility that North America, Australia, and Argentina could produce and transport the surplus food necessary to feed an extra 2 billion people. Therefore, the question is whether a doubling of agricultural output in the developing regions can be brought about by the year 2000.

Taking Latin America, Africa, the Middle East, and Asia as a whole, and looking at their collective performance in agriculture during the 1960's, the answer appears affirmative. This relative optimism stems from the fact that in the 1960's these regions almost—but not quite—maintained a rate of increase of production that matched the rate of increase of consumption. Production increased at an annual average rate of 3.5%, consumption at 3.7%. That apparently small gap between production and consumption was extremely significant; for during the 1960's all the developing regions became dependent on grain imports. Their production could not quite keep up with the effective demand for food. Nevertheless, the fact that the developing countries, taken as a whole, came so close to meeting their own food requirements in the 1960's has led most agricultural experts to conclude that, with enough effort, they could achieve self-sufficiency in the generation ahead. The relative optimism of the experts is strengthened by two facts: there is at least twice as much land physically available for crop production in the developing countries than is now being used; and these regions have not fully applied the technologies of food production which have already proved to be effective in Western Europe and Japan. A 4% annual rate of increase in agricultural production ought not to be beyond their grasp. That rate would provide not merely self-sufficiency but improved nutrition.

The task looks somewhat less easy if we abandon these gross calculations and look at some of the economic constraints which must be overcome and at the situation in particular regions within the developing world.

The expansion of agricultural production in the developing countries will have to depend, in the foreseeable future, on heavily increased application of chemical fertilizers. The price of chemical fertilizers has been radically increased due to the quadrupling of the oil price. In addition, the developing countries have been forced to reduce their imports, due to the increased cost of importing oil. The 1974–75 recession in the OECD world and then the disappointing recovery of 1975–77 have also reduced the foreign exchange available for the import of chemical fertilizers and chemical fertilizer plants. Thus, at precisely the time when the application of chemical fertilizers ought to be expanded in the developing countries, the capacity of those countries to produce them or acquire them from abroad has been made more difficult.

Aside from the foreign exchange problems that must be overcome to achieve an average 4% annual growth rate for agricultural production in the developing world, there are considerable differences among particular developing countries with respect to their resources and prospects. Some food-deficit countries in the developing world can, for example, afford to buy the food they need from abroad, e.g., the OPEC countries, Taiwan, South Korea, China. Other food-deficit countries produced surpluses until recently and command the potential, at least, to regain a surplus position; for example, Burma, Thailand, Brazil. Still others contain large unused reserves of arable land which could quite easily provide them with sufficient food to produce or eliminate imports; for example, some of the Latin American countries. On the other hand, there are nations where a maximum domestic effort will have to be supplemented with substantial external assistance to produce the acceleration in food production that is necessary; for example, some of the countries of South Asia and Africa.

There is, fortunately, a rough but useful international consensus on the correct policy for the time ahead. At the meeting in Rome in November 1974 it was agreed that, in addition to generating international food reserves and facing the problem of diet deficiency in many parts of the world, the developing regions should seek agricultural self-sufficiency.

The degree of tension between the rate of population increase and the world's food supply is the most continuous strand running through the Kondratieff cycles of the past two centuries. A heightening of that tension is clearly one major feature of the fifth Kondratieff upswing, despite the ease-ment brought about by the generally good harvests of 1976 and 1977. But there are several aspects of the contemporary situa-tion which distinguish it from some of the Kondratieff up-swings of the past. First, this is not a period in history where it is possible to open up vast new continents containing large, hitherto unexploited agricultural regions. There is, as noted, still arable land to be brought into production; but there is no new American West, Canada, Australia, or Argentina to be tapped. What is required is an enlarged flow of investment within the developing countries allocated to expand acreage, where that is possible, and to increase productivity. Second, to a degree, the political and even the moral character of the problem of food supply has somewhat altered. In the past generation, the hunger of people who cannot afford to trans-late that hunger into effective demand for food has become a concern sufficiently strong to force governments in the devel-oped world to supply food on concessional terms or as a gift. Such concern is not wholly new. For example, when Britain, during the first Kondratieff upswing, experienced high food prices and the poor faced hunger or worse, the Speenhamland System was created (1795), whereby the poorest workers were guaranteed a minimum wage geared to the price of bread. In the first half of the twentieth century there were charitable responses by individuals and private groups, often through churches, in the face of hunger abroad. After the First and Second World Wars the American government responded generously to the needs of Europe, including the response to the Russian famine which occurred after the Revolution and Civil War. In the third quarter of this century, governments assumed a degree of systematic responsibility for the provi-sion of food supplies to the impoverished hungry. There is a rough communal agreement in a still highly nationalistic and contentious world that the distribution of food cannot be left wholly to the market process. This means that, by one method or another, global reserves and a financial mechanism must be available to provide for occasions of shortage or famine in countries that do not command the resources to buy what they need to avoid mass hunger.

It may be useful to summarize now the policy implications of this brief portrait of population–food prospects over the coming quarter-century when the pressures on the world's food supply may be more acute than at any time over the past two centuries. The question is: What must be done to bring "our most basic human account into balance," and to keep it in balance?

1. Reduction of Birth Rates in the Developing World below 20 per 1,000 by the Year 2000

a) What is required here is, above all, a much expanded investment of political and administrative capital in family planning, accompanied by efforts to create a sustained environment of rapid economic and social progress in the villages as well as the cities. Potentially, the concurrent need for increased agricultural production and productivity converges with the task of bringing down birth rates. The modernization of rural life would serve both vital purposes. Responsibility in family planning obviously rests with the governments and peoples of Latin America, Africa, the Middle East, and Asia.

b) The developed nations can, however, contribute by helping to generate improved birth control technology as well as through policies of aid and trade which contribute to an environment of progress, especially progress in rural areas.

2. Expansion of Agricultural Production in the Developing World at, Say, 4% Per Annum

a) Again, the primary responsibility falls on the governments and peoples of the developing world to expand the flow of investment to agriculture. Investment is required to open new arable land; for irrigation; to bring to bear available technologies relevant to the soil and climate of each region; to expand production of fertilizers and pesticides; to expand local extension services and research facilities.

b) Equally important, and often more difficult, the governments in developing countries need to set price and credit policies and bring about land tenure arrangements which maximize the farmers' incentives to increase output. Here a dilemma exists not unlike that confronted over energy prices in the United States: the need for strong incentives for the producer set against the desire of the consumer for low prices.

c) A larger flow of development assistance from abroad needs to be targeted to expand agricultural production and productivity. In this effort, the OPEC countries, as a matter of equity, should cooperate, given the effects of high oil prices on the capacity of developing countries to expand agricultural production.

d) The developed countries, OPEC, and the developing countries should work together to break the critical bottleneck in chemical fertilizer production and availabilities. The developed countries and OPEC can help with enlarged capital flows; OPEC could help either by offering special lowered prices to developing countries for oil or by special forms of aid for this purpose, to offset the effects of high oil prices; the developing countries could help both by formulating stable policies which would encourage private firms to build fertilizer plants and by devising policies which, without excessive subsidy, make it attractive for farmers to increase chemical fertilizer applications.

e) Some of the most severe forms of environmental degradation have occurred and are continuing in the developing regions in forms which threaten their capacity to produce food: rapid deforestation not only is reducing timber and fire-wood supplies but is also accentuating flooding and erosion problems; the abuse of land, notably by overgrazing, is extending the deserts in northwest India and the Middle East, as well as in several parts of Africa; the same forces are rapidly degrading three major mountain zones and their adjacent lowlands (the Himalayas, the Andes, and the East Africa highlands); inadequate drainage is reducing the productivity of some of the major areas of irrigated land through water-logging and salinity and by the accelerated silting of reservoirs and canals. Large investments are required to halt and reverse these trends. They are unlikely to be undertaken except in a context where developing countries (often in cooperation with one another) have focused sharply on the tasks of agriculture and are being strongly supported by the international community.

3. *Establishment of Buffer Grain Stocks and Stable Food Aid Policies*

Buffer stocks of food and feed grains are needed for two purposes: to avoid excessive price fluctuations and shortages in the international grain trade and, at times, to feed people in nations too poor to finance a large increase in imports. The world of the 1970's and beyond cannot return to the situation of the 1950's and 1960's when American policy and resources generated, almost alone, the requisite surpluses and transferred them in the form of aid in bad years. The task is one which should now be shared among the advanced industrial nations. A good many alternatives can be envisaged. Perhaps the most thoughtful proposal (formulated by Philip Trezise of the Brookings Institution) would provide for an initial reserve of 60 million tons, rising with the increase in world consumption; about one-third would be earmarked as a famine reserve; reserve stocks would be nationally owned, but financed on an agreed burden-sharing basis by all the advanced industrial countries; in times of shortage or famine, stocks would be allocated by internationally agreed guidelines.[1] A 60-million-ton reserve would cost about $6 billion (U.S. $ 1975) and impose annual carrying charges of about 10% of that amount. Proceeds from sales might cover all (or more) of these costs, since sales are likely to occur at periods of bad harvests and high prices. The U.S. share of the financial burden would be about 30%, assuming that the Soviet Union and Eastern Europe participated. By way of comparison, the U.S. share of food aid had fallen from 94% in 1965 to 48% in 1974.

4. Maintenance of the U.S. Agricultural Surplus

The U.S. agricultural surplus is a major national and world asset. It helps cushion the balance of payments at a time of rising and expensive oil imports. The U.S. contributes 60–70% of net grain exports to the world, almost 80% of soybean exports. To maintain that surplus position, however, the U.S. will require enlarged investment in three directions.

a) Conservation of Water. A substantial part of the U.S. agricultural surplus is generated from irrigated land now dependent on declining pools of underground water. Large investments over a long period of time will be required to conserve ground water, now in surplus, and to transfer it to areas where irrigation is required to maintain the productivity of the land.

b) Land Rehabilitation and Preservation. Between 1967 and 1972 U.S. wheat acreage production was cut back from 59 to 48 million acres; coarse grain acreage, from 103 to 96 million acres. The total area subsidized to remain idle in 1972 was 60 million acres. When acreage restraints were lifted in 1973–74, it was discovered that a good deal of land, counted as reserve acreage, could not be profitably cultivated even at the then prevailing high prices. At the same time, the spread of the cities and road-building are taking out of agricultural production substantial amounts of arable land each year. The maintenance of the base of arable land in the United States will require both the nurturing of reserve land (for example, against erosion) and more discriminating policies of land use.

c) *Research and Development*. The rate of increase in the number of persons supplied per farm worker in the United States and in the number of persons supported per harvested acre is levelling off. These are rough indicators that the extraordinary revolution in agricultural productivity experienced since about 1950 in the United States and other advanced industrialized nations is decelerating. With the passage of time this is a normal pattern of evolution for any particular technology or related group of technologies. It means, however, that the maintenance of the previous rate of increase in productivity will require the generation of new agricultural technologies. This need comes at a time when a certain complacency about the American agricultural surplus led in the 1960's and early 1970's to a lessening in outlays for research and development. Basic research will be of particular importance, since the next round of productivity increases may flow, in part, from new scientific concepts in chemistry and genetics. As late as 1973 the National Science Board failed to include food production among twenty-one national problems warranting enlarged research and development outlays. As of 1977 it is clear that omission represented a misjudgment, now corrected, to a degree, by enlarged federal R&D allocations to agriculture.

5. *Future Agricultural Technologies: A Global Perspective*

The need to assure a new scientific and technological base for the continued momentum of American agricultural productivity is, of course, not a problem unique to this country. That requirement is shared among all the advanced industrial societies which have, in different degree, participated in the technical revolution which permitted yields in grain production, for example, to increase at an annual rate of 2.8% in the 1960's. For developing countries, the equivalent rate was 1.9%. As indicated above, the developing regions have the advantage over the next generation of a large backlog of available technologies still to apply. But, as in the case of new technologies for energy production, the lags involved in converting new scientific insights into technically and economically efficient methods of production can be long. The rate of productivity increase after the year 2000 will depend on the creative research and development undertaken between now and then. The appropriate pattern for such research is not identical with that for the presently industrialized countries. Indeed, there are unique problems associated with the soils and climate of each of the developing continents and, often, for regions within them. It is, therefore, a wholesome fact that eight major international institutes for research in agriculture are now at work within the developing continents sponsored by the World Bank, the United Nations, and the World Food and Agriculture Organization. The array of possibilities for the future now being actively explored is long and theoretically promising: the fixation of nitrogen from the air, a capacity commanded by a few plants which, if diffused, would not only economize on energy-intensive nitrogen but also reduce polluting chemical run-off; the crossing of widely different grains; new strategies for pest control; more efficient methods of water and fertilizer use; improved grain quality; treatment of plant substances (e.g., cotton seed meal) for human consumption; improvement of livestock quality, fertility, and disease resistance, etc.

*   *   *

The tension between population growth and the food supply is one of the oldest and most continuous strands in human history. It played an important and often decisive role in the

cyclical pattern which marked the experience of all civiliza-
tions down to the coming of the industrial revolution at the
end of the eighteenth century. Since then that tension has
assumed the form of the recurrent, less cataclysmic Kondratieff cycles reviewed in Chapter 2. On four occasions over the
past two centuries man's technological ingenuity, combined
with the availability of additional land, permitted periods of
high food prices to be overcome before they spiralled into uncontrollable famine, disease, and population decline. The
array of tasks outlined here is more complex than, say, opening the American West with railway lines and encouraging the
migration necessary for those rich acres to be put to work. But
the purpose of the new agricultural agenda is, essentially, the
same; and, as in the four previous Kondratieff upswings, additional capital will have to be generated from consumption or
diverted from other tasks if the job is to be done effectively.

5

Energy: A Test of the Democratic Process

T HE most dramatic feature of the early phase of the fifth Kondratieff upswing was, of course, the quadrupling of the price of oil by OPEC in the autumn of 1973. This brought about a general and sharp relative rise in all energy prices. As noted earlier, that rise was a major cause of the deceleration in the rate of growth and higher levels of unemployment in the OECD world since 1974; and it slowed down the rate of economic and social progress in those developing countries which must import oil. Because energy is a major factor in agricultural production, it has, as noted in Chapter 4, complicated the task of bringing about the accelerated increase in agricultural production required to feed the world's expanding population.

The action of OPEC in 1973–74 was profoundly unsettling for two reasons, quite aside from its narrow economic consequences. First, its suddenness produced a traumatic shock and disrupted all manner of relationships within and between economies. Its effects would have been less severe if the rise had taken place gradually over, say, a five-year period. Second, the event was connected with efforts of the Arab members of OPEC to use their control over supply for political purposes. Thus, the response of importers reflected strategic as well as narrowly economic concerns. Nevertheless, there is a fundamental economic sense in which the price rise was justified. The price of delivered OPEC oil approximates the marginal cost of producing and delivering oil from new major fields, such as those in Alaska and the North Sea. The current price of imported oil is lower than the present marginal cost of certain hydrocarbons on which OECD energy supplies will increasingly depend in the generation ahead; e.g., recovery of tertiary oil reserves, shale, coal gasification, etc. There is some truth in the statements of OPEC spokesmen that they merely forced the world community to face up to the realities of the energy situation, including the reality that OPEC production capacity will begin to decline from, say, the mid-1980's. This outcome is likely to result from a convergence of two situations: a decline in actual reserves in a number of OPEC countries; and an understandable reluctance of Saudi Arabia radically to expand its production capacity to meet world requirements, at the cost of economic development in other directions and of an accelerated running down of its still large but not infinite reserves. Saudi Arabia contains the only truly large reserves within OPEC.

Dr. Samuel Johnson once observed: "Depend upon it, Sir, when a man knows he is to be hanged in a fortnight, it concentrates his mind wonderfully." The quadrupling of international oil prices in 1973 certainly had the effect of concentrating the minds of public servants, energy experts, and economists. The result was a mountainous literature of analysis and prescription. Down to early 1977 the amount of purposeful action that was taken by governments to deal with the energy crisis, while not negligible, failed to match the scale of the problem. This happened because the actual "hanging" proved a bit less imminent than some at first thought. The continued availability of OPEC oil, even at high prices, permitted time for analysis and debate, while governments felt their way towards new dispositions, in an awkward environment of stagflation, foreign exchange constraint, and understandable public resistance to changing patterns of behavior built up in a long period of relatively cheap energy. Meanwhile, the relative rise in the price of energy gave governments an opportunity to observe the extent to which the price system would, by itself, bring about restraints on private consumption, increased economy in commercial and industrial use, and efforts to expand production.

In the United States a series of energy proposals was laid before the Congress between 1974 and 1977; and some measures were enacted: e.g., enlarged resources for energy research and development; the creation of a strategic oil reserve; a mandated limitation on gasoline consumption in automobiles. But, reflecting popular sentiment in a democracy whose voters were overwhelmingly energy consumers, no decisive action was taken either to constrain consumption or to expand energy output. Either course would have required acceptance of higher energy prices in the United States, where price controls still shielded the consumer to a degree from the full impact of the OPEC price increase.

At the time of the oil embargo of 1973–74 the problem had seemed quite clear, and strong political reasons existed in the United States for a purposeful energy policy. The producers had raised the price in an arbitrary and massive way; and some of them were trying to use their control of the flow of oil for diplomatic purposes. The United States was being denied access to a critical margin of a vital raw material. The denial struck at the life of every citizen. Clearly, vigorous action to end such a dangerous dependence was called for. But no such thing happened. When the embargo ended, the nature of the energy problem became more obscure; and, for a time, the political will to face it weakened. Lacking clear and strong leadership from Washington, it was difficult for the public to understand the complex character of the problem. Congress looked for scapegoats and sought to perpetuate by fiat the prices and the life-style to which the nation had become accustomed. The hopes and assumptions underlying projections of U.S. energy production made in 1974 were belied by American performance in the next three years: oil and gas production continued to decline, inhibited by artificially constrained prices; the erection of nuclear power plants was retarded by environmental and other pressures; coal production expanded less rapidly than expected, as the still relatively low prices of gas and oil, plus environmental rules, slowed the conversion of utilities to coal in most parts of the country.

There are, in fact, three energy problems, all real, all serious.

First, and most immediate, is the question of how the OECD world can live successfully over, say, the next decade when there is no realistic alternative to heavy and perhaps increasing reliance on OPEC oil.

Second is the problem of energy supply over, say, the next quarter-century, when the world economy will still primarily have to rely on oil and gas, substantially supplemented by coal and atomic power, further enlarged at the margin by shale, solar energy, geothermal, and other available but hitherto unexploited energy sources.

Third is the most fundamental energy problem; namely, that on a global basis the era of energy derived from hydrocarbons is drawing towards a close. As noted, one major aspect of this process should become apparent in the 1980's and be all too clear by the early part of the next century; namely, that the world supply of oil and gas will run down, just as it has in the United States, even in the Middle East where the largest reserves exist. Reserves of coal in certain parts of the world, including the United States, will last much longer; but for the world as a whole, the era in which hydrocarbons were the energy base for an industrial civilization appears to be ending. Coal had emerged to free industrial societies of dependence on wood, as the timber supply diminished in Britain and its price rose in the eighteenth century. Oil, gas, and hydro-electric power emerged in the last quarter of the nineteenth century as the pace of industrialization threatened to deplete coal supplies from rich and accessible seams.

The human race faces in the generation ahead, therefore, the greatest challenge it has confronted since modern industrialization began in the late eighteenth century: the challenge of creating a new, hopefully infinite and nonpolluting source of energy. The challenge is unprecedented because, as nearly as now can be perceived, the tasks of overcoming the inherent diffusion and difficulties in storing solar energy and rendering fusion power viable are formidable. On the other hand, the nature of the physical world—notably, the fact that energy can be derived from the sun and from matter—means that there is no significant limit to the supply of energy available to man. What we confront, rather, is a pure challenge to man's scientific and technical prowess.

There is what might be called an intermediate option to the creation of effective fusion or solar power—the breeder reactor. The breeder reactor produces more fuel than it consumes by exploiting more than half the potential energy stored in uranium. In theory, it constitutes an answer to the waning of both hydrocarbon and uranium deposits. As with conventional atomic power plants, the breeder poses environmental and other problems considered in Chapter 7. Of the various possible designs, the liquid-metal fast-breeder reactor (LMFBR) is in the most advanced stage of development in the United States. For some years it has absorbed a high proportion of energy research and development funds. It is still uncertain whether or when the LMFBR will prove economically cost-effective. In 1976, the Federal Energy Administration accorded to fusion and solar energy a priority equal to that which the LMFBR had hitherto enjoyed. In 1977, President Carter reduced the funds allocated to this option and postponed the building of a commercial plant. Britain, France, Germany, Japan, and the Soviet Union are, however, proceeding with the commercial development of LMFBR breeder reactors.

Whether the present design of the LMFBR is the correct one to initiate commercial production of the breeder reactor is arguable. But it appears certain that breeder reactors will be—and, in my judgment, should be—developed as rapidly as possible. The fact that they generate uranium, which can be refined to weapons-grade material, will, of course, demand great vigilance. But the notion that the proliferation of nuclear weapons can be avoided by not exploiting breeder technology misconstrues the nature of the nonproliferation problem. That problem is primarily political. A substantial and increasing number of nations are capable of producing nuclear weapons without the aid of breeder reactors. There are strong reasons for them to forego developing such capabilities if their security and status on the world scene can be reasonably assured by other means. The reliability of the United States as a stable ally and friend is, in fact, the key factor which will determine the outcome. A technocratic approach to nonproliferation can be quite misleading and, even, illusory.

Although these three energy problems concern different time periods, they all require purposeful current action if they are to be solved. This is so because time lags of differing lengths decree that all must be pursued with urgency if the nation's energy books are to be balanced without excessive imports or the disruption of the national and the world economy.

Obviously, the problems and policies flowing from the oil importers' painful dependence upon OPEC are now part of daily life in the United States. They include measures to reduce private consumption and increase the efficiency of energy use in industry. The fact that Sweden, West Germany, and Switzerland enjoy levels of real income similar to that in the United States with about two-thirds of our per capita energy consumption is commonly taken as prima facie evidence that great savings are possible without degrading the American standard of living. A sophisticated analysis of comparative energy utilization in North America and Western Europe has roughly isolated the reasons for the difference.[1] According to this study, 28% of the difference is due to relatively higher volume and energy consumption per mile of motor vehicle transport; 6% to the volume of freight transport; 8% to the greater prevalence in the United States of single-family dwellings and the higher temperatures maintained within them; 20% to the intensity of energy use in industry; 38% unallocated. Relatively lower prices for energy in the United States have evidently affected the intensity of energy use in cars, households, and industry; but geography is also important. Both passenger and commercial traffic must transit greater distances than in Western Europe and Japan. In addition, the substantial role of energy-based industries (e.g., petrochemicals) in the American economy plays a part in determining the differential.

The broad conclusion to be drawn from this and similar analyses is that high per capita American energy consumption is not the product of some unique and mindless profligacy but a more or less rational response to relative energy prices, income levels, resource endowments, and geography. On the other hand, the case for energy economy and conservation, given that energy prices will be relatively higher than in the past, is strong. Housing insulation is a familiar example. The substitution of public for private automobile transport will require large capital outlays and take time, as will the now mandated transition to automobiles which consume less gas per mile. The spacious physical layout of parts of the country much less densely populated than Western Europe, reduces somewhat the possibility of achieving similar levels of per capita miles driven in private transport. Much the same is true of Canada, where per capita energy consumption is slightly higher than in the United States. On the other hand, there are large possibilities for energy saving in major industries through the further diffusion of proven technologies already in use; e.g., in the steel, aluminum, and paper industries. Substantial new investment and time will be required to bring about the full use of existing energy-saving technologies and to generate new technologies. As with measures to increase energy production, policies of energy conservation and economy will not produce instantaneous results; and, by themselves, they will not solve the American energy problem. The reality of heavy dependence on OPEC will remain, and, as is argued later in this chapter, the degree of the American dependence on oil imports may well determine the fate of all the OECD economies in the 1980's.

The problems of the period, say, 1985–2000 also require action now because still longer lead times are involved. This is true even for the development of the most familiar sources of energy. The minimum–maximum lead times between the decision to invest and the start of production range as follows in the United States for various energy sources: new on-shore oil and natural gas fields, 1–4 years; existing off-shore fields (mainly in the Gulf of Mexico), 3–7 years; frontier off-shore fields (Alaska, Pacific, Atlantic), 6–13 years; synthetic plants, 5–10 years; nuclear and hydroelectric power plants, 9–13 years; other power plants, 7–9 years; new coal mines, 4–10 years.

Given these lead times and the high stakes involved for the whole OECD world in constraining the level of U.S. oil imports, the virtual wastage of the four years 1974–77 has been extremely costly. In particular, it is important to learn how to generate commercial energy efficiently from the underground conversion of coal to gas, as well as from shale, tar sands, and synthetics based on coal. The United States still contains enormous hydrocarbon reserves in the form of coal and shale. There is a good deal of research and new technology required to translate these possibilities into efficient cost-effective reality. They will probably require some form of public subsidy to bring them initially into commercial production. But if past experience with innovation proves a relevant guide, one can expect significant reductions in cost as large-scale production experience is required.

It will also take time to transform the real but limited possibilities of solar energy, with present technology, into a large, efficient industry, with mass production of the hardware and methods for solving the problem of financing and quality control. Solar energy is now commercially competitive for generating hot water and heating houses in many parts of the United States. Its diffusion is moving slowly, however, because no large American industry has exhibited the initiative required to organize the production and diffusion of solar energy units on a mass basis. The automobile industry, facing the prospect of producing smaller cars, is a good candidate, given its national distribution network and experience in financing the sale of products on a credit basis. Meanwhile, the pace of research and development in solar energy is accelerating and the prospects are reasonably good for the emergence of units capable of cooling as well as heating homes and perhaps (via the photovoltaic cell) for providing some part of the electric supply.

As noted above, three major candidates to solve the long-term energy problem are the breeder reactor, fusion power, and the concentration of solar energy in ways we do not now know how to accomplish. By most estimates, the development of efficient fusion power will require at least another quarter-century's concentrated effort in research and development. The lead time may be at least that long in the field of solar energy, assuming that breakthroughs in concentration and storage occur. Given its more advanced stage of development, it is likely, but by no means certain, that an efficient breeder reactor will be available by the end of the century.

To move forward simultaneously on each of the three energy problems is a many-sided undertaking. The energy problem does not lend itself to concentrated crash programs like the Manhattan Project or Project Apollo. It is inherently more complex and more intimately woven into the fabric of economic life than making an atomic bomb or putting men on the moon and bringing them back. But one enterprise may justify such a special effort: the creation of a motor vehicle powered by an abundant energy source other than petroleum. A more efficient electric battery is an evident possibility, as is a hydrogen-powered car. Given the role of motor vehicle demand in determining oil requirements, success in this venture could significantly ease the tension in the world economy that the peaking out of OPEC's production capacity may create and buy precious time for new energy resources and technologies to be developed.

The preceding observations might be described as something like the conventional wisdom among energy analysts as of Monday, April 18, 1977, when President Carter began the exposition of his National Energy Plan (NEP). In the previous month, the energy experts of the OECD published a study of that group's energy prospects for 1985. The study was more markedly pessimistic than one made in 1974. Despite lower assumptions for the OECD growth rate down to 1985 (4.2% per annum versus 4.9% in 1974), OECD oil imports were expected to be 72% higher in 1985 than was earlier estimated. This judgment flowed primarily from the fact that OECD production for 1985 was estimated much lower in every category than it had been in 1974: 32% lower for oil; 16% for coal; 24% for natural gas; 38% for nuclear energy. In addition, as nearly as it can be separated from the effects of the 1974–75 recession, the rise in energy prices slowed the expansion of energy consumption less than had been hoped. Given its large potential energy reserves and its high per capita energy consumption, the United States, with its poor energy performance between 1974 and 1977, was substantially responsible for the failure of the OECD energy projections of 1974 to come true. The 1976 OECD projections evidently counted greatly on the success of the new American administration in at last fashioning with the Congress an effective program both to constrain consumption and sharply expand U.S. energy production.

The public image of President Carter's plan was shaped by the manner and emphasis of its presentation. That image emerged in the goals incorporated in the draft legislation submitted by the Executive Branch to the Congress:

> The Congress hereby establishes the following national energy goals for 1985:
> (1) Reduction of annual growth of United States energy demand to less than 2 percent.
> (2) Reduction of the level of oil imports to less than 6 million barrels per day.
> (3) Achievement of a 10 percent reduction in gasoline consumption from the 1977 level.
> (4) Insulation of 90 percent of all American homes and all new buildings.
> (5) An increase in annual coal production to at least 400 million tons over 1976 production.
> (6) Use of solar energy in more than two and a half million homes.

In political terms, the emphasis was on slowing the rate of increase in energy use. As the official *Fact Sheet*, issued on April 20, stated: "The cornerstone of our policy is to reduce demand through conservation." The proposal explicitly set aside an all-out U.S. energy-production effort.

For those familiar with energy data, however, it was evident from the beginning that a mighty, unprecedented increase in production must be part of the plan. Only such an effort could reconcile the modestly reduced rate of increase in consumption with the reduction of oil imports. But it was not until a pamphlet of 103 pages was issued nine days later—and until page 96, where a statistical balance sheet was presented, was read—that the production assumptions of the plan could, in fact, be understood.

Table 2 sets out the balance sheet of the National Energy Plan (NEP) along with OECD's 1977 hopes for the U.S. performance by 1985.

Overall, NEP called for somewhat higher net imports than the OECD projection (5.2 millions of barrels of oil equivalent per day [mboed] versus 4.0), even if "additional conservation" measures* are implemented by American citizens. In production structure, NEP provided for more U.S. coal production by 1985 than OECD estimated (14.5 versus 10.9 mboed), much less gas and oil. The target of a virtual quadrupling of atomic power in NEP also was less than OECD projected. Overall, the OECD projection called for an American production level about 3 mboed higher than the Carter plan. Given the tensions widely predicted in the mid-1980's between the global demand for and supply of oil, that difference could be significant.

The NEP target not only fell short of OECD hopes with respect to the reduction of U.S. oil imports, but it also incorporated an extraordinary gap between its own production targets and its implementing arrangements. As presented to the Congress, the NEP laws and administrative arrangements were judged by academic and other experts outside the energy industry as grossly inconsistent with the plan's production

* *The National Energy Plan* describes these additional measures as follows (p. 47): "There are many ways that individual Americans can save energy beyond those specific measures included in the National Energy Plan. Individuals can keep their homes at 78° F. during the summer and at 65° F. during the winter. They can walk or ride bicycles or join carpools, instead of driving alone. They can combine several shopping trips into one. And, they can maintain their energy-using equipment—furnace, car, appliances—in good operating condition, so as to reduce energy waste."

Table 2. Fuel Balances by Sector

(Millions of barrels of oil equivalent per day: Mboed)

	1976	1985 Without Plan	1985 With Plan	1985 Plan plus Additional Conservation	OECD 1985 Projection
Supply	37.0	48.5	46.4	45.2	46.8
Domestic:					
Crude oil[1]	9.7	10.4	10.6		14.5
Natural gas	9.5	8.2	8.8		10.8
Coal	7.9	12.2	14.5		10.9
Nuclear	1.0	3.7	3.8		5.0
Other	1.5	1.7	1.7		} 1.9
Refinery gain	0.4	0.9	0.6		
Total[2]	30.0	37.1	40.0		43.1
Imports/exports (−):					
Oil	7.3	11.5	7.0	5.8	4.3
Natural gas	0.5	1.2	0.6		0.8
Coal	0.8	−1.2	−1.2		−1.1
Total[2]	7.0	11.5	6.4	5.2	4.0

[1] Includes natural gas liquids.
[2] Detail may not add due to rounding.
SOURCE: *The National Energy Plan,* Executive Office of the President, Energy Policy and Planning, Washington, D.C.: G.P.O., April 29, 1977, p. 96.

and consumption objectives for 1985. It therefore risked a much higher, rather than lower, level of oil imports than that which obtained in 1976. The estimates of the gap between NEP's targets and the policies it incorporated led to projections of 1985 U.S. import requirements in the range of 10.8–16.5 mboed.* Expert judgment both inside the Executive

---

* These estimates were done by the Congressional Research Service of the Library of Congress, the Office of Technology Assessment of the U.S. Congress, the General Accounting Office, and the University of Texas at Austin's Council on Energy Resources. In addition, the Congressional Budget Office estimated a shortfall of 20% with respect to the NEP's consumption target.

Branch and outside agreed that a U.S. claim for oil imports within this range in the mid-1980's would probably lead to severe competition among the United States, Western Europe, and Japan for limited OPEC oil supplies, a higher real price for oil, and a grave economic crisis in the OECD world and beyond.

Comments on the major items of the NEP balance sheet follow.

Consumption. The proposed slowdown in the rate of energy consumption is reflected in the balance sheet by the total supply figures; i.e., imports plus domestic production minus coal exports. It is estimated that, without NEP, consumption would have increased at an annual average rate of about 3% over the period 1976–85, as compared to 4.2% for 1960–70. The proposed economy and conservation measures would reduce it to 2.55%. Additional conservation measures might bring the rate down to 2.25%. These average rates indicate that time will be required to bring the rate of increase under 2% per annum—the target set for 1985. And, indeed, it does require time to insulate houses, convert to lighter cars using less gasoline per mile, and to install new energy-saving machinery and processes in industry. As noted above, similar time lags are involved on the production side. With the average annual growth rate of the economy assumed over these nine years (4.3%), this means that NEP envisages some rise in oil imports until new conservation and production measures take effect. The NEP documents do not present estimates of the time-path of energy imports; but the 1977 figure is likely to be 9 mboed.

Coal. NEP calls for an increase of coal production of 84% over 1976 domestic production: an annual average rate of increase of 7%. Coal must move from 26% of 1976 U.S. domestic production of energy to 36% by 1985. The rate of increase over the nine years covered by the plan must be seven times that of the previous nine. There is no doubt that the United States contains the coal required for this expansion.

Coal production in recent years has been constrained by demand, not supply. In 1976 approximately 50 million more tons could have been produced, if a market existed. The demand constraints were, essentially, these:

—The real price of interstate natural gas was only one-half that of coal, the price of oil about three-quarters. The incentive to shift to coal was weak.

—Environmental rules and uncertainties about them also slowed down the switch: among others, uncertainty about interim use of intermittent control systems; reliability and cost of stack gas scrubbers; significant deterioration regulations; compliance deadline extensions; legislative changes in the Clean Air Act; and surface mining reclamation laws.

On the side of supply, productivity (tons produced per man hour) in both surface and underground mines has declined significantly in recent years. An increase in productivity will be required if the 1985 coal target is to be achieved with reasonable efficiency.

NEP proposed to tighten environmental constraints even further; e.g., requiring best available control technology (scrubbers) on all new plants regardless of the sulfur content of the coal burned. These steps were apparently designed to stimulate use of high-sulfur Midwestern and Eastern coal and to reduce the advantage of the extensive low-sulfur coals of the West held largely in lands owned or controlled by the federal government. This action would have significant impact on existing contracts for Western coal held by users in the South and Midwest who have assumed use of low-sulfur coal would preclude the necessity of scrubbers. While lightening the potential burden on the environment, agricultural land, and water in the West, NEP would significantly heighten the environmental burden in the East.

While constraining demand on coal through tightened environmental requirements, NEP sought to stimulate coal demand through a coal conversion program consisting of tax and regulatory measures and by elevating prices of alternative sources of gas and oil, primarily through taxing methods.

Most of the scheduled 84% increase in coal production will not occur until the 1980's simply because of the time required to construct additional coal plants, to open new mines in the East, and to convert existing plants to coal use.

NEP did not address adequately, then, some of the major constraints on the effective exploitation of the nation's ample coal reserves. As Hans Landsberg, a well-known expert on the staff of Resources for the Future, wrote in the *Washington Post* of May 16, 1977:

> . . . not only must mining companies grow, but all facilities associated with coal, including . . . transportation and manpower, must grow apace. State-federal conflicts must be resolved, the aspirations of the Indian tribes controlling large amounts of Western coal have to be reconciled, land-use and restoration practices must be established, and so on.
>
> That in this context the coal industry can raise output by an annual average of 60 million tons is highly unlikely, if not outright impossible.

Nuclear. Although the target was muted in President Carter's public presentations, NEP envisaged the completion or construction of seventy-five nuclear plants by 1985. This compares with the sixty-three which provided in 1977 about 10% of U.S. electricity, 3% of total energy consumption. These figures would rise to 20% and 8%, respectively, by 1985 under NEP. Some calculations indicate, in fact, that 100 nuclear plants would be needed by 1985 to meet the target of 3.8 mboed. This latter estimate assumes plants will be of 1100 MW capacity (the present limit) and function at 65% capacity (present average performance).

NEP spelled out in some detail the administrative problems that would have to be overcome to avoid the costly delays imposed in recent years on the building of atomic energy plants, as well as to deal with environmental and waste-disposal problems. The viability of the nuclear energy target will largely depend on whether and when those problems are, in fact, overcome. As of October 1977, apparent divisions within the Executive Branch still delayed the presentation to Congress of legislation required to accelerate the building of nuclear power plants envisaged for 1985 under NEP.

Gas and Oil. The roles of energy conservation, coal, and nuclear power in NEP are, in conception, quite straightforward, although serious problems must be overcome if the targets set are to be achieved. The role of oil and gas is somewhat more complex.

At first glance, the oil and gas figures for 1985 do not look particularly interesting or striking: a 9% rise in oil production as compared to 1976; a 7% decline in gas; a slight (1%) increase in total of gas and oil production. The drama underlying those figures can only be understood by examining Charts 3 and 4.

Gas and oil production have been in decline since the early 1970's at something like 5% a year. That rate of decline in production from known reserves is expected to continue, as Charts 3 and 4 indicate. Without an heroic effort to establish new reserves, gas and oil production in 1985 will, together, have fallen from about 19 to under 9 million mboed per day. The scale of that heroic effort is roughly measured in Charts 3 and 4 by the area marked "production from New U.S. Reserves," plus the further additions required to bring production up to the 1985 levels marked by asterisks. The rise in oil and gas prices since 1973 led to increased drilling and the finding of some additional reserves down to 1977. Increased production from these new reserves was not on a scale sufficient to compensate for declining production from old reserves, although there was a suggestion that national gas production might be ceasing to decline.

The gap to be filled by the bringing in of new oil and gas reserves turned out to be the largest single element of increased production envisaged in NEP; that is, the plan envisaged an increase of 9.6 mboed from all sources other than oil and natural gas (mainly coal and nuclear), and the finding of sufficient new oil and gas reserves to permit production from these sources to re-attain approximately their 1976 level —a 13-mboed production effort.

There is a consensus that perhaps 2.5–3 additional mboed might come from Alaska oil, an increase over 1976 levels from

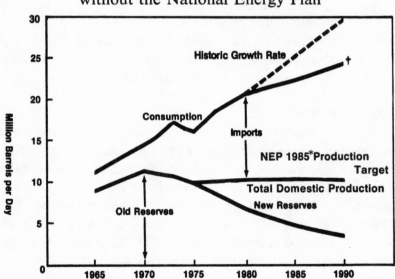

Chart 3. U.S. Oil Consumption*
without the National Energy Plan

* includes Natural Gas Liquids
† assumes implementation of mandatory fuel efficiency standards and reductions induced by higher gasoline prices
SOURCE: U.S. Bureau of Mines and Federal Energy Administration.

Chart 4. U.S. Gas Supply: History and Future[1]

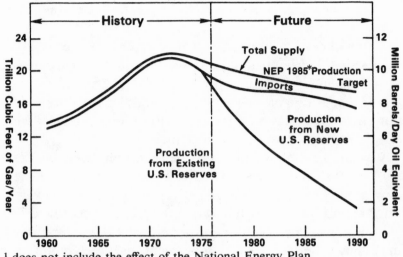

[1] does not include the effect of the National Energy Plan
SOURCE: Federal Energy Administration.

NOTE: Charts 3 and 4 are taken from *The National Energy Plan*, April 29, 1977, pp. 13 and 17. The NEP production targets are added from p. 96.

the Outer Continental Shelf, and oil produced by enhanced or tertiary production methods. The balance would require a massive increase in on-shore drilling and development to fill the gap in oil; a similar accelerated effort, on-shore and off-shore, with respect to gas.

The drafters of NEP apparently believed that the balance of the gap in gas and oil could be generated by private industry responding to the price incentives offered. With respect to oil, producers were offered the current OPEC price (adjusted for inflation) for new oil finds. A wellhead tax on all oil produced would be instituted to bring the national price up to the OPEC level; but the difference between the OPEC price and lower prices set for production from old reserves would flow back to the federal treasury to be rebated to consumers or retained for general revenue purposes. With respect to natural gas, a national price was envisaged of $1.75 per thousand cubic feet (mcf) for new gas, $1.45 per mcf for gas from existing reservoirs.

Although there were many other debatable features of NEP, intellectual and political controversy focused initially on the appropriateness of the proposed price for new natural gas and on the disposition of the proposed wellhead tax on oil production from old reserves. Analytically, the questions were simple in form, complex in substance.

Was the natural gas price set high enough to encourage a shift to coal use at the desired rate and to induce sufficient new drilling to establish the reserves required to achieve the NEP natural gas production target for 1985? Would the diversion of the wellhead tax to consumers (and the federal treasury) deny oil producers the investment resources required to increase drilling rates sufficiently to establish the new reserves required to achieve the NEP oil production target? Behind these questions lay two further issues:

—Would drilling rates be determined by the marginal price of new gas and oil, or by cash flow as determined by the average price received by gas and oil firms?

—What, in fact, is the likely relation between drilling rates and new reserve finds for the period 1977–85?

The Carter Administration, down to October 1977, never revealed the formal basis for its calculations. Its spokesmen, however, took a somewhat paradoxical stance. They argued, on the one hand, that the price and profit incentives offered were ample to induce the drilling rates required to achieve the NEP production targets. This view implied rather optimistic assumptions about the relation between drilling rates and new reserve finds. On the other hand, they argued that drilling rates higher than those they intended to induce would not result in substantial new reserve finds and, in any case, there was a bottle-neck in rigs which would set a limit on drilling rates.

The most explicit and careful published examination of this question concluded—on the basis of past and current relations between prices, drilling rates, and the establishment of new reserves—that the NEP natural gas price policy and its proposed disposition of the oil wellhead tax would yield between 2.2 and 5.0 mboed less oil and gas production by 1985 than called for in NEP.*

The issue, evidently, would be settled by politicians, not by geologists, economists, and econometricians. The Carter Administration, appealing strongly to the desire of consumers for low prices and to the alleged rapaciousness of oil and gas producers, managed to get its NEP legislation through the House of Representatives virtually unscathed. In the Senate, a majority supported the deregulation of new natural gas and the diversion of much of the wellhead tax to energy-related investment. A compromise might assume the form of a gradual freeing of the price of new natural gas and the allocation of, say, half the oil wellhead tax to energy-related investment, including mass-transit in the cities.

Behind this intellectual and political debate, however, deeper forces were at work which promised to alter further the original terms of NEP in the future. First, a widening circle of political leaders, including the state governors, were becoming aware of the dangerous three-sided trap into which the United States was falling: the probable massive production shortfalls in NEP; the probable peaking out of OPEC production capacity in the 1980's; and the dangerously long energy-production lead times. Taken together, they argued for the urgent, all-out U.S. energy-production effort NEP explicitly decried. Second, as the American economy appeared to

* Council on Energy Resources, University of Texas at Austin, *National Energy Policy: An Interim Overview,* September 12, 1977, pp. 8–17.

falter in the second half of 1977, the link between expanded investment in energy production and conservation and a return to full employment began to be more widely perceived. This was the central perception behind both the proposal of the northeast governors for the creation of a Northeast Energy Development Corporation, laid before the Senate in the autumn of 1977, and the backing for regional banks with a still wider mandate (including water, land, and transport development) by the Midwestern Governors Conference and the National Conference of Lieutenant Governors in August 1977. Similarly, former Vice-President Nelson Rockefeller received a warm, bipartisan hearing in presenting before a Senate Committee in September 1977 a proposal coolly received two years earlier for a massive national energy bank to accelerate energy-related investment, notably in the development of energy from shale, *in situ* conversion of coal, and synthetics.

Clearly, as of October 15, 1977, when this book went to press, the United States was still in the process of evolving a national energy policy.

With full awareness that the most conscientious projections, even seven years ahead, can prove faulty indeed, I believe U.S. (and OECD) policy should be based on the assumption that a ceiling on OPEC oil production capacity will, in fact, come into being in the 1980's. Unless U.S. production is rapidly increased and consumption constrained to the degree consistent with a return to full employment, U.S. import requirements either will not be met or met only at the cost of the more dependent economies of Western Europe and Japan. A major economic and strategic crisis would then result, not correctable for some years due to the firmly established lead times between energy investment and new production coming on line.

Given this kind of fundamental danger to the economic and strategic stability of a precarious planet, I see no other rational course than to launch an all-out OECD production as well as conservation effort, including all that is required to achieve minimum lead times. Any other course involves risks that responsible governments ought not to take, notably the government of the democratic nation outside OPEC which commands the largest accessible energy reserves. The problem of an alleged bottle-neck in drilling rigs is evidently manageable if there is a will to manage it, since the Defense Production Act of 1950, as amended in 1975, provides the President explicitly with the power to guarantee the "supplies of materials and equipment in order to maximize domestic energy supplies." Similarly, the alleged danger of abnormal profits in the energy-producing industries can be dealt with, as many have advocated, by an excess profits tax containing provisions which would assure that excess profits be ploughed back into energy-related fields.

What is involved here is a fundamental test of whether American democracy can avoid a classic weakness of democratic governments; that is, to await the onset of acute crisis before acting with resolution. If the political leaders of the nation in the late 1970's fail to act they will deserve Winston Churchill's characterization of the British leaders of the 1930's: "Delight in smooth-sounding platitudes, refusal to face unpleasant facts, desire for popularity and electoral success irrespective of the vital interests of the State."

6

Raw Materials: Cheap or Dear?

IN 1973–74, the explosive rise in food and energy prices was accompanied by a sharp increase in the prices of industrial raw materials. From a level in 1972 of 122 (1967 = 100) prices of industrial raw materials (mainly minerals) rose in the United States to 205 in 1974. In the recession of 1975 they declined to 188, responded sensitively to the limited recovery of 1976, and were back to 214 by the end of that year. They continued to rise in 1977 despite the modest degree of recovery in the OECD world. In short, the prices of non-food, non-fuel basic products have behaved as if they also were caught up in the first phase of a Kondratieff upswing.

Unlike the running down of the world's grain reserves in the 1960's or the degenerating U.S. gas and oil position which helped induce the OPEC oil price decision in the autumn of 1973, there is no single straightforward explanation from the supply side for the price behavior of raw materials in 1973–74. Detailed analyses have been made of this episode; and since raw materials consist of many different commodities, each with unique supply and demand characteristics, there is some variety in the explanations offered. In general, however, three forces appear to have been at work.

First, the industrialized economies experienced a strong simultaneous business expansion in 1971–74. This increase in requirements was heightened by a psychological factor. When increased demand encountered raw material bottle-necks, a shortage mentality swept the international business world. Firms scrambled competitively for raw material supplies in a manner reminiscent of the period 1950–51, when the Korean War induced a similar short-run phenomenon.

Second, investment in raw-material processing had slackened off in the late 1960's, despite low levels of unemployment. This led to high rates of plant utilization—well over 90%. The conventional explanation for this phenomenon is that profit margins came under pressure in this period, and business firms preferred to use existing capacity to the hilt rather than undertake large new investments. Then came the erratic years, 1969–71, when unemployment rose and growth rates slackened. In the United States, there were price controls from the summer of 1971 to the end of 1972. This combination of circumstances is believed to have further discouraged plant expansion. Therefore, the boom of 1971–74 occurred under circumstances of inhibited supply. Explanations of this kind are adduced for raw materials as different as fertilizers, titanium, aluminum, pulp, and paper.

Third, inhibitions on investment in raw material and processing capacity derived from the uncertain state of the economy are believed to have been exacerbated by the introduction of new governmental regulations dealing with the environment, health, and safety.

In the general revival of the economy in 1976–77, anxiety remained that inadequate investment in certain raw material processing sectors could, once again, induce inflationary price increases from the supply side and foreshorten the boom before full employment could be reached. As will emerge, this possibility is heightened by certain international developments in the field of raw materials.

Thus, although there were special forces at work in recent years with respect to raw materials, the behavior of their prices fitted more or less that occurring in agricultural and energy markets. And this fact seemed, as in the other cases, to validate the doctrine of *The Limits to Growth*. The question of the long-run adequacy of raw materials supply was, therefore, re-examined with an intensity not matched since the early 1950's when the Paley Commission was at work. Indeed, a National Commission on Materials Policy reported in 1973, responding both to the current course of raw materials prices and to the challenging argument in *The Limits to Growth;* and a second group, the National Commission on Supplies and Shortages, reported at the close of 1976, with a wide range of policy recommendations (*Government and the Nation's Resources*).

In a rather dramatic table in *The Limits to Growth,* the authors compared the known global reserves of sixteen raw materials with current and projected production. They ended up with a measure of how long these reserves would last at various assumed future rates of growth. The results were not cheerful. If recent rates of growth continued, tin, for example, would run out in 13 years, lead and copper in 21, aluminum in 31. Even abundant iron ore would run out in less than a century. When these growth rates were set against a figure five times currently known reserves, assuming that such additional reserves be found in the future, tin was extended to 61 years, lead and copper to 64 and 48, respectively, and iron to 173. The outcome was the result of classical Malthusian arithmetic: a geometrically increasing number catches up quite quickly with even a large arithmetic increase. If one assumes a steady high percentage rate of growth in annual consumption of raw materials, the amount required each year grows rapidly larger, and even very much expanded reserves can be depleted in a relatively short period.

In *The Limits to Growth* this image of inevitable physical limitations on raw-material supply was reinforced by arguments suggesting that the cost of extracting raw materials would rise and that there are relatively few new geographic areas left to explore except for the seabeds. Therefore, the world economy would have to use progressively lower-quality ores, increasingly expensive to mine and process. The authors also noted that greater insistence on protecting the environment would raise future mineral prices, and that raw material exporters would increasingly act together to raise their revenues at the expense of raw material importers.

The first of these arguments has been vigorously countered along the following lines. "Known reserves" are an essentially economic, rather than a geological, figure. Resources have to be invested to establish the existence of new mineral deposits. This kind of investment takes place in response to expected future demand and future prices. As demand increases and, quite possibly, raw material prices rise, new reserves will be found. Between 1950 and 1970, for example, known reserves of phosphates increased by 4,430 times; potash, 2,360; iron, 1,221; chromite, 675; down to a modest 10-times increase for tin. As for geology, minerals are diffused in the earth's crust and under the sea much more generally than oil or gas. Even in areas such as the United States, the exploration for mineral reserves is incomplete. In short, the earth's crust is likely to prove much more generous than *The Limits to Growth* argument would imply.

Table 3, (p. 102), presents three measures of raw materials availability: the first measure relates known reserves to current annual consumption, as in *The Limits to Growth;* the second estimates recoverable resources in conventional de-

Table 3. World Resource Availability for Important Minerals by Three Measures

	Known Reserves/ Annual Consumption (R/C)	Ultimate Recoverable Resource/Annual Consumption (URR/C)	Crustal Abundance/ Annual Consumption (CA/C)
Coal	2,736	5,119	na
Copper	45	340	242,000,000
Iron	117	2,657	1,815,000,000
Phosphorus	481	1,601	870,000,000
Molybdenum	65	630	422,000,000
Lead	10	162	85,000,000
Zinc	21	618	409,000,000
Sulphur	30	6,897	na
Uranium	50	8,455	1,855,000,000
Aluminum	23	68,066	38,500,000,000
Gold	9	102	57,000,000

SOURCE: U.S. Geological Survey, *United States Mineral Resources,* Geological Survey Professional Paper 820, Washington, 1973, Statistical Abstract, p. 651, as reprinted in William Nordhaus, "Resources as a Constraint on Growth," *American Economic Review,* May 1974, p. 23.

posits; the third, the believed potentialities of deriving minerals from rock in the earth's crust.* In addition, there are the seabeds, which contain a considerable store of minerals awaiting the technologies to render their exploitation economically viable.

It is fair to say, then, that the most knowledgeable assessment is that industrialization will not be inhibited over the foreseeable future by simple physical shortages of raw materials. But the second question remains: will raw materials become increasingly expensive, requiring the diversion of an

---

* On land a single cubic kilometer of average crustal rock contains 2×10^8 tons (metric) of aluminum, over 1×10^8 tons of iron, 800,000 tons of zinc, and 200,000 tons of copper.

increasing volume of investment resources to acquire them? We are back with that old devil, diminishing returns.

The lesson of the past century is that, while the prices of raw materials have varied relative to the general price level, they have fluctuated about a constant or, even, declining trend. Thus far, technology has held diminishing returns at bay, responding to shifts in relative prices. The relative rise in the price of timber, for example, has led to important measures of economy and substitution. In addition, depending on price and technology, there are substantial possibilities for recycling raw materials not available in the case of energy.

The potentialities for substituting one raw material for another which is more scarce (and expensive) have been extensively explored in principle. When minerals are examined one by one and use by use, even present technology suggests that substitutes will be available. H. E. Goeller and Alvin M. Weinberg have generalized their analysis of raw materials prospects (including sources of energy) in the form of three stages which they counterpose to the conclusions of *The Limits to Growth:*

> We can conceive of depletion of resources and substitution in three stages. Stage 1, which almost surely will persist for the next 30 to 50 years, is a continuation of present patterns of use of the nonrenewable resources. During stage 2, when society still would depend on reduced carbon and hydrogen found in nature—that is, coal—there would be little oil and gas, and people would begin to turn away from widespread use of a few of the nonferrous metals and toward much greater use of alloy steels, aluminum, magnesium, and titanium. Stage 2 might last several hundred years. Finally in stage 3, the Age of Substitutability, all the fossil fuel would be exhausted; society would be based almost exclusively on materials that are virtually unlimited. It is our basic contention that, insofar as limits to mineral resources can be discerned, the condition of life in stage 3 would not be drastically different from our present condition: we have the physical possibility of living in the Age of Substitutability and not "completely disrupting our social and

economic structures." To reach this state without immense social disruption will, however, require unprecedented foresight and planning.[1]

Oddly enough, there may be an enlarged role in the future for the forests which, for a long time, have been properly regarded as a scarce resource, requiring conservation. Prices of lumber and wood products have tended to rise more than prices in general: the U.S. wholesale price index rose by 373% between 1929 and 1976; lumber and wood products, 822%. Nevertheless, the most recent analyses suggest that the output of American forests, which still cover a third of our soil, could be greatly increased. Seven methods for expanding the productivity of the forests have been explored and roughly measured: the intense cultivation of fast-growing species; improvement of forest sites through drainage, irrigation, and use of fertilizers; prompt and full seeding and planting of harvested forest land; the full exploitation of the best genetic knowledge in replanting; weeding; thinning; improved protection from fire; and increased commercial utilization of trees, including use of roots, foliage, etc. Theoretically, U.S. forest output might be increased 3–4 times by the application of all these methods.[2]

The conclusion is of importance for reasons which transcend the conventional role of timber as a raw material. Wood can be converted by hydrogenation into liquid fuels and chemical feedstocks, and thus substitute for petroleum. The forests are, then, a potential renewable energy source, perhaps a major source. They can be exploited while maintaining or even enhancing their environmental and recreational roles— although at the moment extreme environmentalists are striving mightily to prevent such rational use.

As one moves from problems of food (where petroleum-based fertilizers remain a critical factor) through energy itself to raw materials, the importance of man's finding a new, essentially infinite (or renewable) and non-polluting energy source emerges as the central challenge of the time ahead. As Goeller and Weinberg conclude:

> Our technical message is clear: dwindling mineral resources in the aggregate, with the exception of reduced carbon and hydrogen, are *per se* unlikely to cause Malthusian catastrophe. But the exception is critically important; man must develop an alternative energy source. Moreover, the incentive to keep the price of prime energy as low as possible is immense. In the Age of Substitutability energy is the ultimate raw material. The living standard will almost surely depend primarily on the cost of prime energy. We therefore urge moving as vigorously as possible, not only to develop satisfactory inexhaustible energy sources—the breeder, fusion, solar and geothermal power—but to keep the program sufficiently broad so that we can determine, perhaps within 50 years, the cheapest inexhaustible energy source.[3]

So much for distant prospects and the gamble on man's creativity.

The fact that the human race can count on the availability of abundant, if not necessarily cheap, supplies of raw materials for the long run does not, of course, mean that raw materials can be dropped from the national and international policy agenda.

There is, first, the question of raw material prices. Must the world economy count on operating over the next quarter-century with a higher range of relative prices for raw materials than was enjoyed in the 1950's and 1960's? This is a matter of some debate.

Some optimistic economists note that, as real income per capita rises into the high ranges attained in North America, Western Europe, and Japan, a smaller proportion of that income is spent in ways which require raw materials. The demand for services, for example, rises faster than for physical commodities containing metals. This relationship leads them to feel that the rate of increase of demand for metals will fall off with the passage of time and that the relative prices of raw materials will actually decline.

Others are less optimistic. They note that many of the most productive ore deposits lie in countries which are politically volatile or where foreign private capital is insecure. Proponents of this view thus argue that the increased nationalist assertiveness of some of the less developed countries which contain raw materials will create an environment of high taxes, price controls, as well as fears of nationalization. These factors could lead to reliance on safer but higher cost sources of supply. In any case, it is inevitable that the developing nations will increasingly process their raw materials before exporting them, as their technological competence expands.

Given the imponderables, no one should be dogmatic about the likely net movement of relative prices of raw materials over the next quarter-century. My own guess is that they will remain relatively higher in price than they were in the 1950's and 1960's, if the world economy resumes the growth rates of that period.

Concern in the United States about price is heightened by the fact that this country faces a future in which its relative dependence on imported raw materials will almost certainly rise. The American net deficit for primary minerals (in $ 1972 prices) was about $2.5 billion in 1950, $7.1 billion in 1972. By the year 2000 the figure might be as high as $40 billion (in $ 1972 prices), with much expanded import requirements for aluminum, iron ore, copper, zinc, and nickel leading the way.

In a secure and reliable world, the balance of payments implications of increased American dependence on imports should prove manageable, if the American economy as a whole maintains its vitality and productivity. For example, the import dependence of Western Europe and Japan in raw materials is—and is likely to remain—higher than for the United States. After all, trade is a two-way street; ultimately, exporters must import. It is the strategic and relative price implications of this increased dependence which pose significant current policy problems.

The United States imports a great many of its raw materials from countries where reliable relations and reasonable domestic stability are currently assumed; for example, Canada, Mexico, Australia, and Brazil. Contrary to a popular view, more than twice the value of non-fuel minerals entering world trade come from industrialized, rather than developing, countries. On the other hand, the United States imports significant amounts of raw materials from areas where political stability is uncertain over the medium run; e.g., Zaire, Rhodesia, South Africa. These possibilities, combined with more conventional strategic considerations, led to decisions in 1976 to enlarge American stockpiles of critically important raw materials.

Stockpiles might also play a limited role in constraining producers who seek to exercise their quasi-monopolistic market position to raise prices. In general, there is considerably less scope for monopoly pricing in raw materials than in oil: there is no equivalent to suppliers (such as Saudi Arabia) prepared to restrain production and sacrifice foreign exchange to maintain price; the problems of political concert among producers is generally more difficult; the possibilities of substitution are greater. Nevertheless, the Caribbean producers of bauxite have managed through export taxes, accompanied by long-term agreements with foreign firms committed to operating in their territories, to achieve an impressive rise in prices; and similar efforts have been canvassed or attempted in other fields, including coffee, phosphates, bananas, and copper. In addition, raw materials production has been nationalized in many developing countries. The cost to all parties of these trends is a sharp drop of foreign investment in the exploration and production of raw materials in, for example, Latin America. The Latin American nations do not yet command the capital, technology, and expertise to compensate fully for this decline. The upshot may be a concentration of raw material expansion in more hospitable areas with less productive deposits, yielding higher prices; for example, the U.S. government is already financing research and development in the production of aluminum from abundant clays in possible substitution for imported bauxite.

As the world slides in the direction of neo-mercantilist policies towards raw materials, stimulated by OPEC's successful exploitation of its monopoly powers, multilateral efforts are being explored to harmonize more rationally the interests of raw material producers and consumers. These include some of the critical issues in the now temperate, but not yet highly productive, dialogue between the industrial and developing nations, centered on the notion of a New Economic Order. (These matters are discussed in Chapter 13.)

More narrowly, the prospects for the supply and prices of raw materials pose a series of foreign and domestic policy issues for the United States, which can be set out under seven headings.

Stockpiles. Stockpiles of raw materials have traditionally been maintained in the United States for straightforward military purposes; that is, to assure that essential needs for military production are met in case wartime circumstances should reduce the availability of imports from abroad. Such stockpiles have also been used from time to time for strictly economic policy purposes; for example, to restrain price increases. The possibilities of supply interruptions (e.g., from Africa), as well as efforts by overseas suppliers to enforce excessively high prices, suggest the need for stockpiles built and used for economic as well as strategic purposes. Whether stockpiles should be used not merely to hedge against disruptions or monopolistic pressure but also as a regular mechanism to stabilize raw material commodity prices was debated within the December 1976 Report of the National Commission on Supplies and Shortages. The majority was against the U.S.

undertaking that task, although a minority position was strongly stated. The case against the use of stockpiles for price stabilization is, essentially, that it places the government regularly at the center of the private markets and tends to place on public stockpiles the total responsibility for maintaining reserves. The argument for assuming that role would assert that relative price stability in raw materials should be a major goal of national economic policy and that, if the upper and lower price limits for government intervention via stockpiles are clearly set and sufficiently wide, the normal workings of the commodity markets would not be unduly inhibited or distorted.

Trade Policy. If the U.S. feared significant disruptions in external supply or effective monopolistic price fixing, tariffs (or direct subsidies) could encourage expanded domestic production at higher cost. For the moment, the advantages of relatively free international trade counsel reliance on positive international agreements which would exclude export restrictions or denial of access to supplies from abroad. The Trade Act of 1974 provides a useful element of bargaining leverage by empowering the Executive Branch to negotiate such understandings and to retaliate in case of their violation. Evidently, the existence of substantial U.S. stockpiles would further increase the possibility of success in such negotiations.

Commodity Agreements. The pressure to negotiate producer–consumer commodity agreements has risen since the recession of 1974–75. The non-oil exporting countries of the developing world which produce and export raw materials found themselves whipsawed by the new high prices of oil imports and the recession in the industrialized world which reduced the demand for and the prices of their exports. The pressure, endemic since the 1950's, for measures to stabilize the foreign exchange earnings of such developing countries increased. The international community acquired considerable experience with the possibilities and limits of international commodity agreements with respect to three commodities: coffee, cocoa, and tin. The lessons to be drawn from the operation of such agreements are equivocal: they may have evened out prices and the flow of foreign exchange in the face of modest supply and demand fluctuations, but they did not wholly shield consumers and producers against major changes in market conditions—witness the 1977 course of coffee prices. An alternative or supplementary approach, which has at times worked well, is the provision of compensating short-term international loans for developing countries experiencing low export prices.

Perhaps the best reason for pursuing international commodity agreements, with all their inherent limitations, is that they educate all participants in their differing perspectives. They can thereby generate a sense of where limited, overlapping common interests lie. This is not a trivial advantage in a world where neo-mercantilist impulses are as strong as they are.

Investment Agreements. One of the most ominous tendencies in the world of raw materials, already noted, is the declining flow of international capital to finance their expansion. Except for creative diplomatic efforts, not much can be done with respect to African areas caught up in or threatened by disruptive conflict. But in Latin America and other areas it is urgent that reliable and equitable terms be found to enlarge such investments. Such arrangements will become increasingly necessary if the world economy as a whole can recapture growth rates approximating those of the 1960's. The drafting of such international investment codes has been attempted by many hands and many committees for some twenty years. No multilateral effort has yet succeeded. This frustration arises for several reasons: the highly charged political and psychological moods generated in large North–South meetings; the inherently overgeneral terms in which such codes must be drafted; and, perhaps most important of all, the real differences in the political as well as economic situations confronted by each developing nation as it faces private foreign firms. Multilateral discussions are worth pursuing because they help clarify the issues which ultimately have to be resolved. But progress is more likely on a bilateral basis or between capital exporters and smaller regional groups of developing countries.

Data and Governmental Organization. The U.S. government was, of course, exceedingly active with respect to raw materials supply during the Second World War. It sought to assure for itself and its allies necessary strategic materials from Latin America, Africa, and other accessible areas, as well as to stimulate the production of synthetic rubber to replace interdicted natural rubber supplies from Southeast Asia. But after 1951, in the fourth Kondratieff downswing, the concern with raw materials largely lapsed in Washington. The Department of Interior published its regular reports on minerals consumption and supplies; but, generally, such matters were not given high-level attention.

Now, and in the time ahead, there is a need to follow closely the raw materials markets, one by one; to anticipate necessary action; and to weave policy towards raw materials into the total fabric of national economic policy. The Report of the National Commission on Supplies and Shortages contains a section with a heading that might serve as well for agriculture, energy, or the environment: "The Need for a Sectoral Analysis Capability Within the Executive Office." The Council of Economic Advisers is restricted by law to a size which has forced it to concentrate on the kind of aggregate Keynesian analysis with which most of its members, in any case, are comfortable. On the other hand, the foundation for a systematic flow of sectoral data on raw materials exists in some of the older Departments; e.g., Interior and Agriculture. The need is for improved data collection and the integration of sectoral analyses into national economic policy as a whole—a theme elaborated upon in Chapter 12.

Recycling. The notion of increasing raw materials supply through recycling is inherently attractive: recycling could conserve virgin minerals; economize on energy needed for ore reduction; save foreign exchange; and cut both the costs of waste disposal and reduce pollution problems.

The recycling of raw materials waste generated within industry is, of course, conventional, running over 50% in steel and copper. The recycling of waste which has passed through the hands of the consumer (postconsumer waste) is also significant, and efforts to increase the raw materials flow from this source (e.g., beer cans) have intensified in the past several years. This happened, in part, as a by-product of efforts to protect the environment. Estimates of the possible further addition to supplies from postconsumer waste range from 2–7% for steel; 6–15% for aluminum; 5–10% for copper; about 14% for paper. These are significant potential marginal savings. Congress has acted in recent years to alter tax, transport, and administrative policy which deterred the exploitation of recycling possibilities; and some demonstration projects have been funded. Changes in attitude towards solid waste disposal, as well as the reduction of jurisdictional barriers at local levels, will be required to exploit fully the considerable possibilities for recycling which exist even at present prices and existing technologies.

Research and Development. Finally, as in every other field examined in Chapters 4–7, there is a heightened case for research and development. And, as in other cases, it is not merely a question of the scale of research and development, but of its direction. In fact, a unified and lucid picture of how federal funds for materials research are spent is only now beginning to emerge. These funds are allocated to fourteen different federal departments or agencies aside from energy.

Co-ordination, both intellectual and administrative, is weak, although somewhat improved in the last few years. The disposition of the much larger resources allocated to research and development by private industry is less exactly known.

Given the time lags inherent in research and development, such investments must be geared to problems where there is a high probability of future relevance. R&D cannot successfully be pursued in response merely to the short-term fluctuations of commodity markets. This is one reason why the public role in research and development is important: the markets do not automatically signal where the most important areas for research and development lie.

The task of government is, therefore, to build up, commodity by commodity, a reasonably firm view of the most important raw materials problems for the medium and long run where research and development could be productive. As in all the other sectors examined, these judgments should be formed by intimate consultation with both the private sector and with expert opinion in other countries.

7

The Environment:
Cost, Benefit, Trade-off

Iɴ 1950, *The New York Times Index* contained one column
of references devoted to water pollution out of the 1,258 pages
which comprise the index; in 1960, about a column and a half;
in 1970, 18 pages in the index were required to reference the
material published on the subject. The equivalent figures for
air pollution were: a little over 1; 2; and 13. As noted in Chapter 1, concern about the long-run resource foundations for
industrial civilization began in the 1960's with anxiety about
the supply of clean water and air.

The Seventh Annual Report of the Council on Environmental Quality, published in September 1976, illustrates both
how ramified the issue of environmental quality is and how
sophisticated the forms of analysis required to devise and to
carry out environmental policy are. Air and water pollution
are dealt with under a number of sharply distinguished categories, depending on their source, the chemical character of
the pollution, and its impact. A whole range of additional
environmental concerns is now embraced: toxic substances in

food, noise, solid waste, land use. Resource issues are addressed in detail as the nation comes to grips with inevitable
conflicts between its economic requirements for water, minerals, and energy and the environmental costs of their further
development. But certain resource issues emerge in their own
right; for example, overgrazed range land, and the decline of
certain Western underground water supplies required both for
irrigated agriculture and expanded energy production. Measures to improve the environment had become so massive by
1976 that a section of the report is devoted to their net effect
on the rate of inflation, the growth of output, and levels of
employment. A whole section is devoted to environmental
diplomacy, bilateral and multilateral. Clearly, the environment has become a big, complex piece of international as
well as national business.

The measures taken in the 1970's to improve the quality of
the environment yielded mixed results, as one would expect.
What is clear is that a popular concern had been translated
into politics, law, administration, and a whole new field of
analysis. College courses on the environment have prolif-
erated; and college book stores contain shelves of paperback
texts catering to the new market.

When a new major issue emerges in public life, it is almost
always possible to look back and find it is not quite as new as
one might think. In 1970, for example, President Nixon was
able to issue an executive order based on the River and Har-
bor Act of 1899 which forbade the discharge of "any refuse
matter of any kind or description"; although the full text and
legislative history of the act casts some doubt on whether the
Congress was then quite as redoubtably environmentalist as
the selected passage would suggest. What the Congress had
on its collective mind was, almost certainly, impediments to
navigation. But at just about the turn of the century, when the
significance of the closing of the frontier in 1890 was altering
the self-image of America, there was thought and action not

only to preserve wilderness areas, through national and state parks, but also to conserve the forests. Still earlier, of course, standards and methods for water supply and sewage disposal were created which markedly improved public health in the cities of the more advanced industrial countries. In 1912, the Public Health Service Act assigned to the Service the responsibility to study and investigate the relationship between water pollution and the propagation of disease. In the same year, the British economist A. C. Pigou first published the basic propositions governing the economics of the environment in *Wealth and Welfare*. He dramatized effectively the limitations of a competitive market economy in dealing with "external diseconomies" (see note, p. 7). And the field of ecology, led by foresters, emerged as a serious intellectual discipline long before the word became a rallying cry for environmental crusaders.

The first national legislation designed to control water pollution was passed in 1948; it was the foundation on which a gathering body of legislation was built in the 1950's and 1960's. The Air Pollution Control Act of 1955 was the first major federal action in that field. Legislation in 1963 and 1965 preceded the 1970 Act which governs, with amendments, current policy.

Despite earlier thought and legislation, it is clear that the United States and other advanced industrial societies transited an historic watershed over the past decade. Never again will the environment be taken for granted as a free good. Air and water, places for recreation and of natural beauty, even species of birds, animals, and fish, have come to be regarded as forms of capital which we have either run down or which might be run down if strong precautionary measures are not taken. Put another way, it is now accepted that significant resources must regularly be allocated or foregone if a satisfactory environment is to be re-established or maintained. Ex-

actly how we define a satisfactory environment and how much
of our resources we are prepared to allocate or forego to
achieve and maintain it is, of course, a major subject of debate; and it is likely to be a lively part of political life, at local,
state, and federal levels, for the indefinite future. As one stu-
dent of the subject has written: "Economic enterprise unin-
formed by a sense of environmental decency has surely led to
misallocation of resources—in particular, to a squandering of
such public goods as clean air and pure water. On the other
hand, slavish adherence to doctrinaire canons of environmental purism leads to equally serious misallocations."[1]
Where and how the United States and, indeed, all the other
nations of the world draw and hold the lines between these
two kinds of resource misallocation are matters now securely
on the agenda of politics and diplomacy. And that is where
they must be, because no narrowly economic analysis, no
matter how sophisticated, can produce an objectively correct
answer to the inevitable trade-offs.

The politics of environmental policy is inherently complex
for three reasons. First, the calculus of individuals and groups
within societies differs as they weigh the costs against the
benefits of resource allocations to improve the environment.
The environmental risks in mining Wyoming coal look somewhat different in Laramie than in, say, Chicago. Second, the
perspectives of nations and governments also differ. Poorer
nations tend to regard environmental quality as a luxury only
the rich can afford. Third, there is a wide spectrum of environmental risks, each of which must be weighed under circumstances where scientific knowledge is often sketchy. Degradation of the environment can, for example, violate amenities
and aesthetic qualities in life. It can destroy significant resources. It can also cause injury or death to individuals or
groups in particular places and threaten with extinction whole
species of animals, birds, or fish. But it is also conceivable

that industrial civilization could so massively disturb the earth's ecological balance as to threaten human life itself over wide areas or over the globe as a whole.

At the moment, the latter mortal concern is also the most obscure. It rests on the possibility that an enlarged industrial civilization might generate profound changes in the weather. In fact, there are two conflicting concerns: the fear that the build-up of carbon dioxide from the combustion of fossil fuel might warm the planet and cause the polar ice to melt, thus raising the sea level; alternatively, the fear that particles emitted into the air from industrial energy and transport might reduce the heat on the Earth's surface derived from sunlight, thus lowering global temperature and inducing a new ice age. The possibility of controlling excessive emission of particles by precipitating them out of smokestacks, has, for the moment, turned scientists towards analysis of a heating, rather than a cooling, of the atmosphere. This concern is heightened because of the possible effects of thermal pollution resulting from man's increasing use of energy as industrialization spreads, with its inevitable discharge of waste heat into either the atmosphere or the ocean.

The consensus on these issues is limited. But scientists do agree that the scale and intensity of energy generation on the Earth is not likely to pose acute problems for considerable time; they agree that they have a great deal to learn about the effects of even vastly expanded industrial activity on the climate; but they also agree, despite acknowledged areas of ignorance, that this possibility, even distant, increases the relative desirability of fusion power or solar energy as ultimate solutions to the energy problem, because they would not involve emissions of carbon dioxide.

It should be noted, parenthetically, that, quite independent of the weather changes that an enlarged industrial civilization might bring about, some sober students of weather cycles believe that we in the northern hemisphere are due for a protracted period of cooler temperatures of a kind not known since the end of the seventeenth century. By these calculations, a mini-ice age (1400–1700) gave way to a warming period which, conceivably, may have begun to reverse about 1940.

The conclusions to be drawn from this area of speculation are that more research on the potentialities of thermal pollution and on the interplay of human activities and the weather is required; and that a long-run energy source that does not emit carbon dioxide is highly desirable.

On the spectrum of danger, the next level down from irreversible change in the climate is the array of problems caused by the use of nuclear fission to generate electric power. They include, at one extreme, the problem of increasing the likelihood of additional nations deciding to produce explosive devices from materials generated by atomic energy plants. This is an inefficient way to acquire nuclear explosives; it has never happened, but it is possible. There is a possibility of theft of nuclear materials from power plants and the manufacture and use of weapons for purposes of terror. There is also the possibility of a major, if localized, disaster caused by a technical failure; for example, the rupture of a main pipe carrying cooling water in the reactor, combined with a failure of the backup cooling system. The chance of a pipe rupture is estimated narrowly between 1 chance in 10,000 per reactor per year to 1 chance in 20,000. If there were 1,000 reactors operational, this means the emergency cooling system would be called upon to perform every decade or two. If the backup system also failed and the overheated reactor melted down and breached, the result would be not an explosion but the release of radiation, which could be dangerous if the unlikely double failure occurred near a densely populated area. The radiation could cause deaths from acute exposure, cancer, and gastric defects for up to five generations. The statistical calculation of risks is a difficult, uncertain business; but even the most pessimistic current calculations indicate that large modern light water nuclear reactors are likely to cause fewer casualties than the generation of electricity from coal.

The breeder reactor (LMFBR) carries with it a different array of problems and potential dangers. These have been identified, and work goes forward to deal with them in the five countries where breeder reactors are being built or contemplated. Safety devices are not sufficiently advanced or tested to provide the basis for a statistical calculation of risk. But the fact that the LMFBR generates near-weapons grade plutonium has led some to seek its postponement, in the hope that a breeder less conducive to nuclear proliferation, using alternate nuclear fuels, might be designed.

At the next level of danger is the problem of endlessly and securely disposing of the radioactive wastes generated by atomic energy plants and avoiding, for example, leakage from the underground storage of such wastes. Many reasonably secure possibilities exist; but the large-scale, long-term problem of waste storage has not yet been solved. However low one may rate the statistical likelihood of the dangers resulting from the generation of electricity by nuclear reactors with existing technology, their reality suggests the priority, in the short run, of expanding energy production, where possible, by other means, and, in the longer run, of achieving efficient fusion or solar power. The harsh fact appears to be, however, that even the United States will have to rely on light water reactors on a very large scale over the next quarter century at least. The proportionate dependence of Western Europe and Japan will be still greater. The scale of the risks associated with nuclear power can, therefore, be limited but not elimininated. The human race is committed to a path which will require endless care and vigilance, as well as efforts to contain nuclear proliferation at its present amply dangerous limits.

I would only add that the containment of proliferation is likely to prove much less dependent on the relative difficulty of acquiring weapons-grade uranium from nuclear power plants than on the creation of a political and security environment in which the increasing number of nations which could produce nuclear weapons decide it is unnecessary for their security or prestige to do so.

As we move from a possible Faustian tragedy brought on by man's altering irreversibly his climate, or not controlling adequately the by-products of nuclear energy, to dirty water, impure air, and other more local forms of pollution, we confront less danger and more expense. In 1970, for example, outlays to contain air and water pollution accounted for 0.4% of gross national product; in 1974, the figure was 2.1%; by 1984, the estimate is that the United States will be diverting 3.1% of gross national product for these purposes.[2] This kind of change in allocation of resources in a growing economy is, as history goes, quite substantial. On this estimate, annual costs for pollution control would rise (in 1975 dollars) from $32 billion in 1975 to $69 billion in 1984.

The building into economic life of regular outlays expanding in this way is bound to have significant effects. Pollution control has, for example, increased costs and prices; and it will continue to make the rate of inflation somewhat higher than it would otherwise be. Pollution control has also become a big enough enterprise to affect the level of employment. In the sharp recession of 1974–75, outlays for pollution control somewhat cushioned the decline in output and employment; but if the U.S. sustains relatively full utilization of labor and industrial capacity over the next decade, the increase in gross national product is likely to be somewhat less than it would be without pollution control expenditures—perhaps as much as 2.2% lower in 1984 than it would otherwise be. The capital requirements for pollution control are now a significant element in total capital requirements for the future; and they may lead to higher interest rates than would otherwise prevail, as well as to a marginally slower growth in national product.

Moreover, the problems posed by pollution control have an uneven impact on various industries. They are particularly important in pulp and paper, metal-working, electric utilities, chemicals, iron and steel. In a period of rapid general expansion of the economy, this uneven impact could contribute to the emergence of capacity bottle-necks which could bring the boom to a premature end.

On the other hand, there are two reasons why calculations of this kind are an insufficient measure of the impact of pollution control on the economy. First, traditional calculations of gross national product have not embraced the serious capital depreciation imposed upon air, water, and other aspects of the environment by growth in the sectors which are measured. There is no doubt that if net national product had been correctly measured in the past, to take account of environmental damage, its rate of increase would be lower than we now calculate. Second, an improvement in the quality of air and water will have certain straightforward, positive economic effects. They are real enough, although difficult to measure with precision. For example, an improvement in air quality will not only reduce certain diseases, but also enlarge the effective amount of work a labor force of a given size can contribute. For example, improved air quality will reduce the amount of damage done to buildings and other structures and thereby reduce the costs of repair and repainting. Similar economic benefits derive from cleaner water; for example, an enlarged commercial supply of fish. Moreover, in affluent nations, where an increasing proportion of the population can afford to travel to beaches, parks, and lakes, these amenities take on an economic as well as an aesthetic significance. In the 1960's, for example, visitors to national parks increased at an average rate of 8 percent, more than twice the rate of increase in gross national product.

In short, the real costs of pollution control are substantially unavoidable if modern societies are not to exhaust certain basic natural resources; and the results of effective pollution control contribute positively to the nation's income, even if those contributions are difficult to measure with precision.

What of the results thus far? Air quality standards are conventionally measured in terms of the concentration of sulphur dioxide (SO_2) and total suspended particulates (TSPS). Chart 5 exhibits the overall progress made between 1970 and 1974 in the United States in reducing these concentrations. Clearly, the national trend has been in a wholesome direction. Data for

Chart 5. Overall National Trends in Daily Observed Levels of Sulfur Dioxide and Total Suspended Particulates

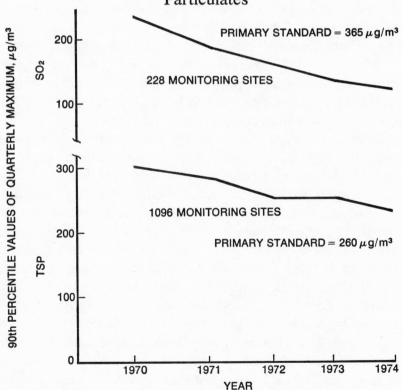

PRIMARY STANDARD = 365 μg/m³

228 MONITORING SITES

1096 MONITORING SITES

PRIMARY STANDARD = 260 μg/m³

SOURCE: *Environmental Quality Seventh Annual Report*, p. 226.

particular cities exhibit different degrees of progress. Some have a long way to go before achieving mandated air quality standards as a normal condition (e.g., Louisville, Birmingham, and Cleveland); by 1974, however, New York, Chicago, and St. Louis were doing very well indeed. There is every reason to believe that, if the nation persists in the effort, the quality of the air breathed in the cities can be substantially improved and gradually brought towards the standards which have been set. Looking to the future, the problem may be complicated by the increased use of coal as a source of energy, requiring expensive measures of emission control, notably in the case of coal with high sulphuric content. On the other hand, the remarkable shift of population to nonmetropolitan areas since 1970 should reduce air pollution in metropolitan areas. The pollution problem may spread to a degree, but it should be easier under present legislation and standards to prevent air pollution levels from rising in nonmetropolitan areas to the degree experienced in the older urban areas. Anticipatory action may also make the maintenance of those standards less expensive.

A high proportion of urban air pollution arises from automobile emissions and emissions from certain large industrial and electric power installations. They have proved reasonably easy, if quite expensive, to control and to monitor. To some extent the problem of water pollution has been reduced by controlling specific fixed sources of pollution; for example, sewage disposal or industrial wastes in the rivers and lakes. Between 1972 and 1975, for instance, there was significant improvement in the quality of water in at least five of twelve rivers chosen for intensive analysis by the Environmental Protection Agency: the Willamette, Colorado, Red, Ohio, and Tennessee Rivers. But the trends are uncertain in the other seven. Considerable future progress is possible with respect to lakes, as well as rivers, if improved methods of disposal for sewage and industrial waste are installed. On the other hand, extensive water pollution derives from more diffuse sources, less easy to control. For example, run-off water from feed lots carries animal waste; run-off from agricultural areas contains fertilizers and pesticides. If the nation continues the programs to control pollution derived from easily identifiable sources, the major challenge in the years ahead will be the control of pollution from these diffuse sources.

Another expanding area of environmental concern centers on chemicals used for commercial purposes, which have been discovered (or are suspected) to have hazardous effects on people or the environment. Vinyl chloride, fluorocarbons, polychlorinated biphenyls (PCBs), Kepone, chloroform, trichloroethylene are now on a lengthening list of substances whose toxic effects were established in recent years, occasionally under tragic circumstances. Many of these chemicals are contained in pesticides on which American agriculture has become heavily dependent. Potential substitutes exist or are being developed in this and other fields, including some in the wide-ranging uses of PCBs. This relatively new dimension of environmental danger requires for its containment methods of pre-testing, monitoring, and control at a time when scientific virtuosity in the creation of chemical compounds is rapidly expanding.

Surveying the whole area of environmental concern, one can take, as in *The Limits to Growth* debate as a whole, a pessimistic or an optimistic view. One can argue, as some have, that the effort to preserve a safe and livable environment for man is simply inconsistent with continued expansion of industrial production in the world. One can portray the efforts being made to contain air and water pollution and to cope with the side effects of reliance on sophisticated, but potentially lethal, chemicals as an inherently losing game in which the human race will divert increasing resources, suffer increasing human and environmental costs, until it accepts a no-growth policy on a global basis. On the other hand, it is possible to argue that the creative capacity of man, as reflected in science and technology, has only now begun to face up to this array of issues. In particular, inventive talent is just beginning to focus on the possibilities of finding nonpolluting or virtually nonpolluting ways of doing things. In energy, priority for work on fusion power and solar energy has only recently been raised. In agriculture, the effort to extend nature's trick, in a few plants, of fixing nitrogen from the air is a promising but still relatively new endeavor. If successful, it might not only reduce energy-intensive fertilizer requirements but also reduce pollution in the waterways. One can easily envisage a nonpolluting automobile engine (say, an efficient battery) to supplant the rather expensive and cumbersome present methods for reducing pollution from automobile emissions.

There is no simple policy conclusion to be drawn in this exceedingly complex field. Virtually no one in the United States now doubts the legitimacy of a public policy designed to protect the environment. All but environmental purists would accept the fact that this objective must be balanced against others in the making of public policy. That reconciliation has been only slowly, painfully, and partially achieved in some cases; for example, in the exploitation of off-shore oil and gas in the Atlantic and Pacific. The knotty problems involved in the use of on-shore public lands for resource development have hardly been confronted. What will be required in the future are more swift and firm methods for settling, in politically responsible ways, the inevitable trade-offs between the quality of the environment and other legitimate economic and social objectives.

8

Productivity: Decline or Transition?

A rather ominous story is told by Charts 6 and 7. Chart 6 shows how the United States has fallen off its long-term productivity* curve since 1966. Over the previous eighteen years, output per labor-hour had increased at an annual rate of 3.3% per year. Over the next seven years, the erratic course of productivity averaged an increase of only 2.1%.

---

* Productivity can be defined in a variety of ways of which three are most often used: labor productivity, measured as output per worker or man-hour; capital productivity, measured as the percentage increment in total output, associated with the percentage of total output invested (the marginal capital–output ratio); and total factor productivity, measured by relating the increase in real output to the inputs of labor and capital (including natural resources). It should be noted that a rise in labor productivity may be caused by forces making capital more productive (e.g., more capital per worker, or new production techniques), while the capital–output ratio can fall due to a rise in the level of education or skill of the working force. Modern productivity analyses, recognizing these interconnections, seek to isolate and measure the qualitative as well as quantitative factors at work with respect to labor and capital (including natural resources).

127

Chart 6. Productivity in the Private Business Economy

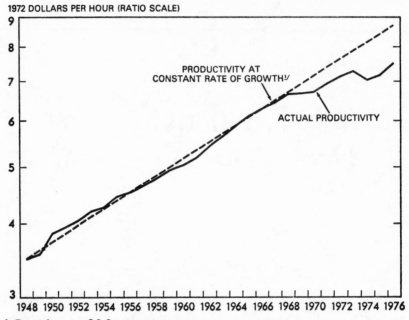

1972 DOLLARS PER HOUR (RATIO SCALE)

PRODUCTIVITY AT CONSTANT RATE OF GROWTH[1]/

ACTUAL PRODUCTIVITY

1948 1950 1952 1954 1956 1958 1960 1962 1964 1966 1968 1970 1972 1974 1976

[1] Growth rate of 3.3 percent per year.

SOURCE: Department of Labor, in *Economic Report of the President*, January 1977, p. 46.

Chart 7 exhibits a major effect of this change, if it persists. The potential expansion of GNP at full employment of labor and full utilization of industrial capacity is lowered significantly: its rate of growth drops from 3.9% a year to about 3.5%. At least two-thirds of this downward shift in the economy's capacity to grow is estimated to result from the slowdown in the rate of increase in productivity.* The increase in

* The other two principal factors which have caused this downward revision in potential growth are: the assumption that the enlarged role of youth and women in the working force makes 4.9% rather than 4% unemployment the lowest level attainable without inflation; and a decline in average hours worked.

productivity is the major factor causing rising real incomes per person; and the rate of expansion of real national income is the principal source for expanded government revenues. For example, the new lower curve implies that at full employment the federal government would take in some $30 billion (1972) less than if the economy had stayed on the old curve. Thus, both levels of private affluence and the nation's capacity to sustain public services are shadowed by the decline in the economy's rate of productivity increase. In addition, a slow-down in productivity imparts an inflationary bias to the economy. A given increase in money wages will cause a greater increase in prices when the rate of productivity increase declines. Or, put another way, stable prices would require a lower increase in money wages.

Chart 7. Gross National Product, Actual and Potential

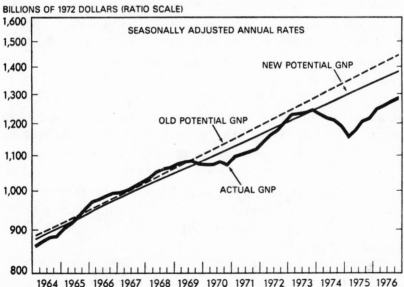

BILLIONS OF 1972 DOLLARS (RATIO SCALE)

SOURCES: Department of Commerce and Council of Economic Advisers, in *Economic Report of the President*, January 1977, p. 55.

The rather abstract lines in Charts 6 and 7 thus reflect forces which could affect adversely the economic prospects of every American family. We economists know something, but not nearly enough, about what determines a society's average rate of productivity increase. For example, we have some reason to believe that the scale of prior investment in research and development helps increase productivity; but we don't know how to measure that connection. We are certain that the productivity of labor can vary widely within countries and between countries, and even within the same industry, depending on the quality of entrepreneurship and management; but we don't know how to calculate this factor for an economy as a whole. It is diffused among the factors productivity experts think they do know how to measure. Since productivity increase varies greatly in different parts of the economy, it follows that an economy's structure affects the average productivity of its workers; for example, the proportion of the working force in rapidly expanding high-productivity sectors incorporating new technologies, as opposed to older sluggish sectors; the proportion of an economy's equipment and technology that is up to date rather than obsolescent. We can measure these structural factors only up to a point. Then, of course, the rate of investment affects the rate of productivity increase by determining how fast the amount of capital per worker is expanding. But there is a catch here. The relation between the rate of increase in the capital stock per worker and productivity varies a good deal over time, as between countries, and as among an economy's sectors. Finally, there are the educational level, skill, health, and motivation of the workers. They surely matter, but we have trouble measuring just how they matter.

The complexities involved in explaining the productivity of labor are, perhaps, best illustrated by taking a case in comparative analysis. It is now generally acknowledged that, overall, the productivity of British labor is relatively low. The estimates suggest that labor productivity in the United States may be over 50% higher than in Britain; Sweden, about 50%; Germany, 33%; France, 25%. When analysts seek to explain these differentials, here are some of the factors they adduce to account for the British situation:

—overmanning (i.e., feather-bedding);
—greater fear of unemployment and a willingness to trade job security for higher pay (and productivity);
—less modern machinery (i.e., low and misdirected levels of investment);
—less competent entrepreneurship and management;
—a more fragmented and less disciplined labor union structure;
—deeper class schisms and greater difficulty in finding labor–management consensus.

The list could be extended, of course. But it does illustrate two fundamental truths about productivity analysis. First, the productivity of labor is inextricably connected with the pace of investment and innovation, as well as with the quality of management. Second, labor productivity is linked in ways hard to measure to the social and institutional structure of a society, its politics, and to a sense (or lack of it) of national direction and purpose.

In addition, productivity has varied with business fluctuations: it generally rose most rapidly towards the end of a business contraction and the early stage of expansion; it often slowed down towards the peak of a boom; and it slowed down even more or actually declined in the early stage of contraction. The decline in productivity in the recession of 1974–75 was unusually severe. Chronic unused industrial capacity and relatively high unemployment can be expected to depress the average rate of productivity increase.

Despite the number and complexity of the factors bearing on productivity, and difficulties in measuring the importance of each, there is a certain shapeliness in the average course of productivity in the American economy since 1889, when reasonably good measurement begins.

The story begins with a marked slowdown in productivity in the period from about the beginning of the twentieth century to the First World War. This slackening was, in different degree, a characteristic shared by the three most advanced industrial economies of the time: the United States, Britain, and Germany (for special reasons, France did better). In the American case, productivity in agriculture (output per unit of labor input) marginally declined, as the limits of the frontier were reached and no striking new technologies were substituted for the flow of farm labor to the cities. There was a retardation of productivity increase in mining, manufacturing, and transportation. I am inclined to attribute these trends mainly to the ending of the railway-building age and the coming to maturity of the initial phase of the steel revolution which had begun in the 1870's. The extraordinary influx of immigrants in the period may, in the short run, have reduced average labor productivity, but this is by no means certain. The one component in the economy whose productivity accelerated in the pre-1914 period was the area of communications and public utilities. The telephone, electric utilities, and manufactured gas were coming in rapidly and exhibiting high rates of productivity increase. As we shall see, the productivity retardation of this period bears a family relation to that experienced since the late 1960's.

A new, higher productivity trend emerged around 1917 and lasted until 1929. The acceleration was quite general, but not uniform. The tractor and other mechanized farm machinery lifted agricultural productivity and there were wide-ranging technological improvements in many other sectors from food canning to chemicals. But at the heart of this surge was the coming of the age of automobiles and electric-powered durable consumers goods. The automobile carried with it tech-

nological revolutions in new types of steel, rubber, and petroleum refining, all of which exhibited rates of productivity
increase far above the average. The United States pioneered
in developing this group of sectors and, virtually alone among
the major industrial economies, enjoyed relatively full employment in the 1920's.

There was, as one would expect, a marked general retardation in the rate of productivity increase during the years of
depression, partial recovery, and war. But there were a few
exceptions; for example, air and truck transport, and pipe-
lines; electric utilities and natural gas; and beverages.

From the late 1930's a remarkable productivity revolution
in agriculture began which involved not merely the mechanization of cotton production, but also the intensive application
of fertilizers, pesticides, and new seed strains in the production of a good many crops.

In the period 1948–66, the high average rate of productivity
increase was (as Chart 6 shows) the result of an above-average
surge in the early 1950's; some sagging away in the late 1950's
and the early 1960's (when there was considerable under-
utilized capacity); a recovery in the mid-1960's as the economy moved to full employment. Agriculture exhibited a 5.6%
average annual increase in product per man-hour—almost
twice the average for the whole economy. Electric and gas
utilities, communications, and mining also experienced high
rates as did chemicals, plastics, instruments, and electrical
equipment. Contract construction was the worst performer in
the productivity league, falling away from a reputable 4.4%
increase in 1948–53 to absolutely declining productivity per
man-hour since 1960.

John Kendrick, the senior American scholar in this field,
has summarized his explanation for the slowdown in productivity since 1966 as follows:

> Changes in labor force mix, particularly the accelerated
> growth in proportions of youth and women; accelerating price-

inflation; some deceleration in the rate of economic growth; a substantial decline in the ratio of research and development outlays to gross national product; negative social tendencies; and increased governmental intervention in the economy, including certain mandated social outlays and wage and price controls during the period 1971–74.[1]

The increased role of young people and women in the working force affects productivity measurements because they are paid less than the average, and this differential is assumed to reflect their productivity performance. The bulge in youth entering the working force is a result of the post-1945 surge in birth rates which ended towards the close of the 1950's. From about 1980, therefore, there will be a decline in the flow of young people into the working force and this retarding factor will no longer operate. The working force will become progressively more mature and, presumably, more stable and efficient. The increased role of women entering the working force may reflect smaller family size, new attitudes among women, and efforts to cushion family income against declines in real income brought on by inflation and the real wage impact of the fifth Kondratieff upswing. When the surge in women entrants into the working force will end cannot be predicted, but presumably it will level off at some percentage of working force participation higher than in the past. Experts attribute about 30% of the productivity deceleration to the changed composition of the working force.

Kendrick believes that accelerated inflation after 1966 may well have diverted capital resources from their most productive uses; although formal measurements of the expansion of capital per man-hour continued to show an increase at past rates. The expansion of capital per worker, however, slowed down. This difference reflects a decline in average hours worked and leads to a factor which all analysts regard as important: the erratic short-period behavior of the economy, especially after 1969. The United States experienced in the period 1969–76 a slower average growth rate, higher average unemployment, lower average utilization of productive capacity, and fewer hours worked per employed person. The minimum estimate for the productivity loss from these closely related factors is 36%.

The proportion of the nation's resources invested in research and development declined in these years: from 2.92% in 1966 to 2.25% in 1976. But this trend is hard to evaluate for two reasons: a good deal of the decline came in military and space; and there is some question as to whether a relative decline in R&D outlays would translate itself so promptly into decelerated productivity in the economy as a whole. Although it is an uncertain measure of inventiveness, patents granted peaked out, for the time being at least, in 1966. The question of research and development is explored at greater length in Chapter 9.

Kendrick leaves place in his analysis for another range of factors, impossible to measure, but perhaps of significance: the increased drug abuse of the 1960's, crime, and the anti-establishment sentiment generated by the Vietnam War and other developments of the period. One operational reflection of these moods among the young was a relative decline in those opting for education in science and engineering during the second half of the 1960's.

Government policy may have retarded productivity increase in a variety of ways. The period of price controls (1971–73) may have squeezed profits and reduced outlays for productive investment. Federal legislation to protect the environment and increase workers' health and safety may have reduced the productivity of investment, as conventionally measured. As suggested in Chapter 7, investment of this type can be productive in certain measurable ways over a period of time, but it is also productive in ways which escape present methods of national-income accounting. In addition, the rise in energy prices since the autumn of 1973 may have reduced the productivity of current investment outlays and rendered a part of existing capital, dependent on low energy prices, obsolescent.

Efforts have been made to estimate the factors decreasing productivity from the side of capital rather than labor. For example, the Council of Economic Advisers, in the January 1976 *Economic Report of the President,* summarized a study done within the government which concluded that in the 1970's business investment would be about 15% less productive than it was in the 1960's. Table 4 shows the factors to which the authors of that study attribute the deceleration in the productivity of investment. The table includes estimates for industries where the capital–output ratio (c/o) is believed to be rising and falling. The capital–output ratio roughly measures the increase in output brought about by a unit of investment. Thus, a rising capital–output ratio suggests declining productivity; a falling ratio, increasing productivity.

By these tentative and rough calculations, pollution control causes 26% of the decline in the productivity of capital outlays in the 1970's; the lower productivity of energy investment, 31%; but 43% is caused by a factor not dealt with in Kendrick's analysis and similar estimates of the deceleration in the rate of increase of output per man-hour; that is, the decline, on balance, of the productivity of capital investment in the economy (a rising capital–output ratio).

This element in the story is examined later; but I believe it is a major factor. Just as the deceleration of productivity in the pre-1914 generation was caused by the ending of the railway age and waning productivity in steel and all its many new uses, I believe a substantial part of the decelerating productivity of investment in recent years is due to the waning of the age of the automobile (and all its related sectors) and of energy-intensive durable consumers goods; the relatively low productivity of services, to which the economy has radically shifted; and the deceleration of productivity gains from the technologies which have carried agriculture forward so rapidly over, say, the past thirty-five years. But before exploring further the implications of that hypothesis, let us turn to the debate about the future of productivity in the United States.

Table 4. Factors Affecting the Cumulative Total Business Fixed Investment Required from 1971 through 1980

(Billions of U.S. dollars)

Factor	Total	Percentage Change Pre–1970 Versus 1971–1980
A. Assumed fixed 1970 capital output (c/o) ratios and pollution control requirements limited to pre-1970 law	1,283	
B. Estimated total business fixed investment actually required ...	1,473	
Difference between A and B ..	190	15% of which:
Of which: *Add* for actual Pollution Control Laws passed in 1970 and 1972	48	25%
Add for industries with c/o ratios increasing for reasons other than the achievement of greater energy independence	118	62
Subtract for industries with decreasing c/o ratios	−36	−19
Add for additional capital required for greater energy independence	58	31
Add for increase in pollution control investment induced by additional investment in energy	2	1

SOURCE: Adapted from *Economic Report of the President*, January 1976, p. 45.

Here, as in so many other areas examined in this book, there are optimists and pessimists. Kendrick is a relative optimist. In part, his view is based on a judgment about American society: ". . . there are cybernetic forces in the economy and in the broader society which lead to the correction of unfavorable tendencies either through built-in stabilizers, or as a result of conscious policies to reverse the negative trends once they are recognized as such."[2]

Turning to the proximate factors to which he attributed the productivity slowdown after 1966, he notes that the surge of youth into the working force was a transient demographic factor. He expects a higher and more regular utilization of productive capacity in the future than since 1969. He believes the negative social factors which may have operated in the late 1960's have, on balance, altered for the better; and the related shift of students away from science, engineering, and business administration of the late 1960's appears to have been reversed in the 1970's. The short-run effects of pollution control, safety and health measures will not increase and may even begin to yield labor productivity increases. In quantitative terms, the proportion of real investment devoted to health, safety, and energy-conservation purposes may level off or even decline and, with the passage of time and increased experience, they may become more productive. He acknowledges that a retardation of productivity in mining, agriculture, and energy production may continue, but judges the net effect will be small. He concludes that the rate of productivity increase in the decade 1976–86 will be higher than in the previous decade, if not quite as high as between 1948 and 1966.

One of the pessimists about the future of productivity, Edward Renshaw, assembled a useful, eclectic summary for presentation to the Congress. His central theme is: ". . . the United States and the more industrialized nations of the world can [not] avoid a fairly rapid and inevitable decline in the future rate of productivity advance. . . ."[3] His most basic hypothesis is that science itself—man's creativity—is subject to diminishing returns. He argues that the fact that labor productivity and other measures of technical progress have historically increased at a fairly regular compound rate does not mean such rates will continue in the future. An S-shaped curve is more likely; that is, a path of acceleration followed by deceleration. And he believes the human race may have just passed the half-way mark in the golden age of technological change and, therefore, confronts a slippery, decelerating slope in the time ahead.

Specifically he argues that we are coming up against natural limits to certain basic factors which accounted for the pace of increased productivity in the past: speed in travel and machine operations; the scale of plants and machines; automation; the efficiency of converting energy to useful purposes. He is conscious that his argument may hinge substantially on whether man can find a new, cheap, unlimited energy source; but he is skeptical that fusion power will prove economical.

Turning to specific sectors, Renshaw quotes authorities who suggest that the work going forward in certain hitherto productive scientific and technological fields is yielding smaller and smaller returns; e.g., synthetic fibers, antibiotics, medical science in general, agriculture. He evokes explicitly the doctrine of the 1930's that the United States may be approaching a technological maturity from which it can only escape through radical, new innovations; and he sees no such innovations on the horizon. As an increasing proportion of the working force shifts to services, he believes the prospects for productivity further dim, despite some possibilities for higher productivity in service sectors (e.g., no-fault insurance, automatic checkout systems at supermarkets, do-it-yourself divorce, more extensive group insurance policies, a pill or toothpaste that really prevents dental cavities).

And, as one would expect, the whole of his argument is set against a background of expected diminishing returns and higher relative prices for energy, food, and raw materials.

With Renshaw and those who share his perspective, we are

back to a version of *The Limits to Growth* argument. And, somewhat in the spirit of that book, he argues that, while accepting the inevitability of a progressive retardation in productivity, we should act vigorously in various directions to improve the quality of life and to reduce the boredom of repetitive tasks.

Evidently, no one can arbitrate with confidence the difference in underlying assumptions which yield Kendrick's optimism and Renshaw's pessimism. They come to rest ultimately on speculation or judgment about the productivity of man's creative powers and the resilience of the modern societies he has built over the past two centuries. Chapter 9 speculates on these large matters. But there is some limited insight to be gained by examining briefly the state of innovation in the American economy as viewed in early 1976 and then looking back at that year as a whole.

The February 16, 1976, issue of *Business Week* carried an article entitled: "The Breakdown of U. S. Innovation." Its subtitle: "No-risk, super-cautious management is one of the prime villains." At first sight, the picture drawn strongly supports Renshaw's view that the United States has passed from a golden age of innovation to the decelerating slope of his S-curve. The following quotations give the flavor of the piece:

> . . . from boardroom to research lab, there is a growing sense that something has happened to American innovation. Some say it is in rapid decline. Others claim it is taking new forms. Either way, the country's genius for invention is not what it used to be.
>
> "For 25 years after World War II, we saw some of the most dramatic commercial innovations in our history," says Jerry Wasserman, senior consultant with Arthur D. Little Inc. "There was television, computers, the transistor and integrated circuit, containerized shipping, microwave ovens, Polaroid 'instant' photographs, Xerox copiers, automatic transmissions —things that changed our basic way of life." Now, says Wasserman, most so-called innovations build on existing technol-

ogies and simply extend the state of the art. "This is true whether you're talking pocket calculators, digital watches, or whatever," he notes. "For proof, just look at what's happened to research budgets."

"Put succinctly, who needs another new plastic?" asks William E. Bonnet, vice-president of technology for Sun Oil Co. "There are already so many around."

. . . nearly all leading companies, whether strong innovators or not, share one response: Their broader corporate approach to innovation is becoming more defensive.

. . . says Philip D. Aines, vice-president of research and engineering at Pillsbury Co., "It's much more difficult to come up with a synthetic meat product than a lemon–lime cake mix. But you work on a lemon–lime cake mix, because you know exactly what that return's going to be. A synthetic steak is going to take a lot longer, require a much bigger investment, and the risk of failure will be greater."

"Just look at it in terms of a single major postwar innovation, the office copier, and what our economic life would be without it," says market researcher Solomon Dutka, president of Audits & Surveys Co. The first Xerox copier, he notes, led to a $4.5 billion industry that employs more than 150,000 persons. "Knock a couple of very innovative industries like this out of our economy," Dutka warns, "and you begin to see how much impact a slower rate of innovation might have."

. . . the public's attitude toward industry and its products also began changing. Consumers became more conservative in their buying and more suspicious about what they were buying. As pollster Lou Harris put it recently: "After three decades of hearing about the miracles of American knowhow, the public feels cheated. Consumerism represents shaken confidence in American technology."

[Richard S.] Morse goes on to warn that new high-technology growth companies are no longer being formed "in sufficient numbers to provide the jobs and technical products for export which will be needed in the decades ahead." That would mean less economic growth, fewer jobs, a loss of foreign markets, greater import competition in domestic markets, and finally, of course, a potentially devastating rise in trade deficits.

This no doubt accurate portrait of the state of mind and of policy in American boardrooms early in 1976 might well be read as solid proof that diminishing returns were rapidly closing in on the innovative capacity of the American private sector. And on November 25, 1976, *The New York Times* reported starkly in a lead paragraph to a long article: "American innovation and ingenuity have lost their momentum, the chairman of the President's Committee on Science and Technology told the National Academy of Engineering in Washington last week." Renshaw and the pessimists can, clearly, mobilize a lot of vivid evidence for their proposition.

But there is a quite different way to look at this evidence and the underlying situation it reflects. From 1973 to 1977 the American economy experienced a shocking rise in energy prices; a sharp recession; and a sluggish, disappointing recovery. Per capita real disposal income actually declined in 1974 and only regained its 1973 level in 1976. Between 1961 and 1974 it had increased at an average annual rate well over 3%. Business and the consumer were understandably shaken and made cautious by the manner in which the fifth Kondratieff upswing arrived, for it carried with it the usual damping effect on real wages.

Moreover, it was wholly natural for research and development priorities to change in the altered environment. The innovational behavior reflected in the passages quoted above may represent not the coming of a long-term decline in creativity and innovational zeal as a whole but a transient interval when the institutions of a still resilient but somewhat befuddled society pause to find their bearings under sharply changed circumstances. Indeed, by June 27, 1977, *Business Week* was publishing data on R&D expenditures in American industry exhibiting an 11.6% increase in R&D outlays for 1976 as opposed to 6.5% for the previous year. The latter figure represented a decline of real R&D outlays, given the 9% inflation rate in 1975. The figure for 1976 was more than twice the inflation rate (5%). *Business Week* could conclude (p. 62): "Industry is returning to its pattern of healthy growth in spending on future products and processes." And elsewhere in the same issue (pp. 52–58) was an article that supplied part of the explanation. It described the rapid rise in private as well as public R&D outlays on energy production and conservation.

We cannot predict a priori whether Renshaw's pessimism will prove correct, or whether we are merely observing a change in the directions of R&D required and rendered profitable by the contours of the fifth Kondratieff upswing. But it is worth noting that the assessments of the 1930's that the United States and other industrial countries had arrived at maturity and exhausted the possibilities of industrial innovation proved false. In a post-1945 environment of relatively stable full employment, Western Europe and Japan, as well as the United States, moved forward rapidly by elaborating technologies already familiar in the 1930's: the automobile, durable consumers goods, chemicals, and the unfolding applications of electricity and electronics. This time, it is quite possible that the particular leading technological sectors of the past half-century may have lost their capacity to carry forward economic growth in the advanced industrial world. That has happened before in history: with cotton textiles, the railroads, and steel. But that familiar phenomenon is quite different from the arrival of diminishing returns to science and technology as a whole.

One way to put the matter is to raise the possibility that Renshaw is confusing the inevitable arrival of diminishing returns to one batch of technologies with the running down of the human capacity to innovate in productive, economic ways.

To a degree, the issues at stake in this debate can be clarified by examining in more detail the potential role in the time ahead of science, technology, and innovation, which is done in Chapter 9. But putting these critically important matters aside, what can usefully be said about policy designed to accelerate or slow the decline in the rate of productivity increase?

The conventional prescriptions, in terms of the economy as a whole, are three.

First, we should return to relatively full employment and sustained high growth rates. Although, as noted, productivity gains slacken off towards the peak of a business cycle, sustained periods of high growth and low unemployment are accompanied by high rates of productivity increase. Note again, for example, in Chart 6 (p. 128) that the high rates of productivity increase in the early 1950's and mid-1960's as compared to the lower rates of the late 1950's and early 1960's, when there was a good deal of slack in the economy. And, one can add, private investment in R&D, like other forms of investment, is sensitive to the overall fluctuations of the economy.

Second—and related, of course, to sustained full employment—is the need for an environment of reasonable stability and predictability for business and labor, the farmer, and the consumer. Business will be more innovative, labor less defensive and given to feather-bedding if the prospects for sustained high levels of employment are good. But there is more to it than that. The rate of inflation and its variability affect productivity performance, although measurement of their impact is difficult. So do the scale, character, and predictability of the government's role in the economy.

Third, we should seek a rise in the proportion of income invested. A rise in the investment rate may be required to sustain previous growth rates if, as Table 4 suggests, a variety of factors have raised the American capital–output ratio. A rise in the investment rate would carry with it, in the normal case, an expanded flow of more modern technology because capital investment incorporates the latest equipment judged to be efficient. A variety of tax measures have been proposed to bring about an upward shift in the investment proportion.

As the reader will have gathered, my approach to these legitimate objectives differs somewhat from that which is conventional. In my view, one must first ask: How will full employment be achieved? I believe sustained full employment can only be brought about by a large expansion of investment in particular directions decreed by the structural characteristics of the fifth Kondratieff upswing. If a combination of private–profit incentives and public policy can bring about a reordering of the directions of investment, I believe a reasonable approximation of the three conventional objectives, described above, is attainable. It should be emphasized that what I am recommending here is a set of changes at the margin. In my judgment, the margin is extremely significant. But if those marginal changes in the directions of investment are achieved (in energy, energy conservation, water development, transport rehabilitation, etc.) and the economy reattains rapid growth on a new structural basis, investment should increase in more familiar directions; e.g., housing (now to be systematically insulated and equipped with solar units), industries supporting the production of both nondurable and durable consumers goods, and services. I come to this conclusion because I believe a resumed rise in real private income per capita is possible despite the continuing pressures on real income that may be exerted by high energy prices and the other constraining forces at work in the fifth Kondratieff upswing.

It should be noted that one institutional change in the federal government has been made bearing on productivity: the creation of the National Center for Productivity and Quality of Life. It is governed by a Board of Directors containing representatives of business, labor, government, and the citizenry at large. Its recommendations have been confined to limited areas of consensus, mainly in the field of labor–management cooperation. The creation of this unit reflects an awareness that the issue of productivity is serious, of national concern, and hitherto not well examined by existing government agencies. But, as the analysis in this chapter suggests—and Chapter 9 as well—a heightened concern for productivity should, in the end, suffuse the work of all branches of government concerned with the nation's economic and social welfare, and all sectors in the private economy.

One reason why the nation needs an across-the-board improvement in productivity relates to the U.S. balance of payments. Our overall import requirements are likely to increase during the foreseeable future, notably in energy and raw materials. We shall have to pay for them with exports and do so in an environment of acute competition. The ultimate basis for an economy's competitive status in international trade rests on the productivity of its export industries; but these industries, in turn, depend on flows of materials, components, and service support from a wide range of non-export sectors in the economy. One can observe in Britain and, to a degree, in the American Northeast and Middle West the degenerative process that can be set in motion if a nation or a region falls behind in the productivity race.

But behind the question of a possible productivity acceleration in the American economy lies the deeper forces at work in science, invention, and innovation, to which we now turn.

9

Science, Invention, and Innovation: Is Human Creativity on the Wane?

As has been evident from Chapter 1 forward, the debate about the future of the world economy and, within it, the American economy comes to rest on the prospects for invention and innovation. Those prospects partially depend, in turn, on the results to be derived from an expanding scientific base which, in complex ways, sets the framework for invention and innovation. This is the case whether one looks down the road at the prospects for agriculture and, to a degree, for birth rates in the developing world; energy and energy conservation; raw materials; and the environment. The pace and fruitfulness of science, invention, and innovation also emerged in Chapter 8 as a critical factor in assessing the future rate of productivity increase in the American economy, with fundamental implications for real income, inflation, and the balance of payments. Within the framework of what science and invention yield, Chapter 10 argues that the pace of innovation is likely to be a critical factor in coping with the various regional problems of the United States, notably in the Northeast and industrial Middle West, but also in the currently more dynamic states of the South and Southwest.

Among futurologists, it is often conventional to take a broad view of the technological prospects and possibilities ahead and, in effect, to lump together science, invention, and innovation. Behind either optimistic or pessimistic projections lies the assumption that the progress of basic science will (or will not) yield insights leading to highly productive (or less productive) inventions which, through the process of innovation, will be effectively introduced into the day-to-day workings of the economy, successfully defeating (or failing to defeat) diminishing returns. And in the debate about the limits to growth over, say, the next century, this is understandable. Over a long span of time it may well be proper to assume that men and institutions will not only create the technologies that science and their own ingenuity permit but also apply those which prove cost-effective. This is, for example, the procedure used in *The Next 200 Years,* by Herman Kahn, William Brown, Leon Martel, and their colleagues at the Hudson Institute.

This temperately optimistic study of the human prospect establishes the case for a levelling off of global population in the next century; for a gradual deceleration in economic growth rates, as an increasing proportion of the human race comes to enjoy affluence; and for the capacity of known or likely technologies to supply the energy, food, and raw materials to support this universally affluent population while protecting it from gross environmental degradation.

The focus of the present book is somewhat different. While recognizing the possibility of the hopeful prospects explored in *The Next 200 Years* and similar studies, I have concluded that their coming to pass depends greatly on a successful passage through the critical next quarter-century. At one point in *The Next 200 Years* (pp. 187–88), the authors note that, if one projects forward the economic and technological trends that occurred between 1890 and 1910, the world economy, as of

1960, appears to be, more or less, on the projected curve. They also note that between 1910 and 1960 there were two world wars, a spate of bloody revolutions, and a catastrophic depression. They observe (p. 187): "The forces behind technological and economic growth had a surprising staying power and intensity that enabled them to make up in prosperous years for deviations from basic trends in troubled ones." As a historian, I am prepared to agree with that spacious, philosophical judgment on long trends in the twentieth century. But, like everyone else, I would greatly prefer to see us transit the next quarter- or half-century without great wars in a nuclear age, without bloody revolutions, and without passages of economic catastrophe. And the possibilities for economic and even bloody catastrophe in the next quarter-century are real enough. For example, the international study organized by Carroll Wilson of MIT on the global prospects for energy, published in May 1977, drew a vivid portrait of a possible desperate international scramble for limited oil resources in the 1980's which might easily yield "confrontation and conflict."[1] The field of energy is not alone in posing such neo-mercantilist dangers. Therefore, the present book descends from the grand debate about the ultimate limits to growth to nearer-term issues of policy—to the problems of how to get from here to there without excessive troubles.

In that narrower context, it is necessary to look more closely at the three kinds of human activity which are involved in creating and diffusing new technologies: the pursuit of knowledge about the physical world; the creation of new practical devices and processes capable of rendering the economy more productive; and the cost-effective introduction of such new devices into the economy. Rarely—very rarely—one man has successfully conducted all three of these activities. Edwin Land of Polaroid is a contemporary example. But generally they are conducted in our times in separate domains, by different men and women working in separate institutional settings.

It was not always so. One of the most striking characteristics of the germinal period in the late seventeenth and eighteenth centuries which led to the beginning of modern economic growth was the close osmotic linkage of scientists, inventors, and innovators. As T. S. Ashton, the great historian of this period and process in Britain, has written:

> The sciences were not . . . as yet so specialized as to be out of contact with the language, thought, and practice of ordinary men . . . there was much coming and going between the laboratory and the workshop, and men like James Watt, Josiah Wedgwood, William Reynolds, and James Keir were at home in the one as in the other. The names of engineers, ironmasters, industrial chemists, and instrument-makers on the list of Fellows of the Royal Society show how close were the relations between science and practice at this time.[2]

But then and now the linkage between basic science and invention was oblique, not direct. Inventions did not flow in a straightforward way from the propositions of basic science. They were often pragmatic achievements whose scientific foundations were not even understood. Nevertheless, science —its spirit, methods, and insights—was important to their creation. For example, James Watt wrote of Prof. Joseph Black:

> Although Dr. Black's theory of latent heat did not *suggest* my improvements on the steam-engine, yet the knowledge upon various subjects which he was pleased to communicate to me, and the correct modes of reasoning, and of making experiments of which he set me the example, certainly conduced very much to facilitate the progress of my inventions. . . .[3]

Surveying the relation between basic science and invention in the twentieth century Jacob Schmookler came to a similar conclusion:

> The negligible effect of individual scientific discoveries on individual inventions is doubtless due to the orientation of the typical inventor, even those well trained in science and engineering, to the affairs of daily life in the home and industry

rather than to the life of the intellect. The result, however, does
not mean that science is unimportant to invention, particularly
in recent times. Rather it suggests that, in the analysis of the
effect of science on invention, the conceptual framework of the
Gestalt school of psychology is perhaps more appropriate than
is that of the mechanistic, stimulus–response school. The
growth of the *body* of science conditions the course of invention
more than does each separate increment. It does this by making
inventors see things differently and by enabling them to imagine
different solutions than would otherwise be the case. The effect
of the growth of science is thus normally felt more from generation to generation than from one issue of a scientific journal to
the next.[4]

Thus, despite the obliqueness of the linkage of science to invention, the connection remains fundamental.

There is, however, a second complexity in this linkage.
Science has had (since, say, Copernicus) a life, an inner logic,
a sequence of its own. In part, this sequence is closely related
to the development of increasingly sophisticated tools for
observation, measurement, and experiment. These tools and
methods set limits on the areas of the physical world that
could be fruitfully explored and on the profundity of that
exploration. In part, the sequence in which each branch of
science unfolded was the product of the great hypotheses
which emerged from men's minds. These captured the imagination of successive generations, were probed and refined
until some new revolutionary hypothesis set scientists off in
another direction. The scientific base from which practical
applications might be derived or stimulated has, therefore,
varied over time; and, at any moment of time, it is fixed in
ways which may or may not correspond to man's most urgent
requirements. It is quite true that necessity is the mother of
invention; but all necessities are not always matched by inventions. One reason for this partial sterility is the structure,
limitations, and focus of the body of basic science which
exists at any period of time. This means that, if one is trying

to estimate the potentialities for invention and innovation over any future time period, one must guess, at least, about the probable areas of scientific progress.

The connection between the inventor and the innovator is equally important. Inventions do not pass automatically into the economic system. Some entrepreneur must take the risk of introducing the new invention: building or financing the machines, training the working force to use them, working out the bugs, and sometimes persuading the market to try a new or significantly modified product. Matthew Boulton performed all these functions for James Watt and his improved steam engine, as well as financing and nursing Watt through many technical and psychological tribulations. In a few major American industries, that kind of intimate and sympathetic linkage between the laboratory and the business end of the firm has been institutionalized rather well; e.g., the more sophisticated and modern branches of the chemical industry; electronics; aerospace. In others, the potential linkage between inventor and entrepreneur has been exceedingly weak; e.g., the automobile industry; steel; machine tools; construction. What this distinction reflects is the fact that innovational capacity—the ability to understand and nurture the inventor and the will to introduce his new technologies or processes into the economy for the first time—varies greatly among sectors and, indeed, among business firms within sectors.

In short, if one seeks to explore or guess about the future rate of productivity increase, he must take into account three distinct kinds of human activity: the pursuit of basic knowledge; the capacity and will to invent; the capacity and will to innovate.

Before considering the prospects for the future in these terms, it may be well to set the stage by summarizing briefly the changing scale and character of activity in these domains in the recent past.

The essential facts about the evolution of research and development since the 1960's are these.

First, from a peak in 1964, U.S. R&D expenditures declined as a proportion of GNP from 2.9% to about 2.25% a decade later. The proportion rose in a number of other advanced industrial nations over these years, including Japan, West Germany, and the U.S.S.R., the latter two allocating a higher proportion of GNP to R&D than the U.S. in 1974.

Second, the proportion of total U.S. R&D expenditures devoted to both military purposes and space declined sharply. Nonfederally funded R&D as a proportion of GNP continued to rise, in fact, until 1969–70, when a slow decline occurred. Table 5 shows the changed distribution of federal R&D expenditures between 1961 and 1977 for selected periods

These figures capture rather well some major responses of R&D to changes in public policy over those turbulent years: the decline from the post-Sputnik peak in defense R&D; the

Table 5. Distribution of U.S. Government R&D Expenditures among Areas, 1961–1977
(*fiscal years*)

National Objectives	Percent Distribution			
	1961–62	1966–67	1971–72	1977
National defense	70.7	49.0	52.6	51.0
Space	11.8	31.5	18.1	12.5
Nuclear energy	7.3	5.2	5.1	8.6
Economic development	3.3	4.7	8.1	11.5
Health	4.8	5.7	8.5	9.7
Community services	1.0	1.9	4.5	2.5
Advancement of science	1.1	1.8	2.9	4.2

SOURCES: 1961–62 to 1971–72 from National Science Foundation, *Science Indicators 1974*, Report of the National Science Board, Washington, D.C.: G.P.O., 1975, p. 156. 1977 derived from Appendix B, National Science Foundation, "An Analysis of Federal R&D Funding by Function," (NSP 76-325), Washington, D.C.: G.P.O., September 1976.

rise and fall of R&D in space; the sharp response of R&D energy outlays to the rise in the oil price in 1973; the doubling in relative R&D outlays for health, although a decline occurs in 1976–77; a considerable increase also in economic development R&D outlays, including in the latter the environment, natural resources, and agriculture; the drop after 1972 in R&D outlays for community services (education, income security, housing, etc.).

Third, total R&D outlays (in real terms) peaked out in 1968, declined by about 7%, but exhibited some increase in 1976–77, for the first time in several years. The total number of scientists and engineers employed follows, as one would expect, a similar path: a rise of about 13% in the 1960's, peaking out in 1969; a subsequent decline of about 7%, mildly reversed since 1973. In 1969, for the first time, the number of scientists and engineers employed in Soviet R&D exceeded those so engaged in the United States, as did the proportion of GNP diverted to R&D.

Fourth, basic research expenditures in the U.S. more than doubled in real terms between 1960 and 1968, declined by about 10%, and are now again slowly rising.

Fifth, within industry, the following sectors account, as they have long done, for the bulk of R&D expenditures (about 70%): electrical equipment and communication; aircraft and missiles; motor vehicles; and chemicals. As a proportion of net sales, funds allocated to R&D range from 3–5% in the most R&D-intensive sectors to as low as 0.4–0.8% in food, textiles, lumber, primary metals, and other less technologically dynamic sectors.

The results of R&D are, of course, extremely difficult to measure. Calculations of the rate of return over cost of R&D outlays are inherently difficult given the powerful but oblique effects of basic research, complexities in measuring the returns on new products, etc. Efforts to approximate the results in conventional economic terms suggest that investment in

R&D and innovation yields a rate of return as high as, and often higher than, the return on other investments. For specific innovations, such investment yields returns in the range of 10–50% per annum; productivity growth in innovating industries has been calculated in the range of 30–50%. In agriculture, R&D led to breakthroughs where the rate of return has been calculated as high as 300–600%; e.g., hybrid corn and new methods for accelerating poultry output.

A serious effort to develop indicators of R&D results has been made by the National Science Board, an arm of the National Science Foundation. The results, at first sight, appear to lend credence to a somewhat pessimistic assessment of the course of American scientific and technological creativity in these domains.

Chart 8 shows, for example, the course of American patents granted from 1960 to 1973. It exhibits since the mid-1960's a declining trend for U.S. individuals, a static trend for U.S. corporations, a rising trend only for foreign residents of the U.S. On the other hand, foreign patents granted to U.S. nationals have declined somewhat since the late 1960's. In the basic sciences and engineering, the proportionate contribution of Americans declined in a number of fields over recent years, with a sharp dip in the early 1970's. The proportion of major technological innovations contributed by the United States dropped from about 80% in the mid-1950's to less than 60% in the early 1970's. The proportion of total U.S. major innovations judged to be "radical breakthroughs," as opposed to "major technological advances" or "improvements of existing technology," declined over the same period from 35% to 18%.

What is one to make of data of this kind?

First, it appears to be a fact that the absolute as well as relative scale of resources devoted to basic science and technology in the United States has diminished since the 1960's.

Second, it is natural that the relative scientific and techno-

Chart 8. U.S. Patents Granted
for Inventions, 1960–1973

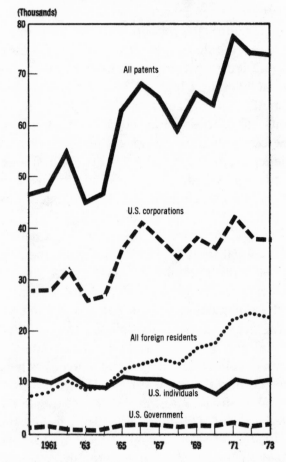

(Thousands)

All patents

U.S. corporations

All foreign residents

U.S. individuals

U.S. Government

1961   '63   '65   '67   '69   '71   '73

SOURCE: U.S. Patent Office, Chart from *Science Indicators, 1974,* National
Science Board, 1975, p. 97.

logical role of the U.S.S.R., France, Germany, and Japan
should have risen over the past generation. They all had to
reorganize their societies after the destruction of the Second
World War. They have all enjoyed relatively high growth
rates, allocated large resources to education and basic sci-

ence, rapidly absorbed technologies pioneered elsewhere, and carried them forward on their own. Put another way, the immediate post-1945 dominance of the United States in science and technology was the product of unnatural circumstances and was bound to subside as expanded, well-trained cohorts of scientists and engineers emerged into maturity in other advanced industrial countries. Moreover, the pace of innovation in the United States is not wholly dependent on the creativity of American science and technology. It is the expansion of the global pool that matters, and the energy and imagination with which American entrepreneurs exploit that pool. On the other hand, the continued rise in the proportion of Soviet GNP devoted to R&D (to over 3% in 1973–74) is an important fact with possible strategic significance.

Third, it is hard to avoid the conclusion that the substantial net decline in total and relative U.S. R&D outlays is related, no doubt in complex ways, to the deceleration in the nation's productivity since the late 1960's. The complexities include the fact that the decline in federal military and space outlays bore heavily on allocations to basic research; the decline in private R&D outlays since 1969–70 may be both a result of the subsequent erratic course of the American economy and a partial cause of its decelerating productivity; the decline in "radical breakthroughs" in American R&D may reflect the fact that the economy was, during the 1960's, elaborating vigorously certain basic innovational possibilities opened up in the first postwar decade. As these were brought to maturity, and the economy entered a new phase, inventive momentum decelerated. But in the time ahead R&D may generate another phase of "radical breakthroughs" in the new directions rendered important and profitable by the strains of the fifth Kondratieff upswing in such fields as energy, agriculture, and raw materials.

Fourth, the focus of R&D at the federal level has shifted three times since the late 1950's: to military outlays and space in the post-Sputnik period; to the quality-of-life sectors of the late 1960's and early 1970's; to energy and resources since 1973. Since R&D investment can have a long period of gestation, with considerable lags between the allocation of talent and resources and results, it is too soon to assess the results which may be forthcoming from this latest shift.

Bearing in mind that the connections between basic science and invention are rarely direct, what can one say about the areas of scientific pursuit which may open up new possibilities bearing on the productivity of the world's economies? I put this question to a small group of scientists and professional observers of science.* They responded generously with their own observations plus extensive recommended readings. Here is an amateur's conclusions from this limited exercise in guided self-education.

The first proposition that emerged was that a number of areas in basic science are experiencing such extraordinarily rapid development that the character of additions to knowledge and their practical implications cannot be confidently predicted. John Wheeler's observation on astrophysics appears to hold for several other major scientific domains: "We would call today the golden age of astrophysics if all the signs of the time did not tell us that ten years from now would be closer to the golden age of astrophysics."† Harvey Brooks put it more generally: "The fact of the matter is that almost all areas of fundamental science at the present time are moving very rapidly, and many of the most exciting developments continue to be ones that were not anticipated only a few years previously."‡ In fact, the expectation of the unexpected is a quite general characteristic of these evaluations. For example,

---

* I am particularly indebted to the guidance on this matter of W. O. Baker, Harvey Brooks, William Brown, Paul Olum, Gerard Piel, and John Wheeler.

† John A. Wheeler, in an unpublished talk, "A Few Faces of the Future of Physics," at the National Academy of Sciences, Washington, D.C., 26 April 1976.

‡ In a letter to the author, 28 April 1977.

Paul Olum: "One thing I feel pretty sure of . . . is that there will certainly be in the next 25 years at least one (and probably several) development which will produce profound changes in our society totally contrary to those now being predicted and planned for by our governments."*

Second, there is a rough consensus about the areas of high momentum and great expectation. Although each breaks down into many subfields, at least four broad areas are evidently undergoing revolutionary change or the rapid elaboration of revolutionary insights:

—*Developmental biology,* where the discovery of deoxyribonucleic acid (DNA) set in motion a wide spectrum of study and application ranging from the origins of life itself to genetic engineering—the transplanting of blocs of genes across species and genus lines.†

—*Astronomy and Astrophysics,* where "the discovery of the existence, almost omnipresence, of a high-energy, explosive universe" has transformed knowledge and defined challenging areas of ignorance; e.g., the phenomenon of "black holes."‡ Although nature may continue to prove elusive

* In a letter to the author, 2 May 1977.

† Although summaries of the prospects for contemporary science date rapidly, "Frontiers of Biology" (Chapter One in *The Life Sciences,* Washington, D.C.: National Academy of Sciences, 1970, report of the Committee on Research in Life Sciences, National Research Council) captures well the dimensions of change in this field.

‡ See, notably, *Astronomy and Astrophysics for the 1970's,* Vol. 1, Report of the Astronomy Survey Committee, National Research Council, Washington, D.C.: National Academy of Sciences, 1972. The quoted phrase is from page 3. For an exciting brief account of the evolution of certain frontier dimensions of astronomy and astrophysics, more or less accessible to the layman, see Kip S. Thorne, "New Objects in Space: From Quasars to the Black Hole," *Bulletin of the American Academy of Arts and Sciences,* December 1974, Vol 28, No. 3, pp. 16–36. Thorne emphasizes the dependence of the revolution in this field on improved technology of observation and instrumentation. See, also, D. W. Sciama, "The Limits of Space and Time: Exploding Black Holes and the Origin of the Universe," *Daedalus, Discoveries and Interpretations Studies in Contemporary Scholarship,* Summer 1977, Vol. I.

and enigmatic, one cannot read this literature without sensing that the life scientists feel themselves hot on the trail of the origins and nature of life; the cosmologists, the origins and nature of the physical universe.

—*The Human Brain.* Biologists, neurologists, psychologists, and computer scientists are moving together towards an understanding of how the brain and nervous system work. The development of ultra-small components in electronics, with many immediate practical applications, is here playing a significant scientific role.

—*Measurement.* As noted earlier, the evolution of modern science has, from its beginnings, been significantly linked to the capacity to observe and measure. One central characteristic of modern science, as opposed to the science of earlier times, is the two-way linkage of the scientist and tool-maker. It appears to be a characteristic of contemporary science that all its major dimensions are being strengthened by an explosive increase in our capacity to measure. William Brown, of the Hudson Institute, has produced (from NASA data) the predictive forecasts in Table 6.

No one can now define confidently the scientific and practical meaning of these generally large-order-of-magnitude improvements in the capacity to observe and measure. Similarly, we do not know what it will mean to move from computer units aboard spacecraft with a data storage capacity of 2000 books (of 300 pages each) in 1975 to half the Library of Congress in 1990, to ten Libraries of Congress in the year 2000. In the inelegant language of computer scientists, this is a progression from 20 gigabits to 8,000, to 160,000: an 8,000-fold increase in a quarter-century. Perhaps, when we gain perspective on the extraordinary growth of modern science, we shall perceive that the computer was a central feature of its momentum. Laymen like myself instinctively think of the computer in its variety of now familiar applications in manufacturing, commerce, space exploration, and economic research. Its

Table 6. Some Forecasts for Improved Sensors or Instruments

	1970	1980	1990	2000
Microwave radiometers				
Noise temp. (°K)	2000	300	30	30
Aperture (meters)	1	2	10	40
Radio telescope:				
Sensitivity at 1-GHZ	1	.02		.01–.001
Radar resolution, from Earth				
orbit (meters)	5	3.5	2	1
Space telescope:				
Aperture (cm.)	50	200		350–450
Laser absorption spectrometer,				
ABS. COEFF.	4	10	12–100	10^2–10^4
Multi-spectral imagers,				
resolution (micro-rad.)	100	25	10	7
Solid state camera (CCD)				
resolution (no. of elements,				
millions)	—	1.1	5–7	11–30
Photon sensitivity				
(micro-joules/M^2)		.8	.3	.2
Electron sensitivity				
(micro-joules/M^2)		.02	.01	.008
X-ray telescope (20–300 K.E.V.)				
sensitivity	1	.2	.03	.006
X-ray spectrometer (20–300				
K.E.V.) sensitivity	4	.2	.01	.001
Superconducting magnetic				
spectrometer, index	1.5	7–8	25–50	90–250
Magnets (kg. per kilogauss)	1.5	.5	.1	.04
Gravity gradiometer	1	.01	.001	.001

SOURCE: William Brown, "New Technologies: Emphasis on Space Exploration," Hudson Institute, October 1976 (HI-2515-BN/2/4). Data derived from *Outlook for Space,* Washington, D.C.: NASA, 1975, Vol. III.

most profound applications, however, may well be in basic science—virtually every field of basic science.* The capacity quickly to solve problems whose solutions would involve drudgery and time beyond the human capacity if traditional means of calculation were used may be the engine which continues to drive science forward at an exponential if not accelerating rate.

These four areas by no means exhaust those where scientists survey their prospects with a mixture of high excitement and a touch of vertigo. There is, for example, the whole area of materials substitution, where physics and chemistry merge. But I, at least, emerge with the clear impression that, so far as basic science is concerned, J. M. Clark's dictum appears still to hold: "Knowledge is the only instrument of production not subject to diminishing returns."[5] There is, as yet, no sign that human creativity in basic science has passed over an inflection point to the decelerating slope of an S-curve.

Even if that impression is correct, it does not, in itself, guarantee a flow of technological change in industry and agriculture at a pace sufficient to solve efficiently the key resource problems of the next quarter-century. This is so even though the time lags between scientific insight, invention, and innovation appear to have been narrowing. The odds are that, over the next quarter-century, the technologies which evolve and are actually introduced into the economy are likely to be based not so much on new findings of basic science but on the turning of inventiveness in new directions rooted in already familiar scientific propositions or on the further elaboration of technologies which currently exhibit high momentum. Indeed, circumstances in the market sometimes render relevant very

* This point is made by W. O. Baker in "Computers As Information-Processing Machines in Modern Science," in *Daedalus,* Fall 1970: *The Making of Modern Science: Biographical Studies,* Vol. 99, No. 4, pp. 1088–1120. It was strongly reinforced in a conversation with William Brown of the Hudson Institute.

old technologies. For example, the flat-plate solar collector, now diffusing quite rapidly in a world of high energy prices, was probably first devised by an eighteenth century Swiss scientist, Nicholas de Saussure. In Chapters 4–7, some of the possible, or even likely, fruits of inventive enterprise in new directions required by the fifth Kondratieff upswing have already been suggested. Here, again, is an illustrative list of possibilities:

Birth Control.—Long-lasting suppression of fertility by vaccination.

Agriculture.—The extension of nitrogen fixation in plants.

—The crossing of plant types (e.g., wheat and rye) and other methods for developing crops of higher yield, higher protein content, and greater disease resistance.

—Hydroponic agriculture.

—Single-cell protein (SCP) for animal and perhaps human consumption, derived from petroleum or cellulose.

Energy.—Rendering competitive at likely levels of energy cost of: *in situ* coal conversion; wind power; bioconversion of trees, crops, solid wastes (biomass); the photovoltaic cell and other refinements in solar energy; ocean thermal power; geothermal; the breeder reactor; nuclear fusion.

—Energy conservation: more efficient power transmission; more efficient motor vehicle engines; heat pumps; productive use of waste heat; improved insulation techniques.

Raw Materials.—Substitution and recycling; seabed mining; deeper level mining; more efficient processing of low-grade ores.

Environment.—Nonpolluting efficient motor-vehicle engines (e.g., electric); conversion of polluting coal into gas or low-sulfur crude oil; other technologies which reduce pollution (e.g., nitrogen-fixing plants, solid-waste energy conversion).

Obviously, no one can predict with confidence the pace at which creative inventiveness will render these and similar possibilities cost-effective. Nevertheless, these three propositions can be asserted. First, a concentration of talent and resources on this array of problems and possibilities is a product of the past few years in the case of energy and raw materials, not much longer in the case of agriculture and the environment. A sharp change in the directions of research and development takes time, notably in the highly bureaucratized settings within which a good deal of contemporary invention occurs. Moreover, the process of purposeful invention itself takes time, as it always has done. A seventeenth-century English writer captured well the painful, stubborn, protracted process involved:

> Now not one [invention] of a hundred outlives this torture, and those that do are at length so changed by the various contrivances of others, that not any one man can pretend to the invention of the whole, nor well agree about their respective shares in the parts. And moreover this commonly is long a-doing, that the poor inventor is either dead, or disabled by the debts contracted to pursue his design; and withal railed upon as a projector, or worse, by those who joyned their money in partnership with his wit; so as the said inventor and his pretences are wholly lost and vanisht.[6]

Bankruptcy may be somewhat more rare in a world of government grants and large industrial laboratories, but it remains true that definitive breakthroughs tend to be the final result of the work of many hands and minds; and breakthroughs take time.

The second relevant proposition is that the pace of progress in some of these directions is already quite promising, despite the short periods of sharply focused effort involved. Moreover, inventive effort is proceeding simultaneously, in a good many centers, in a number of countries. The chances of breakthroughs are enhanced by this diffusion of effort, so long as reasonably ample resources are available.

Third, the outcome will depend not merely on the scale of the human and physical resources invested in the process of invention, but also on the environment society creates for the potential inventors. John Wheeler's observation on this matter has much historical evidence to support it, although press, pundits, and the man in the street have not always been the ultimate source of morale:

> What a difference in morale and productivity one sees in any upper echelon man at the Los Alamos Scientific Laboratory or the Lawrence Livermore Laboratory between the times he feels needed and wanted by the American people and the times—that come and go—when press and pundits tell him, in effect, get lost. No research man is a sausage machine that automatically turns out good new developments merely by being cranked. He belongs to government or industry or an independent research institution or university. Whatever the place, however, his work is a work of the imagination and his drive comes from feeling needed and appreciated.
>
> The man in the street may suppose that this and that new discovery, new way of doing business, new drug, new history, new engine, new fabric "just happens," when in truth nothing did more to slow or speed its arrival than his indifference or support, his alienation or sympathy.*

As for the elaboration and more effective application of existing technologies that have a high natural momentum of their own, the laser and communications appear most promising.

The laser—with its extraordinary concentration of energy, combined with pinpoint sharpness even over long distances—lends itself to many different applications. The breadth of its potential use has probably played a part in its relatively slow introduction, which is suggested by the following incomplete list of its present or likely roles: eye surgery; the precise measurement of continental drift (by bouncing laser beams off the moon); the drilling of extremely fine holes in metal (e.g., 20,000 holes in a steel sheet the size of a postcard); the align-

* John Wheeler, "The Morale of Research People," *Discovery,* Vol. 1, No. 3, March 1977, p. 2.

ment of tubes, pipes, and tunnels in construction; and, potentially of greater significance, in communications and information handling.

The coming of a new communications revolution, like the future ubiquity of the laser, has been widely heralded. It includes, again, a good many different dimensions. There is, for example, the possibility of transmitting images as well as speech in private and commercial communications, including, in the former, charts and designs as well as human forms. High-capacity mobile telephone systems also appear on their way, as well as the capacity of machines to approximate credibly the human voice. In another direction, the storing and communication of data appear to be developing in ways which might permit production units to be smaller and more widely diffused, helping give rise to Norman Macrae's engaging but not wholly persuasive portrait, in the London *Economist* of December 25, 1976, of a future where large manufacturing and commercial units will have become part of the past.

Evidently, as in the case of basic science, any conclusions about the prospects for inventions must be impressionistic. My own impression is that there is a good deal of momentum already in resource-related fields relevant to the fifth Kondratieff upswing, including resource conservation; momentum is likely to accelerate as inventive minds, only recently diverted to such problems, are given time to produce results; but the most important potential invention remains uncertain —that is, a cheap as well as essentially infinite and relatively non-polluting source of energy.

Now, what about innovation? Can we assume that the private sectors of the American economy will, in fact, effectively absorb the technologies which are generated by human inventiveness?

As of October 1977 one would have to describe the zeal of the private sector in the United States in mixed terms.

On the one hand, business expansion had been under way

for two years; private investments in general (as well as R&D outlays) lifted a bit after a deep and disturbing decline in 1974–75; but all the major OECD economies exhibited abnormally low investment levels, by past standards. The computerized models used for predicting short-run economic change held out hopes for a much larger expansion of investment on the basis of the increased profits of 1976 and the improved cash-flow position of firms. The immediate prospects for the American economy were subject to uncertainty and debate; but they were much better than in most of Western Europe. One had the sense that, to a degree, the American business community might be beginning to get its bearings in the altered setting of the fifth Kondratieff upswing.

On the other hand, there was another, darker strand in the mood of American private enterprise: uncertainty about the longer future; fears of a recurrence of acute inflation and a recession renewed before full utilization of capacity and low levels of unemployment were reached; anxiety about the course of events in Britain, Italy, and France and the sense that, in some way, the United States might be moving down a similar path; a continued brooding about the tendency of some members of Congress to use private enterprise as a scapegoat for the energy crisis—a mood not relieved by the tone and content of the National Energy Plan laid before the Congress on April 20, 1977, and later pronouncements from the White House attributing opposition to sinister special interests. To these anxieties was added a disturbing fact: a combination of high oil imports and a greater degree of recovery in the United States than elsewhere was producing large balance of payments deficits.

As will emerge in Chapter 10, these moods were heightened because of the divergent paths of the American regions, notably since 1973. The atmosphere of caution and apprehension was most marked in the Northeast and industrial Middle West. Those regions not only still contain a high proportion of the nation's industrial plant but a still higher proportion of its head offices, financial institutions (including the volatile stock exchanges), and the centers for R&D. Subscribers to some respected expert analyses of the American economic situation were being told to expect a future described in terms like these: accelerated inflation followed by serious deflation lasting two decades, "wreaking great havoc and culminating in a trough war, at which time the cleansing process is complete and a whole set of new values have been instilled in society."[7] Men subjected to apocalyptic predictions of this kind, harassed by the political process, without a lucid understanding of the economic environment which has enveloped the world economy since the end of 1972, were not likely to take the creative risks a rapid pace of innovation required.

It is here in the domain of private innovation and its relation to public policy, rather than in the alleged deficiencies of science or invention, that the greatest danger to the future appears to lie—a theme to which Chapter 12 returns.

10

Regional Change:
Conflict or Reconciliation?

Wᴵᴛʜᴵɴ the general perspective of the fifth Kondratieff upswing, Chapters 4–9 considered a series of major sectoral problems confronted in the American economy; and, where relevant, they were placed in their international context. In this chapter, these and other domestic issues are examined as they emerge from a brief survey of problems and prospects in the major regions of the United States.

In February 1976, *The New York Times* published a series of articles on the relative shift of population, industry, and income towards the states of the South and Southwest. The May 17th issue of *Business Week* carried on its cover the following title of a special report: "The Second War Between the States." The subtitle was: "A bitter struggle for jobs, capital, and people." In June, *The National Journal* included a section entitled: "Federal Spending: The North's Loss is the Sunbelt's Gain." These articles reflected a prior political fact. Over the three previous years, various members of Congress and several Northern governors had become aware that average unemployment rates were higher in the North; that the Northeast and Middle West were, relatively, losing population to other regions; and that industrial jobs were declining absolutely in the North while continuing slowly to increase in the Sunbelt despite the post-1974 recession. They began to look to a relatively enlarged flow of federal funds for redress. But 1976 was clearly the year in which America's regional problems began to attract the nation's attention and pose sharply some difficult policy issues.

Recent regional trends in the relative growth of population, real income, and industry, as well as North–South unemployment differentials, are to be understood in terms of three phenomena: the tendency of late-comers to modern economic growth to catch up with those who industrialized earlier; the differential impact on American regions of the first phase of the fifth Kondratieff upswing; and the overall inadequacy of national economic policy in dealing with the problems posed since the end of 1972. The failure to generate an effective energy policy or to devise policies of sustained full employment has rendered regional problems and tensions more severe than they had to be.

Economic historians have long been aware that, in the early stages of a country's development, regional differences in growth rates and real income are likely to increase. This happens because modern industrial technologies are picked up and applied, sector by sector, in areas endowed either with appropriate resources, location, or particularly creative entrepreneurs. In the United States, for example, New England led the way with a modern textile industry in the 1820's; Pennsylvania, with a modern iron industry in the 1840's and 1850's; Chicago, with farm machinery; and, later, Detroit with automobiles. The northern regions of a number of countries industrialized before the southern: in Britain, the United States, France, Germany, Spain, and Italy. Hence Stephen Potter's gamesman's ploy for breaking a flow of pretentious exposition at a cocktail party: 'Ah, but it's different in the south.' Brazil was an interesting exception: São Paulo and Rio, in the south, led the way, while the Brazilian north, initially committed like the American South to a single crop (sugar), lagged. But with the passage of time and the availability of a diversified pool of unapplied technologies, the lagging regions began to exploit their opportunities and to catch up. As one analyst of this problem concluded: "Rising regional income disparities and increasing North–South dualism is typical of early development stages, while regional convergence and a disappearance of severe North–South problems is typical of the more mature stages of national growth and development."[1]

What has been true within countries has also been true among countries. The familiar cliché that the poor get poorer and the rich get richer is simply not true. Both historical and contemporary evidence suggest the opposite. I have recently reviewed and analyzed that evidence in an article whose subtitle is: *Reflections on Why the Poor Get Richer and the Rich Slow Down.*[2] For example, the average growth rate in income per capita of Britain, from the beginning of its industrialization in 1783 to 1967 was 1.3% per annum; for the United States, for the period 1843 to 1972, 1.8%. On the other hand, Japan, which started in 1885, and Russia, starting in 1890, both averaged 2.5%. Mexico, starting in 1940, has done even better: 3.4%.

The same broad result emerges if one looks at growth rates, in cross-section, for the 1960's. The poorest countries (under $100 per capita in 1967 dollars) averaged only 1.7%. The rate rises steadily to a peak at about $1,000 per capita, where growth rates were 6.5%. The growth rate then declines for the richer countries, with the U.S. averaging in that decade only 3.2%.

There are two basic reasons for this pattern: first, the latecomers to industrialization have a large backlog of unapplied modern technologies to absorb, whereas the more advanced nations must depend on the flow of new technologies while carrying a heavier weight of old or obsolescent industrial plant; second, as countries (or regions) get richer, they allocate more of their income to services which, in general, do not incorporate technologies of high productivity to the same extent as manufactures.

The relative rise of the Sunbelt flows, then, from the fact that it was late in moving into sustained and diversified industrialization and the modernization of its agriculture; but once the process took hold, the South moved ahead faster than the older industrial areas because it had a larger backlog of technologies to bring to bear. Its consequently more rapid increase in income and accelerated urbanization amplified the process.

In the long sweep of the South's history, the turning point clearly came between 1930 and 1940, in the period of recovery from the Great Depression after 1929 (see Table 7).

Focus for a moment on the South Atlantic and East South Central states. Their relative income per capita declined between 1840 and 1860, as the North as a whole experienced its first rapid phase of industrialization; but, still, the Southern regions stood at about two-thirds the national average in 1860, roughly the same level as the East North Central agricultural states. The Southern states lost ground seriously after the Civil War. This was a result not only of wartime destruction and the vicissitudes of Reconstruction but also because of a sharp decline in cotton prices and a slowing down in the expansion of the world's cotton consumption. There was some recovery from the mid-1890's to 1920, as the cotton price improved and some modest industrial development occurred in the South, centered on the textile industry. In the 1920's the region again lost ground relatively, as agricultural prices sagged. In 1930 relative income per capita was only about half the national average. From the mid-1930's, however, four decades of sustained relative progress occurred. The West South Central states followed a similar path, although their

Table 7. Per Capita Income as Percent of U.S. Total, by Regions: 1840–1975

Year	USA	New England	Middle Atlantic	East North Central	West North Central	South Atlantic	East South Central	West South Central	Mountain	Pacific
1975	100	108	108	104	98	90	79	91	92	111
1970	100	108	113	105	95	86	74	85	90	110
1965	100	108	114	108	95	81	71	83	90	115
1960	100	109	116	107	93	77	67	83	95	118
1950	100	106	116	112	94	74	63	81	96	121
1940	100	121	124	112	84	69	55	70	92	138
1930	100	129	140	111	82	56	48	61	83	130
1920	100	124	134	108	87	59	52	72	100	135
1900	100	134	139	106	97	45	49	61	139	163
1880	100	141	141	102	90	45	51	70	168	204
1860	100	143	137	69	66	65	68	115	—	—
1840	100	132	136	67	75	70	73	144	—	—

SOURCES: 1840–1970, *Historical Statistics of the United States, Colonial Times to 1970*, Washington, D.C.: Department of Commerce, 1975, p. 242; 1975, *Survey of Current Business*, August 1976, Vol. 56, Table 2, p. 17.

relative income position in 1930 was a bit higher than that of other parts of the South.

The rise of the Sunbelt in terms of relative income is, then, a phenomenon some forty years old. It was accompanied by a large flow of black migrants to the North. Between 1940 and 1970, for example, the white population of the South increased by 59%, the Negro population by only 21%. In the Northeast and North Central regions the Negro population more than tripled in these years, and increased more than tenfold in the West.

The process which brought about this striking movement of the South towards income equality with the rest of the country had these specific features:

—A remarkable decline in agricultural employment accompanied by the technical modernization of agriculture, including a shift to the West and mechanization of cotton production.

—A more than doubling of manufacturing employment, with a marked relative shift towards the production of durable as opposed to non-durable goods (e.g., textiles).

—A large shift of labor to construction as the region's population moved into the cities and suburbs (37% of the population in the South was urban in 1940, 65% in 1970).

—Rapid expansion of public and private services, including education. In Texas, for example, the proportion of the population in 1940 in institutions of higher education was .6% as opposed to the national average of 1.2%: in 1970 the proportions were 3.1% and 3.4%. Much more than the gap in income was narrowed between North and South in those thirty years. And these social changes, including especially a rise in the educational level, were a necessary condition for the effective absorption of the backlog of sophisticated technologies.

In broad terms, then, the structural differences between the South and the rest of the nation were rapidly reduced over the period 1940–70. It could no longer be said in the old way and to the same extent: 'It's different in the south.'

There were, of course, great differences among the Sunbelt states. Florida, for example, enjoyed a relatively high per capita income in 1940 (86% of the national average) and improved its position only modestly (1970, 94%), lacking either a substantial manufacturing structure or energy resources. It has remained disproportionately dependent on tourism and retirement. Primary metals are a major source of income only in West Virginia, Alabama, and Kentucky. Energy production is a major export of Kentucky, Oklahoma, Louisiana, Texas, and West Virginia. Other Southern states face energy problems similar to those in the North. The proportionate role of agriculture, services, and industry as a source of employment varies greatly among the Sunbelt states. For example, 37% of employment in North Carolina is industrial, 13% in Florida. Mississippi, Arkansas, South Carolina, and Alabama remain still relatively poor states as compared, even, to the rest of the South and Southwest.

As of 1970, the uneven movement of the South towards rough homogeneity in income and structure with the rest of the country was a phenomenon little studied in the North; and, when noted, it was a source of gratification rather than anxiety. In particular, the success of the South in adjusting to the Civil Rights Acts of 1964 and 1965—ending Jim Crow and permitting a rapid increase in voting among Southern blacks— was widely, if not universally, regarded as a victory for the nation as a whole in dealing with its oldest and most difficult problem. It was the coming of the fifth Kondratieff upswing which suddenly converted a benign pattern of regional development into something of a national problem. This was the case because the relative rise in food and energy prices accelerated the development of a good many Sunbelt states which exported energy and agricultural resources to the rest of the country; while the relative price shift decelerated the already slower rate of expansion in the Northeast and North Central industrial states. The population shift to the Sunbelt picked up momentum, although about two-thirds of the recent population increase in that region is due to somewhat higher birth rates than in the North. But the fact is that more than half the nation's population increase between 1970 and 1975 was in the South. And the flow of blacks from South to North reversed.

In the sharp recession of 1974–75, unemployment averaged in the latter year over 9% in New England, the Middle Atlantic, and East North Central states; 7.9% in the South Atlantic states, with Florida, dependent on tourism, as high as 10.7%; 6.9% in the South Central states. Texas experienced in 1975 only 5.6% unemployment. The relatively higher levels of unemployment cut tax revenues and increased requirements for compensating social services at precisely the time the tax base was also being weakened by the initial impact of the fifth Kondratieff upswing on real income and the accelerated flow of people to the South.

The impact of the fifth Kondratieff upswing is, perhaps,

Table 8. Percent Change in Nonagricultural Employment and Location Quotients[a] for the United States, the Northern Industrial Tier, and the Sunbelt-South: 1970–1975

| Industry | Percent Change in Employment: 1970-75 | | | Location Quotient | | | |
| | U.S. | Northern Industrial Tier | Sunbelt-South | Northern Industrial Tier | | Sunbelt-South | |
				1970	1975	1970	1975
Total Nonagricultural	8.6	1.3	16.7	—	—	—	—
Mining	19.6	13.6	21.5	.44	.40	2.0	1.90
Construction	-2.2	-13.6	14.1	.84	.80	1.18	1.29
Manufacturing	-5.2	-12.7	1.6	1.17	1.16	.96	.96
Transportation and Public Utilities	-0.1	-5.7	9.0	.95	.98	1.02	1.03
Wholesale & Retail Trade	12.7	6.4	21.6	.96	.97	1.00	1.00
Finance, Insurance & Real Estate	14.5	6.7	29.1	1.04	1.04	.90	.95
Services	20.4	14.6	30.8	.99	1.01	.88	.89
Government	17.3	11.8	23.5	.87	.89	1.06	1.04

most vividly seen in Table 8, showing the startling decline of manufacturing jobs in the North between 1970 and 1975, while the South continued to gain, despite the sharp recession of 1974–75.

Thus, the shift in relative prices since the end of 1972 did not create the problems of the Northeast and North Central states; but it converted a slow-moving erosion of their relative position into something of a Northern crisis.

Table 8, exhibiting the structure of employment shifts as between the Northern industrial states and the Sunbelt, reflects the role in the process of the energy producing sectors, with oil and gas included in "mining."

The role of the relative price shift in bringing about these changes is underlined by looking beyond the Sunbelt. Between 1970 and 1975, both the agricultural states of the West North Central area and the coal-rich Mountain states also enjoyed a rise in relative prices, a favorable relative shift in income, and lower than average unemployment. The Mountain states, in fact, experienced the highest rate of population increase (16.3%) of any of the nation's regions over those five years.

We turn now to the pattern of development since 1940 in the Northeast and East North Central states, and to the reasons for their peculiar vulnerability to the coming of the fifth Kondratieff upswing.

---

a A location quotient is the ratio of the proportion of a region's total employment which is located in a particular industry to the proportion of the nation's total employment which is located in the same industry.

SOURCES: U.S. Department of Labor, Bureau of Labor Statistics, *Employment and Earnings,* May 1973, Vol. 19, pp. 128–137, and May 1976, Vol. 22, pp. 49 and 126–135. Table 2 was compiled by C. L. Jusenius and L. C. Ledebur, "A Myth in the Making: The Southern Economic Challenge and Northern Economic Decline," prepared for U.S. Department of Commerce, Washington, D.C., November 1976, p. 34.

There is a substantial consensus on the characteristics which have marked the evolution of these regions over the past three decades. Here, for example, is one statement of the situation of the East North Central region:

> It is a region in trouble:
> —National economic shifts are causing the region to lose more jobs than it is gaining;
> —A substantial outflow of talent is now occurring as a result of out-migration toward the South and West;
> —This outflow is leaving behind a large population of poor who migrated into the industrial cities in earlier decades;
> —Many cities are dominated by one industry and have highly specialized, vulnerable economies;
> —These conditions have led to substantial financial trouble as cities try to meet the rising costs of public services out of dwindling tax bases;
> —These problems are compounded by fragmented government and taxing capacities in many of the metropolitan areas;
> —These fiscal difficulties are reinforced by a highly unfavorable "balance of payments"—poorer than any other section of the country—with respect to federal taxes paid and federal funds received;
> —It is at a disadvantage in competing with other sections of the country in terms of recreational and climatic amenities; and
> —It is a region with a high percentage of obsolescence in its manufacturing plants, housing, and public facilities.[3]

This array could constitute a conventional statement of the problems confronted in the Northeast—chronically in the 1950's and 1960's, acutely in the past five years. The Midwest has, however, an additional concern: the peculiarly important role of the automobile industry which ramifies back from the assembly plants in Detroit to steel, rubber, and the other industries which furnish components. A 25% reduction in the demand for automobiles (or reduction in their size) might cause a loss of 400,000 jobs and increase unemployment in the region by 3.2%. The Northeast is somewhat more diversified. There is no single equivalent of this massive but now vulner-

able industrial complex, although a good many cities throughout the Northeast are dependent on particular plants for a
significant proportion of their employment.

There is another way to look at the matter: in terms of old,
slow-growing sectors and sectors based on newer technologies, experiencing rapid growth. The former include not only
textiles, shoes, and the classic non-durable consumers goods,
but also steel, machine tools, and, I would now add, automobiles. The more dynamic sectors include the electronics industry, in all its many facets, and certain technologically vital
branches of the chemical industry. By and large, the industrial structure of the Northeast and Middle West is heavily
weighted by history towards the older sectors. Those parts of
the Northern region linked to the newer sectors have systematically fared better than others. It is in the mature sectors
that obsolescent industrial capacity has mainly emerged. In
Ohio, for example, 21% of plant and equipment is classified as
obsolescent as compared with the national average of 12%;
but in the older primary metals and non-electrical machinery
sectors, obsolescence is over 40%. But the new high technology sectors of the 1950's and 1960's may also be decelerating
in the 1970's, a tendency dramatized by IBM's use of its cash
surplus in 1977 to purchase its own stock rather than to invest
in new directions. As noted in Chapter 8, the private sector is
almost as bemused as federal policy as to where productive
investment should be undertaken in the changed context of
the fifth Kondratieff upswing.

In the Northeast, a rather remarkable job was done between
1950 and 1970 in supplanting older, non-durable industries
with durable goods industries, often linked to new technologies. A loss of some 338,000 jobs in the former category was
just about balanced by 312,000 new jobs in the latter. The rise
of federal spending on military and space hardware helped.
The Northeast benefitted greatly from its comparative advantage in first-class educational, engineering, and research and

development institutions. The decline of national security outlays has retarded these sectors. To a significant degree, however, the comparative advantage of the North in high technology fields remains. In 1974, 33% of total industrial outlays
for R&D (federal and private) was in the Northeast, containing about 23% of the nation's population; 22% in the North
Central states (27% of the population). By way of comparison,
the total figure for all three regions of the South (32% of the
population) was only 14%.[4] The task of the North is to bring
this capacity to bear on the resource-related sectors whose
importance has risen in the fifth Kondratieff upswing: energy
and energy conservation, transport, agriculture, raw materials, and pollution control. All this will not be easy. The
North contains a relatively old working force; and, like investment in general, movement is held up by unresolved
national policies for energy and the environment as well as by
rather discouraging local tax structures. But if my analysis is
correct, the sophisticated R&D and industrial capacity of the
North will be greatly needed by the nation in the time ahead.

There are also both mature and new sectors in the South
and Southwest. Both have generally expanded more rapidly
than their northern counterparts, mainly because of relatively
higher rates of both population and income growth. But in
certain sectors (e.g., textiles) the South has felt the competition of overseas suppliers. Overall, however, its mix of industries is newer and the problem of obsolescence less acute.

The problems of the Northeast and North Central states
were complicated in the 1970's by the rise in the role of services relative to manufacturing. Included under services are a
wide variety of quite different economic activities: wholesale
and retail trade; finance, insurance, and real estate; government; education; health services. As nearly as we can measure productivity in services, it is systematically lower, on
average, than in manufacturing, because it is somewhat less
subject to technological innovation. Some services are auto-

matically required as population, industry, and income expand, and urbanization takes place. Thus the large expansion
of service sectors in the South as well as in the North. Others,
notably education, health services, and welfare outlays are
subject over a significant range to public policy.

The disproportionate growth of services relative to manufacturing rendered the Northeast and North Central states
vulnerable to a situation where the increase of income and
population was slowing down and other parts of the country
were developing a capacity to generate financial and other
services in support of their regional economies. This tendency
was exacerbated by the development of a good road-transport
system in the South and the national shift towards light, high
technology industries, less dependent on the dense railroad
network which was once a special asset of the North.

Against this background, the coming of the fifth Kondratieff
upswing hit hard the two Northern regions. Somewhat like
slow-moving Great Britain of the 1960's, the high-income
North had committed itself to enlarged public and private
services at a time when its manufacturing base, with high
obsolescence in certain sectors, was waning, its rate of population increase was slowing down, and population was actually declining in some major urban areas. The unfavorable
shift in the region's terms of trade, as in Britain, reduced real
income at just the time it confronted unemployment rates
about 2% higher than those in the South and Southwest. The
fiscal problems posed for state and local government were
only in degree less acute than for New York City. Meanwhile,
as noted earlier, the relative rise in energy and agricultural
prices accelerated the flow of population to areas producing
these products, widened growth rate differentials, and still
further weakened the foundations of the economies in the
Northeast and North Central states.

As this situation became apparent, the initial reaction of
politicians in the North was to seek redress by inducing the

federal government to reallocate federal expenditures from South to North. That theme dominated the literature of early 1976 on the subject of regional change. In crude terms, the argument was: the rise of the Sunbelt was a product of disproportionate outlays of the federal government financed by Northern taxes; now is the time for the South to contribute disproportionately to the rehabilitation of the North. As experts dug into the data on federal tax and expenditure flows, the evidence suggested a less straightforward picture of the past and less simple remedies for the future.

For example, when federal tax contributions are calculated as a proportion of income per capita in the states (rather than per capita), the relative contribution of the Northern states to federal revenues is much reduced. On the other hand, when present (inadequate) cost-of-living indexes are applied to the regions, the North–South real income per capita differential is further narrowed. For example, when the flow of federal grants is systematically correlated with various indicators of economic development in the states, no significant association emerges; and, in the case of rapidly growing Texas, federal spending and federal taxes are almost exactly equal. For example, when federal expenditures are analyzed by categories and measured in terms of outlays per capita in the various states, the Northeast appears to have been drawing more from Washington than the South in: defense contracts, welfare programs, and, marginally, retirement programs. On the other hand, with respect to defense contracts, it is impossible to trace where the subcontractors are and where the outlays (allocated to the location of corporate headquarters) are, in fact, spent. The more rapidly urbanizing South acquired somewhat more for highways and sewers, and a great deal more in defense salaries due to the location of military bases. The East and West North Central states fared worse than the South in all categories except highways and sewers; but the West (a high-income area) far outstripped all other regions in defense contracts and salaries, and in highways, the latter mainly because of the still expanding interstate highway program in the Mountain states.

The analysis and debate about federal tax flows and expenditures can be expected to become more complex but to remain a lively part of the national political scene. My own view is, quite simply, that the major regional changes in the country have been only marginally determined by the balance of federal tax and expenditure flows; and that the future of federal policy and outlays in the regions should be determined by the requirements of the several regions, seen in terms of their deeper structural problems and the larger interests of the nation as a whole. It is a wholesome fact that, as analysis of the nation's regional problems has gone forward in 1976–77, this is the direction of thought and prescription.

When, for example, the Northeast Governors Conference met in Saratoga in November 1976 they did, indeed, point to the apparent imbalance between tax revenues and federal expenditures from which the South and West profit at the expense of the North. But they went further to propose measures which would enlarge investment in energy production and conservation; to rehabilitate the region's transport system; and to expand and modernize industrial capacity in areas of particularly severe unemployment. They proposed manpower training and public works programs, exhibiting considerable sensitivity in assuring that the latter were undertaken in sectors where investment would prove productive over the long run; e.g., transport rehabilitation, solid waste disposal plants, etc. The conference also considered the complex problem of welfare reform on a national basis, but with an understandable emphasis on the extent to which slow growth, the long prior period of South to North migration, and higher than average unemployment since 1973 have converged to make the welfare problems of the Northeast particularly acute. The institutions and policies, regional and national, do not yet exist to translate these directions of thought into lines of action; but the governors of the Northeast have taken a major step. They formulated in detail a plan for a Northeast Energy Development Corporation and persuaded the Senate to open hearings on such regional institutions in the autumn of 1977. In their present formulation, the federal role would be limited to guaranteeing the bonds of the regional banks.

In 1976–77 similar analyses were emerging in the North Central states; for example, the studies of the Academy for Contemporary Problems in Columbus, Ohio. The academy has surveyed extensively the structural changes and problems of the whole East North Central region and prescribed a detailed program for Ohio. Its policy agenda includes special measures to expand local coal production and to reduce energy consumption; a modernization of the transport system; special incentives to stimulate high-growth manufacturing and export industries as well as to rehabilitate aging or obsolete plants. As in the Northeast, there is a call for redirected federal tax revenues, a national welfare plan, and intensified regional cooperation between the public and private sectors to stimulate investment in the directions necessary for further development. In August 1977, the Midwestern Governors' Conference threw its support behind the concept of regional development banks which would stimulate public–private investment in transport and water development, as well as soil conservation and energy.

The South and Southwest confront what may appear in the North an easier future; but analysis of its serious structural problems is also increasing. The excellent report of the Task Force on Southern Rural Development, for example, measures the scale and character of poverty in the South relative to the rest of the country. In 1974 there were still 10.8 million poor Southerners and 13.5 million poor persons outside the South. Fifty-four percent of the southern poor are rural; only 38% are rural outside the South. Evidently, a massive problem of poverty still exists in the rural South, roughly matching in

scale the more visible urban poverty of the North, but consti-
tuting a higher proportion of the total Southern population,
which was only a third of the national total in 1975. One out of
six Southerners lived in poverty; one out of eleven outside the
South. The recommendations of the task force, notably with
respect to retraining and bringing the poor effectively into the
working force, are similar to the manpower proposals of the
Saratoga program of the Northeast Governors Conference.

As the South and Southwest look to the future, analysts are
beginning to perceive a set of investment and policy tasks
quite as challenging, in their way, as those in the North and
Northeast. For example, the whole irrigated area of the High
Plains, from Northwest Texas to Nebraska, is endangered by
the decline of the underground water basin which supplies it.
The region produces a significant part of the American agricultural surplus. Large investments in surface water conservation
and transfer will be required to preserve it. In addition, the
oil and gas reserves from conventional sources are almost
certain to run down over the next generation in Louisiana,
Oklahoma, and Texas. Like the nation as a whole, they face
a transition to coal; atomic energy; geothermal, solar, and
other forms of energy, but they do so with a disproportionately
high percentage of their economic structure linked to petrochemicals and other energy-based industries.

On March 31–April 2, 1977, a conference of the Southwest
American Assembly was held in Texas on "Capital Needs of
the Southwest: The Next Decade." Its agenda was familiar
to analysts in the North, including among the major investment fields: energy and raw materials; plant and equipment
for manufacturing; pollution and environmental controls;
housing, public facilities, and education. In September 1977,
the Governor of Texas launched a commission to examine the
state's problems and possibilities down to the year 2000. Its
mandate includes study of the problems of energy and water
supply.

The challenge to the Sunbelt is, of course, to complete its

transition to modernization; to develop further its resources in energy and nurture its agricultural base; and to deal with its social problems, under conditions of rapid population increase, while avoiding as much as possible the environmental degradation which marked the urbanization of the North. The problem of the North is to bring to bear its enormous potentials in technology, finance, and entrepreneurship; to exploit its energy resources in the new price environment; to rehabilitate its transport system in cost-effective ways; and to modernize the industrial sectors which hold greatest promise for the future. This will require a new regional sense of purpose as well as intimate public–private collaboration.

It is worth asking bluntly: Do the Northeast and industrial Middle West have a future? If this analysis is correct, the situation of the Northern states is the result of deeply rooted structural problems which have resulted in a greater relative load of obsolescent industries, a heritage of sizable commitments to expensive social services, and a large concentration of poor in the central cities (reflecting a prior South to North population flow over a protracted period). There are those who have concluded that the North, after a century and a half of leadership, should gracefully decline and surrender economic leadership to the South and Southwest. From newspaper accounts, a gathering of economists at Rutgers University in March 1977 developed some such consensus.

I do not share that mood of passive pessimism about the North. For one thing, as the case of Britain illustrates, economic decline is not a graceful process. It is painful, socially contentious, and potentially quite ugly in the political moods and problems it generates. Nations or regions which choose to go down in the style to which they have become accustomed find it a difficult or even tragic path to follow. Moreover, I believe it is unnecessary. Surely, the pattern of economic development in the North will have to change. Surely, the North cannot go on doing what it has been doing if it is to cope with the special pressures of the fifth Kondratieff upswing. Surely, the antiseptic, easy devices of fiscal and monetary policy will not cure the ills of the North. But the lesson of economic development in many parts of the world is that it hinges mainly on the human resources available, mobilized around the right tasks. The North commands both the material and human resources for a great revival; and it contains half the nation's population.

There are a good many examples of nations which successfully recaptured momentum after falling behind under the weight of mature industries with substantial obsolescent plant. Post-1945 France and Belgium accomplished such a transformation as, indeed, did post-World War II New England. The initial assessments of postwar Germany, its economy split in an historically unnatural way, burdened with refugees and great war damage, were exceedingly gloomy. Every Northern business, labor, and political leader ought to read Chapter 10 in Jean Monnet's *Mémoires*. Its title: "France Modernizes Itself." It describes how France found itself in a state of severe industrial and agricultural obsolescence after the Second World War and how, through public–private collaboration, led and inspired by a minuscule bureaucracy, it underwent a total technological renovation. Perhaps the two Monnet dicta most relevant from that experience to the situation of the North are: "We do not have a choice. There is no alternative to modernization except decadence"; and "Modernization is not a state of things but a state of mind [esprit]."[5]

Structural transformations are clearly possible if there is a common will to accomplish them, a sense of direction, and a general environment of rapid economic growth. Only those who live in the North can generate the common will, the sense of direction, and the requisite institutions for communal action.

This brief survey of regional change and of thought about future development is, of course, too simple. It cannot be overemphasized that there are great differences among states and even within them. There are special problems and prospects in the Mountain states and Far West, Alaska and Hawaii. But six large, general conclusions stand out which fully mesh with those which emerged when American problems were viewed on an undifferentiated national basis.

First, a return to sustained full employment and high-growth rates on a national basis would greatly ease the special problems of the Northern states by simultaneously reducing welfare requirements and expanding tax revenues. Further, analysis of the national situation in terms of the regions strongly reinforces the central argument of this book that sustained full employment is to be achieved by expanded investment in energy and other resource development and conservation fields, combined with outlays to re-accelerate the growth of productivity. Without full employment and rapid growth, it will be exceedingly difficult to sustain welfare services and deal with poverty problems.

Second, economic as well as social and human considerations require serious and sustained efforts to bring into the working force the large number of Americans now trapped in urban and rural poverty, North and South. The nation should look with equal concern at the problem of the central cities and the impoverished margins of life in the Southern countryside. Except for energy, we do not yet command the data to measure the scale of the nation's special investment requirements over, say, the next ten years in basic resource fields: agriculture, raw materials, the environment, the rehabilitation of obsolescent industrial and transport facilities, research and development. Clearly, however, the tasks confronting the nation will require it to use its manpower resources to the hilt.

Third, the case for a national energy policy which would both enlarge production in all the regions and economize energy use is greatly heightened as one observes the differential regional impact of the energy crisis which has had us by the throat since the autumn of 1973.

Fourth, a national welfare policy is required which would establish more uniform criteria for public assistance. President Carter's proposals of 1977 are an interesting effort to achieve that objective. But they will prove viable only in an environment of full employment and rapid growth.

Fifth, within the states and regions—as well as at the national level—new forms of public–private collaboration will be necessary. Obviously, the kinds of problems reviewed in this chapter cannot be dealt with by conventional devices of fiscal and monetary policy. If the nation is to mitigate or solve its problems, public policy must deal with particular sectors, regions, cities, and rural areas. Americans do not have and do not want a fully planned and directed economy. On the other hand, a public role is inescapable. We have no other course than to learn how to make the public and private sectors work together, along the lines suggested in Chapter 12.

Finally, it seems clear to me, at least, that these problems cannot be dealt with if the states and regions look merely to Washington for salvation. The basic analyses, investment plans, public–private consortia must be developed within the states and regions. Local capital and entrepreneurship must be mobilized. In the end, however, there is scope for federal assistance in the form of tax incentives, investment capital, manpower retraining programs, and the direction of public-service job programs towards areas judged to be of high priority within states and regions.

Although the creation of state and regional development corporations should certainly have a role, it is likely that a national development bank will be required, like the old Reconstruction Finance Corporation. Its authority should extend not only to the fields of energy and energy conservation (where such an institution was proposed to the Congress by the Ford administration in 1975 and again laid before the Senate in September 1977 by Nelson Rockefeller), but also to the financing of water development, transport rehabilitation, and other projects believed to be of top national priority.

Wherever possible, such a bank should use its authority to guarantee or marginally to subsidize funds raised privately or by state or local governments, rather than engage in full direct financing.

In addition, it would be wise, in the phase ahead, for both state and federal governments to organize their budgets in ways which would separate authentic investment outlays from conventional expenditures and transfer payments.

There is a warning to be made about any proposal for an increased government role in the investment process: high standards of priority and productivity must be preserved. The experience of Great Britain and other countries with nationalized industries and with government loans to industry suggests that there is an inherent danger of confusing criteria of productivity and simple job maintenance or creation. The latter can lead to increasing public subsidy and the drawing off of scarce investment resources to low-productivity tasks. Public authorities tend to persist with lines of investment, even if of low productivity, because they do not face the competition of the market place and because political vested interests rise up around such public ventures. If my analysis is roughly correct, the United States and the other industrialized nations have ample opportunities to generate full employment through high-priority and essential investment tasks. None can afford to compound existing tendencies towards declining rates of productivity increase in the advanced industrial world by committing public funds to largely wasteful enterprises.

11

Inflation: Its Cause and Cure

T HE fifth Kondratieff upswing heightened the endemic problem of inflation, which had much deeper roots. The experience of the world economy with inflation since the end of the Second World War is, in fact, unique in modern economic history. In a period without major war, including the falling or relatively low prices for basic commodities of the fourth Kondratieff downswing (1951–72), there was a strong inflationary trend. It was climaxed by the price explosion of 1972–74 and the high but lesser inflation rates of the subsequent three years. Chart 9, exhibiting a British price index from 1661 to 1974, indicates how odd the post-1945 experience has been when compared to the longer past: the relatively well controlled price inflation of the Second World War gives way not to a typical postwar deflation, as after the Napoleonic and First World Wars, but to a protracted inflation of a kind never before known in a time of relative peace.

It should be noted that the classic era of modern economic growth (1815–1914) was, contrary to popular image, a period

Chart 9. The British Price Level: 1661–1974

SOURCE: Phyllis Deane and W. A. Cole, *British Economic Growth, 1688-1959*, Cambridge: At the University Press, Second Edition, 1967, end paper following p. 350, updated from official British data.

of overall declining prices. From its Napoleonic War peak, the British price level quickly fell 35% by 1820. In 1913, after many fluctuations, it was 20% lower than it had been in 1820. Despite two world wars, it was only about twice the 1913 level in 1946. In the subsequent quarter-century the British price level tripled. Although the annual average rate of inflation in this quarter-century was somewhat higher in Britain than in, say, Germany or the United States, Chart 9 captures pretty well the unique inflationary experience of the whole indus- trialized world in recent times.

The analysis of inflation in its post-1945 setting is a complex art. It involves the interweaving and interaction of three major elements: the intensity of effective demand for labor in rela- tion to supply, including, on the side of demand, fiscal and monetary policy, and on the side of supply, the potentialities for drawing labor from rural areas and abroad; the extent to which foodstuffs, raw materials, and energy are relatively scarce or abundant on a world basis, and a nation's degree of dependence on imported supplies; and the extent to which implicit or explicit disciplines within societies link money-wage increases to the average level of productivity increase. In short, there can be three types of inflation: demand-pull, raw-materials push, and wage-push. We have seen them all since 1945.

But these distinct types of inflation interact. For example, the leverage of labor unions in wage bargains is obviously related to the tightness of the labor market. Demand-pull and wage-push inflation cannot wholly be separated. On the other hand, there are significant differences among nations in the response of wages to degrees of unemployment; and there are changes in the relation between unemployment and wage increases within nations over periods of time. In addition, the pace of inflation has been affected by currency revaluations. These reflected, in part, the prior relative success of the various nations in controlling inflation on a national basis; but, in lowering the prices of exports and raising the prices of imports, devaluations affected, in turn, the subsequent course of inflation. Germany, for example, was thus doubly rewarded for its capacity to constrain wage-push inflation better than most: its domestic price increases were less; and the upward revaluation of its currency relatively reduced the cost of its imports, making the control of inflation easier at home. On the other hand, Britain was doubly punished by its difficulties in controlling inflation. Its series of devaluations raised import prices. There was, even, an element of triple jeopardy for Britain vis-à-vis Germany. The necessity for stop-and-go policies imposed by relatively high inflation rates lowered the level of domestic industrial investment, helped cause lower rates of increase in productivity, and, therefore, further reduced export competitiveness relative to Germany.

The role of the three types of inflation in the story of post-1945 prices, and the interactions among them, varied.

For example, all three types of inflationary pressure were involved in the initial phase of readjustment and reconversion, down to 1948: tight labor markets, high raw material prices, and (in the United States, at least) wage increases in excess of the average productivity increase, raising unit labor costs. By 1948–49, the initial postwar readjustment was about completed in Western Europe (excepting Germany) as well as in the United States. The latter experienced a sharp recession in 1949 which cut wage increases sufficiently to lower unit labor costs. Then came the Korean War boom which involved a brief passage of demand-pull, raw materials-push, and, with a typical lag, wage-push inflation. From 1951, as noted earlier, foodstuff and raw material prices entered a protracted phase when they were relatively low. This background eased the problem of inflation over the following fifteen years in the advanced industrialized areas of the world. Nevertheless, excepting the period 1961–66 in the United States, when reasonably effective wage-price guideposts operated, the element of wage-push inflation was present as well as a demand-pull inflation, generally more acute in Western Europe and Japan than in the United States.

The acceleration of inflation from the mid-1960's involved in the United States both demand-pull inflation, as unemployment fell below 4% in the period 1966–69, and a related weakening of wage guideposts. Unit labor costs averaged a 3.7% annual increase in the last three years of the Johnson administration and surged to 7.1% in 1969 when wage-price guideposts were formally abandoned. The movement of foodstuff and raw material prices exacerbated the problem in the sense that, by the late 1960's, they had generally ceased their relative decline. The American farm parity ratio, measuring the relative prices farmers are paid against the prices of the goods and services they buy, had, for example, fallen from 107 in 1951 to 76 in 1964 (1910–14 equals 100). It averaged 75.6 for the period 1965–69. In these years of increased inflationary expansion, real wages in the nonagricultural sector came under pressure, averaging a small net decline (0.1% per annum) when spendable weekly earnings are calculated in constant dollars. This heightened the natural thrust of the unions to increase money-wage rates in negotiated settlements.

F. W. Paish captures vividly the interweaving of the various types of inflation in Britain from 1969 to 1974:

Up to the end of the third quarter of 1969 there is a clear relationship . . . between the level of unemployment and the rise of incomes from employment. After the third quarter of 1969, however, this relationship disappears, and between then and 1972 the main cause of the faster rise of employment incomes was the use of their monopoly power by the trade unions. The reason for this change seems to have been the success of the government's policy between 1967 and 1969 of holding down real disposable personal incomes in order to divert resources from consumption to exports. It is tragic that, just as this policy had been successful and it was becoming possible to allow consumption to resume its rise, the trade unions felt obliged to adopt a more militant policy in order to raise the real disposable incomes of their members. . . .

Towards the end of 1972, the already large effects on the rate of rise of prices of the over-rapid rise of wage rates were reinforced by a rapid rise of import prices, especially of food, feeding-stuffs and industrial raw materials. For most of the period between the collapse of the Korean war boom in 1951 and the third quarter of 1972, import prices had risen much more slowly than home costs, so that the effect of imports was to slow down the rate of rise of total prices. . . . In the last quarter of 1973, the rise of total import prices was greatly accelerated by the monopolistically-imposed quadrupling of prices of imported oil, so that between the second quarter of 1972 and the second quarter of 1974 average import prices of all goods and services rose by nearly 90 per cent, causing British internal prices to rise faster than home costs for the first time since 1972.

The faster rise in consumption prices in turn caused the trade unions to increase their wage demands further, so that, although the rise of import prices greatly slowed down after the second quarter of 1974, mainly as the result of a fall in the prices of many industrial raw materials, the rise of consumption prices has continued to accelerate, and may well accelerate further.[1]

Paish's fear of further acceleration was justified: in the late spring of 1975 British inflation was thoroughly out of hand, and proceeding at an annual rate of 40 per cent, a momentum broken to a degree in the second half of the year by a strong deflationary government policy executed with belated support from the labor union leaders.

What Paish describes is a sequence in which demand-pull inflation, accompanied by some wage constraint, sets off a subsequent phase of determined wage-push inflation, which then is reinforced by the almost universal boom of 1972–73 and, in particular, by the dramatic rise in the relative prices of basic materials, starting at the end of 1972, which, in turn, exerted severe pressure on real wages. This resulted in a further round of wage-push inflation. The British case proved to be extreme, in that wage-push inflation resisted the cyclical downturn of 1974–75, with its temporary softening of food and raw materials prices. But the fact is there was a rough doubling of inflation rates in the industrialized world as between 1965–72 and 1972–74. The sequence described by Paish for Britain has several special features; but in catching the convergence in the latter years of all three types of inflation, it is generally illuminating.

The problem of inflation was perceived from the early postwar years to be a potential time bomb in an era of relatively steady, rapid growth. Summing up the papers written for a conference at Oxford in September 1952, D. H. Robertson posed the issue well:

> What of . . . the tendency of wage–rates to climb steadily upwards, even . . . in face of temporary flickerings of demand? Is this also a potential cause of "an industrial depression of the traditional form"? Or is it rather . . . a potential cause of something quite different—a complete break-down of monetary stability, leading to a naked choice between totalitarianism and chaos? Has this result been hitherto prevented . . . by the occurrence of the mild price and employment recessions of 1949 and 1951? And if so, can we rely on an indefinite succes-

sion of these beneficent slumplets, not severe enough to generate widespread distress but sufficient to prevent the reputation
of money as a store of value from being irretrievably under-
mined? Or does anybody know of a "wages policy" which will
purge a "full employment" regime, not of its manifold ineffi-
ciencies and injustices—that is too much to hope—but of its
propensity to ultimate suicide?[2]

The best analysts of Western European growth in the 1960's
noted the penalties high growth rates and low unemployment
levels exacted in political democracies and also expressed
their anxiety for the future. The governments themselves were
not wholly passive. In the United States the control of inflation was part of the national agenda from the Truman administration forward. And virtually all the Western European
governments experimented with versions of incomes policy
which would, by negotiation, constrain money wages and the
bargaining power of unions in the face of chronically tight
labor markets, while assuring that labor self-discipline would
not result in unjustified price increases and a relative shift of
income to profits.

For brief periods these policies appear to have had some
benign effect; e.g., in the Netherlands down to 1963, the
United States from 1961 to 1966 and in 1971–72, and, generally, in Germany, where for most of this period the unions
exercised self-restraint out of old memories of inflation and a
lively sense of the connection between wage increases and
their nation's capacity to export.

The fact is, however, that, over the whole span of the postwar boom of 1946–74, the political and social task of constraining money wages became increasingly difficult. In part,
perhaps, the reasons are technical: the labor surpluses to be
drawn into the urban working force pool from the countryside
or from abroad diminished; and the post-1951 damping effect
of relatively low raw material and foodstuff prices ceased to
operate as the 1960's wore on and then gave way to a mighty

phase of raw materials-push inflation which has typically marked the first phase of a Kondratieff upswing. In part, the reason is psychological: the tendency of inflation to accelerate set up expectations of further inflation which led union leaders to try, in their current negotiations, not merely to correct for past pressures of inflation on real wages, but to achieve settlements which would hedge their clients' real income against expected future inflation. In a sense, failure bred failure: the breakdown of successive incomes-policy efforts consolidated inflationary expectations in business and labor. And so these rich, comfortable, and rapidly expanding economies became —so far as wages and prices were concerned—like a dog chasing his tail. The process was chronically exacerbated by wage drift among non-union workers, achieving in tight labor markets greater increases than those negotiated by unions; and it was virtually always complicated by varying degrees of fragmentation among the unions, leading to competition in wage settlements by the various contending union leaders as well as difficulties in getting the rank and file to accept the pacts their leaders negotiated. The latter was, for example, a factor in the breaking of the U.S. wage guideposts in the airline machinists' strike of July 1966.

Behind it all, of course, was the triumph of the Keynesian revolution. At the insistence of their electorates, democratic governments no longer regarded periods of cyclical unemployment as acts of God to be accepted passively. Rather, governments assumed the responsibility for maintaining low levels of unemployment. And the elaboration of the Keynesian revolution supplied the tools of fiscal and monetary policy needed to reach that goal. With high levels of employment more or less assured, labor leaders could count on an excellent bargaining position in their wage negotiations. Business firms could count on relatively high levels of demand for their products, and on a setting in which wage increases could be passed along in higher prices without excessive penalty. All this contributed, of course, to the fact that the overall growth rates in the industrialized world were higher in the three postwar decades than at any time over the past two centuries. But it also posed the problem D. H. Robertson defined in 1952: would the inflation accompanying a full-employment regime lead to "ultimate suicide" in the advanced industrial societies?

The costs of inflation are of two kinds. First, within a society, inflation erodes private savings, including pensions, insurance policies, and social security payments; it saps the resources of private foundations and educational institutions which often lack the capacity to expand their income as fast as the rate of inflation; it raises interest rates and thereby the cost of residential houses; it distorts the investment process, by rendering uncertain costs and returns from large projects requiring long periods to complete; and, generally, it leads firms to use their resources to hedge against inflation rather than seek the optimum paths for investment; it distorts the tax system while simultaneously lifting the cost of local, state, and federal government. Various devices to hedge against these inflationary distortions have, of course, been created; for example, raising social security payments more or less in line with inflation, government subsidies to housing, altering tax structures. But few would deny that a protracted environment of inflation has been a corrosive force in democratic societies, even if it has not yet proved suicidal.

The second effect of inflation is international; and for some countries this has proved very dangerous indeed. The danger arises because, even with the floating exchange rates of the past six years, the value of a national currency is inversely linked to its rate of inflation as compared with that of other countries. Look, for example, at Table 9.

The first phenomenon that emerges from Table 9 is, evidently, the disturbing phenomenon of acceleration: for each period the inflation rate is higher than in the previous period,

Table 9. Inflation Rates in Consumer Prices
in the United States and Other Major
Industrial Countries, 1955–1976
(*Average annual percentage increase*)

	United States	Canada	Japan	France	Germany	Italy	United Kingdom
1955–65	1.5%	1.7%	3.8%	4.9%	2.3%	3.4%	3.1%
1965–72	4.1	3.8	5.5	4.7	3.4	3.6	5.6
1972–76*	8.8	10.0	15.1	11.6	6.6	17.3	17.5

* Third Quarter
SOURCE: Calculated from *Economic Report of the President*, 1977, p. 305.

excepting the slight deceleration of France in 1965–72. Second, is the peculiar situation of Japan. Because of the high rates of productivity increase in its export industries and various policy devices to shield its export prices from domestic inflation, Japan has managed systematically to reconcile a strong balance of payments position with a higher than average rate of domestic inflation. Third, for the period 1972–76 the relative strength of the national currencies and their general economic position (again excepting Japan) is inverse to their inflation rates. The economic situations in Italy and the U.K. have been notably precarious, in France only a little less so. All three countries have consequently confronted difficult political problems. The German position has been strongest. In North America, Canada has been under somewhat greater strain than the United States; but both occupy an uneasy intermediate position in the perverse inflation race.

What, then, can be done about inflation?

In writing his *General Theory,* Keynes was conscious that a regime of full employment posed the problem of inflation. He dealt with the issue seriously, but in a highly stylized way. With respect to demand-pull inflation, he noted that, as full employment approached and the limits of industrial capacity were reached, prices would rise. Therefore, he acknowledged a limit on the extent to which public policy could safely stimulate effective demand. With respect to raw materials-push inflation, he had little or nothing to say. This was understandable in the 1930's, at a time of exceedingly cheap food and raw material prices; although, as noted earlier, he had been sensitive to this problem in the pre-1920 years of the third Kondratieff upswing (see above, pp. 14–15). With respect to the avoidance of wage-push inflation, Keynes considered two policies: a regime of constant money wages with prices falling as productivity increased; a regime of money wages rising with the economy's average increase in productivity, yielding a constant price level. Although he understood the advantages of the former (which roughly conformed to historical experience during the first and second Kondratieff downswings), he opted, by and large, for the latter as the better solution. He did so because, writing in the depressed atmosphere of the 1930's, he feared that a falling price trend would not stimulate sufficient private investment.

What Keynes did not consider was the political, social, and institutional setting in which either form for disciplining money wages could actually be brought to pass in modern democratic societies.

What can we say now, forty years and many wound stripes later, about policy that might bring inflation under more or less steady control? Evidently, a serious policy must confront all three forms of inflation and the connections among them.

So far as demand-pull inflation is concerned, there is a reasonable consensus among economists. They would now acknowledge that full employment, realistically defined, must fall some distance short of zero unemployment if strong inflationary pressures are to be avoided.

As noted earlier, 4% unemployment was, for some time, taken in the United States as a measure of that critical level; and some would argue that the additional role of young people and women in the working force may now make the appropriate figure something like 4.9% (see above, p. 128*h*). These figures allow for the fact that in a large continental economy like ours there are bound to be many workers in the process of changing jobs; and there will be differences in job opportunities within regions and states. Inflationary labor bottlenecks can be experienced in certain places and industries while there are pools of unemployed labor elsewhere. It follows from this perception that better information about job opportunities, facilities for retraining labor for jobs that are available, and the provision of productive work where chronically unemployed labor exists could lower the overall unemployment level associated with inflationary danger.

It is also true that the limits of industrial capacity are not reached uniformly. Inflationary bottle-necks can be experienced in one sector while idle capacity exists elsewhere. Therefore, policy to extend the limit set by demand-pull inflation should address itself to the supply situation in particular industrial sectors, as well as in the economy as a whole.

There is also agreement that demand-pull inflation can be mitigated by effective public policy against monopolistic price-fixing, which would, through enforced competition, prevent prices from rising prematurely during a business expansion.

Despite these significant refinements in thought and policy addressed to the structure of the working force and the economy as a whole, there is consensus that effective demand should be held within limits which avoid demand-pull inflation.

Most contemporary economists, like Keynes in the *General Theory*, have given little thought to raw materials-push inflation. In the formative years of the 1930's this was not a central problem in the United States, except for those concerned to raise agricultural prices and incomes. The years of the Second World War and the period down to 1951 tended to be thought of as an aberration. And most economists took for granted the comfortable situation for industrial societies of the fourth Kondratieff downswing, with its relatively cheap food and raw materials.

How, then, does one conduct an anti-inflationary policy in the context of the fifth Kondratieff upswing, a period when we shall probably have to live with relatively high and perhaps even rising prices for food, energy, and raw materials? The answer comes in two parts.

First, the battle must be fought hard on the supply side. The diversion of increased investment resources to energy, food, and raw materials supply, the increased allocations to research and development, the increased attention to productivity—all of which are the steps to resumed high growth rates and structural adjustment—are also the correct route for containing raw material-push inflation. In that process, the development of stockpiles of oil, raw materials, and food could play a useful, stabilizing role, as could the kind of international raw materials agreements considered in Chapter 13.

Second is the problem of preventing a surge of raw materials-push inflation from setting off a reinforcing round of wage-push inflation. To the extent that automatic cost-of-living adjustments are built into wage contracts, that battle has, to a degree, been lost, and we are thrown back on the struggle for expanded supplies, new technologies, higher productivity, and stockpiles to contain raw materials-push inflation. But there is a lesson of the period 1972–74 which labor leaders, businessmen, and government should contemplate together. The convulsive rise in raw material prices during those years set in motion a second round of inflation through wage increases which aimed to fend off the effects on real wages of the rise in living costs. In the United States, for example, wage rates in new bargaining agreements were running at 5.5% increases in the first quarter of 1973, at 12.1% two years later. In those two years, unemployment rose from about 5% to 8%; and the real value of earnings in the private nonagricultural sector declined about 5%. The effort to counter raw materials-push inflation by higher money wages both failed to prevent a fall in real wages for those employed and caused unemployment to be higher than it might have been. The exaggerated rise in prices—with wage-push piled on raw materials-push inflation—brought about increased unemployment by frightening the public authorities into more restrictive policies than they would otherwise have pursued. Moreover, once ratchetted up, money-wage increases are difficult to bring down, despite high unemployment rates. In the mild economic recovery of 1976–77, new wage settlements in the United States were still running at 8–10% increases, and, with output per hour showing a temporarily high 3.6% increase, typical of the first phase of recovery, a basic inflationary rate of 5–6% was built into the economy. Some such underlying element of wage-push inflation persisted in 1977.

The points to be made here, then, are that raw materials-push inflation must be fought redoubtably on the supply side and that efforts to respond to an inflationary raw materials-push by a round of wage-push inflation are likely to prove self-defeating; that is, costly for the working force and the economy as a whole.

That brings us to wage-push inflation itself. If the pattern of the fifth Kondratieff upswing follows that of its predecessors, the initial explosive phase of raw materials-push inflation of 1972–74 need not recur. It might recur if the whole OECD world, and notably the United States, fails to adopt an effective energy policy and thereby confronts in the 1980's a global oil shortage under circumstances where the intervening period has not been used to develop alternative energy sources. But, even under the best of circumstances, the OECD world will probably experience a phase when raw material prices fluctuate in a relatively high range, with some erratic tendency to rise, unless that tendency is contained by vigorous supply and stockpile policies. Under these circumstances, the underlying basic inflation rate will be determined in the various advanced industrial societies by success or failure in dealing with wage-push inflation.

I believe that, for our times, the optimum solution would be a regime of fixed money wages, with prices falling with the increase in productivity. Keynes' objections to this policy no longer appear cogent; that is, modern industrial nations palpably command the fiscal, monetary, and other tools to stimulate demand sufficiently to maintain full employment, even if the price trend were downward. And the advantages of such a regime are great: workers would be granted increases in real wages automatically through the market place; the focus of the working force, as well as the consumer, would turn to productivity, where it ought to be; in societies where public services now absorb so much of the working force, real-wage increases would be automatic and the danger of public-service strikes greatly reduced. As those knowledgeable in labor history are aware, periods of constant money wages and falling prices were marked by rising real wages and, relatively, by labor peace. It is also true that the real value of debts would rise; but this trend would be countered by falling interest rates.

My view is, however, generally regarded by my economist colleagues as radical and somewhat eccentric. When they face up to wage-push inflation, they tend to think in terms of average money-wage rates rising with the average increase in productivity, yielding, in theory, a constant price level.

But the real questions at stake here are not to be settled by abstract debate on one or another theoretical formula for avoiding wage-push inflation. We are up against one of the most profound and complex issues democratic societies have ever encountered. Without exception, every American administration, from Truman to Carter, has confronted the problem of wage-push inflation. There were only two periods of relative success in dealing with it: the pattern President Kennedy set in 1961–62 in dealing with the automobile and steel wage negotiations, confirmed by his reversal of the steel price increase in April 1962; and President Nixon's more rigid price-wage controls of 1971–72. But the first effort was not sufficiently institutionalized to stand the strains of 1966; and the second was an explicitly transient effort to meet an acute balance of payments crisis and would, in any case, have been disrupted by the price explosion of 1972–74. Other democratic nations have also had periods of limited success with agreements which contained wage-push inflation; but none has yet been able to build such arrangements steadily into the workings of its society.

Why is the record of the past thirty years so littered with failures? The short answer is that wage-price agreements require that both labor and business accept restraints which clash with their conventional ways of operating.

For labor there are two problems. The first is that, except in a few countries, the unions are fragmented. This means that wage contracts are negotiated at different times in different industries. It also means that each union leader and the workers he represents are determined to do at least as well in wage contracts as other leaders and groups have done recently. It also means that if a government wishes to stop inflation at a given time (for example, with a wage freeze), there is a real problem of equity: some unions will have made settlements recently and are relatively satisfied for the moment; others are counting on catching up in future negotiations. The complications in labor structure do not end here. In some democratic countries, union leaders may press excessive wage claims for political reasons. In some unions the leadership may not be able to impose on the rank-and-file workers the settlements they have negotiated.

What is needed on the side of labor to negotiate a non-inflationary regime is, ideally, a single union (or coalition) negotiating with business and government wage settlements covering the bulk of the working force for a fixed time ahead, with sufficient authority and legitimacy for those settlements to be accepted by the workers. And, indeed, some of the relative success stories in this field are in countries which have unified labor movements or coalitions; e.g., Sweden. An alternative way to solve the problem, after agreement in principle with labor has been achieved, is to allow a catching-up period at the beginning of a long-term wage-price agreement, in which upward wage adjustments for the negotiating laggards would be permitted.

The second problem for labor is profits. How can labor leaders be assured that its wage discipline will not result in business making excessive profits by either raising prices or failing to pass along to the consumer, in lower prices, the productivity increases in the industry?

On June 20, 1961, these two central problems were dramatized by Walter Reuther in these questions he put to me when I was sounding him out, at President Kennedy's instruction, on whether he would accept a 2½% wage increase (then viewed as the average annual rate of productivity increase) in the forthcoming negotiation with the automobile industry: "If I'm damn fool enough to accept 2½%, what about Dave McDonald?"[3] McDonald, head of the steel union, was scheduled to negotiate shortly after Reuther. "If McDonald and I are damn fools enough to accept 2½%, what makes you think you professors in the White House can keep the steel industry from raising prices?"

In the upshot, the assurances were given; Reuther's anxiety about the steel industry proved prescient; and President Kennedy, if not his professors, proved capable of holding the steel price. A pattern was set in this rough-and-ready way, backed by explicit wage-price guideposts, which checked wage-push inflation for more than four years. That pragmatic piece of business illustrates rather well the abiding problems involved for labor in dealing with wage-push inflation; but it is by no means a satisfactory model in the more complex American environment of the 1970's. And it is certainly no model for other countries, with quite different political and institutional arrangements.

There are, of course, difficult problems for business. Any such arrangement requires that the public authorities interest themselves in their productivity, prices, and profits. How can even able, dispassionate, and technically knowledgeable bureaucrats or politicians decide when prices and profits are excessive? If prices and profits are kept too low, necessary investment in new plant and technology may not take place, as some allege was the case in the 1971–72 period of price control. Is there not a temptation to apply jawboning to an industry that may be peculiarly vulnerable to government pressure; for example, if the industry depends heavily on government contracts or the government commands a stock-pile whose release would arbitrarily increase supply?

When wage-price controllers and jawboners, from the Truman to the Nixon administrations, gathered in Boston to share their reflections on these matters, in November 1974, they were creditably candid in expressing their concerns about the equity as well as the efficiency of what they had done in their respective times of responsibility.[4] And it is not difficult to despair in the face of limited past success, multiple failure, and the irreducible complexities of negotiating and maintaining an equitable non-inflationary wage-price regime in a democratic society. Indeed, most economists, as well as businessmen and labor leaders, would accept chronic inflation for the indefinite future, with all its costs, as opposed to fully administered and mandated wage and price controls of the kind applied in wartime.

I, for one, do not believe our society should accept the risks of living indefinitely with a 5–6%, or higher, annual inflation rate. I believe that we must try again, with a wage-price control system that is essentially voluntary, although backed with legal reserve powers. I believe agreements should be negotiated on the understanding that the system will remain, for the indefinite future, a part of our economic and political life. Only a long-term agreement will provide an opportunity to move the system equitably into operation, given our wage-negotiation cycles. Only a long-term agreement has a chance of breaking the inflationary expectations, in business and labor, which take on the force of self-fulfilling prophecies.

I believe such an outcome is not beyond our grasp for three reasons. First, in American public opinion polls inflation emerges consistently as the issue of highest concern among citizens—higher than unemployment. There is, without question, a strong, if diffuse, public desire to bring inflation under control. Indeed, even formal price and wage controls are quite popular in public opinion polls, compared with their ill-repute among businessmen, labor leaders, and economists. Second, every serious businessman and labor leader knows that inflation over a period of time is costly to the interests he seeks to protect. In the short run, businessmen can generally pass along wage increases in higher prices. In the short run, a labor leader can emerge proudly from a negotiation yielding, say, a 10% per annum wage increase when productivity is increasing in his industry at, say, only 3%. And these converging short-run interests contribute to the fact of inflation. Business and labor leaders, by taking the easy next step, can, in effect, connive to get by until the next negotiation in the style to which they have become accustomed, at the expense of the society at large, including their own workers and stockholders.

But businessmen also know that inflation leads to stop-and-go policies, and that profits are exceedingly volatile. A policy to maximize profits over a reasonably long period of time should be non-inflationary. Similarly, labor leaders know that, even if wage settlements manage to keep up with the cost of

living (which is not by any means always the case), the real
income of labor will suffer over a reasonably long period of
time from the higher average unemployment and reduced
rates of productivity increase that are brought on by stop-
and-go policies. Third—and perhaps most important—the circumstances we face, in any case, require that we generate in
American society the most important single ingredient for
successful wage-price policies: a sense of common purpose.
Commenting on early post-1945 efforts at wage-price agreements in Europe, an American analyst (Mark Leiserson)
wrote that such agreements, to succeed, must be "part of a
coordinated effort to achieve a clearly defined national objective. . . ."[5] If my analysis is roughly correct, such a coordinated national effort is clearly called for: in energy, water,
agriculture, raw materials, and the environment. As Chapter
12 argues, this effort requires a form of national planning,
joining the public and private sectors in sustained partnership.
In that setting, the uniting of business, labor, and government
to create and manage non-inflationary wage-price guidelines
should be easier than otherwise.

The reason that a program short of full price and wage controls can work is that many sectors of the economy are effectively competitive. If, for example, wage increases geared to
the norm of the average rate of productivity increase were
accepted, the monitoring of prices, productivity, and profits
could focus sharply on the less competitive sectors or on
sectors where abnormal circumstances exist; e.g., health
services. One of the key failures of wage-price agreements in
the past, for example, has been the failure to insist that prices
decline in sectors where productivity is rising faster than the
national average; for example, the automobile industry after
the 1961 wage settlement. Moreover, a good deal of flexibility
is required in any such regime to permit labor to move towards
rapidly expanding sectors or sectors with high rates of productivity increase. Similarly, less than average rates of wage

increase are justified in stagnant or declining sectors or sectors with low rates of productivity increase. No one conversant with the complexities of an essentially voluntary wage-price control system, with residual powers for selective intervention, believes that its management would be easy. But they would also tend to agree with Arnold Weber's conclusion that the greatest failure of the past was ". . . a consistent failure to develop a national consensus on the objectives of and rules governing wage-price policy."[6] The whole enterprise would thus require a good deal of statesmanship at the highest political levels of our society, as well as a pervasive equity and common sense in administration. But the stakes appear too great for us not to try.

12

Reflections on Sectoral Planning in a Democratic Society

I n American society and its politics, planning is a contentious word. It summons up visions of a vast bureaucracy deciding in detail what should be produced and consumed, imposing its private statistical vision on an economic system where individuals, households, farms, and business firms cherish the right to make their own decisions, take their own risks, experience the satisfactions or disappointments, gains or losses that ensue. Discussions of planning easily slide into ideological confrontation where the freedoms of private capitalism are seen as threatened by the road to serfdom.

In dealing now directly with the question of planning, which emerged naturally in one after another of the preceding chapters, I bring to the argument two prejudices.

First, I believe a private, competitive, free enterprise system is intrinsically better than a system of public enterprise. It is more consistent with human freedom; it is generally—not always—more efficient; and it has the great virtue of forcing the society to cut its losses when resources don't pay their way. Public enterprises have a considerable capacity to survive even when they are using resources inefficiently, as Britain and a good many other countries have demonstrated in recent times.

Second, unlike Milton Friedman,[1] I believe Adam Smith was right when he defined an area for public enterprise in these terms: "The duty of erecting and maintaining certain public works and certain public institutions which it can never be for the interest of any individual, or small number of individuals, to erect and maintain, because the profit could never repay the expense to any individual or small number of individuals, thought it may frequently do much more than repay it to a great society."[2]

The fact is that our great society has evolved, since Alexander Hamilton won President Washington's backing, by a kind of partnership between the public and private sectors. The public sector not only created a setting of trade and financial policy within which private enterprise could flourish, it also built the Cumberland Road and Erie Canal; subsidized the long-distance rail lines; provided mass public education and then the agricultural and technological colleges which have proved so useful. It engaged the Corps of Engineers in massive public works programs of the kind Adam Smith envisaged. It leaned against monopolies or regulated them. In the wake of the Great Depression of the 1930's, it assumed responsibility for the level of employment, using, in part, the Federal Reserve System created earlier for other public purposes. It enlarged our educational systems, provided an approximation of equal opportunity for higher education, provided health services to elderly citizens and the poor, and took other measures of equity an affluent people judged to be morally right. Moreover, many of the nation's most important enterprises—from rebuilding the centers of our cities to putting a man on the moon—were accomplished by public–private collaboration almost too subtle and complex to describe, a kind of collaboration that rarely makes its way into the textbooks on economics or government.

Every one of these operations had its flaws and costs, as we are all aware. Since Hamilton jousted with Jefferson, there were always, and there remain, legitimate reasons for debate at the margin concerning the appropriateness of one or another form of public intervention in the economy. Some were clearly disastrous, like the NRA during the New Deal and the fixing of the gas price in the 1950's. But I believe we were correct to build our society through a public–private partnership; and I believe we would be well advised to set aside the notion of a polar choice between the public and private sectors, accept the verdict of our history and that of other advanced industrial democracies, and go on from there, arguing policy case by case.

There is also a question of fact which should be promptly introduced. After making the positive case for sectoral planning in a gathering at the Chamber of Commerce in Washington in November 1975, I made this observation:

> . . . I could, of course, debate the matter much more simply. The fact is governments are in the sectoral planning business, including the government of the United States. Indeed, bad sectoral planning, here and abroad, accounts not for the existence but for the severity of our current agricultural and energy problems. Governments are deeply involved in R&D. There is no indication governments are about to get out of the sectoral planning business. The objective, therefore, is to do the best job intelligence and a sense of proportion permit.[3]

The pragmatic case for planning is, then, the same as that made in Chapter 3 for the inadequacy of neo-Keynesian economics. It is inherent in the problems of the fifth Kondratieff upswing that they cannot be wholly solved by the workings of private competitive markets. In different ways, this is true of the problems of food and population, energy, raw materials, water, transport, and pollution control. Therefore, planning is inevitable. It is being done; but it is not being done very well.

What, then, are the criteria for good planning and how can they be brought to bear in the United States?

The first criterion is that planning be informed by a doctrine. As Winston Churchill once said, "Those who are possessed of a definite body of doctrine and of deeply rooted convictions upon it will be in a much better position to deal with the shifts and surprises of daily affairs than those who are merely taking short views, and indulging their natural impulses as they are evoked by what they read from day to day."[4] This is an important observation, although I would immediately add Keynes' caveat: "Words ought to be a little wild, for they are an assault of thought upon the unthinking. But when the seats of power and authority have been attained, there should be no more poetic license. . . . When a doctrinaire proceeds to action, he must, so to speak, forget his doctrine. For those who in action remember the letter will probably lose what they are seeking."[5]

At the present time, the fundamental problem with American economic policy is that no relevant Churchillian doctrine, even tempered by Keynes' pragmatic proviso, is at work. The policy debates of 1977 are still controlled by the doctrines of the 1960's, with antecedents reaching back three decades further.

The conventionally debated issues are by now of classic simplicity: bigger or smaller federal deficits; more or less welfare spending; lower or higher central bank interest rates. To these classic neo-Keynesian issues has been added a pure product of the 1960's: the passionate thrust of the environmentalists to make their criteria for policy overriding. Excepting the environment, the old debates about effective demand —and its relation to employment, welfare, and inflation— dominate the field.

While the Executive Branch and the Congress conduct their central discourse in these terms, the structural problems of the fifth Kondratieff upswing are substantially neglected. No doctrine is now at work which would illuminate systematically the supply side of the nation's problems. Thought and action on energy, agriculture, water, raw materials, pollution control, R&D, are fragmented specialist fields, treated ad hoc. There is an awareness of the link between the balance of payments position and energy policy; but, as noted in Chapter 5, for whatever reasons, the stated objective of reducing U.S. oil imports was not backed in President Carter's April 1977 proposals by policies which might credibly produce that result.

Until a lucid consensus emerges which would relate the tasks of sectoral planning to the twin objectives of sustained full employment and structural adjustment to the imperatives of the fifth Kondratieff upswing, an effective planning effort will be impossible. In a vast bureaucracy it is easy to underestimate the role of a unifying intellectual perspective or doctrine. But it is a primary condition for effective action. After all, planning is a purposive effort to get from here to there. It is impossible usefully to define either here or there outside an arbitrary but relevant intellectual framework.

There is a second useful view of planning, well captured by Eugene Black:

> Between the idealists, who are more interested in imposing solutions than in illuminating choices, and the cynics who distrust planning in all its interpretations, lies, I think, a rational definition of the concept which should be nourished. Planning, simply defined, should be the place where the political leader is faced with an awareness of the consequences of his decisions before he makes them instead of afterwards. Taking the definition one step further, it should be the means by which the lines of communication are kept open between those who make decisions, those who illuminate them, and those who carry them out.
>
> Whatever form planning takes, if it does not keep these lines of communication open, there will be a mess.[6]

From this view of the planning process flow a procedural and a technical imperative.

The procedural rule that follows from Black's notion of

planning is that, in a diffuse democracy like ours, those who will have to carry out a plan should have a hand in shaping it. That is the fundamental wisdom of Jean Monnet's observation in his *Mémoires*. Speaking of the principles on which the post-war French modernization plan was to be based, he said to General de Gaulle towards the end of 1945: ". . . I am sure of one thing. One cannot transform the French economy without the French people participating in the transformation. When I say the people, it is not an abstract entity. I am referring to the unions, business firms, government departments, all those who will be associated with the plan. . . ."[7] In our great sprawling continental society, Monnet's dictum is even more relevant than for more centralized France.

President Carter's energy plan was a rather pure case of violation of this procedural dictum. It was formulated and sent to the Congress without effective consultation with those inside or outside the federal government who would, in fact, largely bear the burdens and consequences of its execution.

The technical imperative which flows from Black's definition of planning relates to the need for the political leader to be aware "of the consequences of his decisions before he makes them instead of afterwards." The reason this is now so difficult in economic policy is that we lack the data, the intellectual tools, and even the governmental staffs needed to relate what happens in one sector of the economy to others and to the economy as a whole. And although our knowledge of what has happened and is happening in the various regions of the country is improving, much the same weaknesses exist in assessing the regional consequences of any course of action. This serious technical limitation is another result of the Keynesian revolution. Our best data and most sophisticated techniques for analyzing them are highly aggregated; that is, they permit us to deal with large variables like investment, consumption, government spending, and the overall balance of payments position at the national level. But there is no place in the federal government where detailed knowledge of the

sectors or the regions of the country is systematically interwoven with the aggregate analysis of the economy. I shall
return to this problem when considering some organizational
aspects of planning later in this chapter.

A third rule for planning in a democracy is that the direct
interference of the government should be the minimum necessary to accomplish the desired result. The dynamics and institutions of the economic system as it already exists should be
used to the maximum. For example, the great power of the
price system should be exploited wherever possible to achieve
the results which are sought. A high energy price, for example, reflecting accurately the marginal cost of additional
energy production, is certainly the most powerful tool available to induce both economy in energy use and enlarged
energy production. For example, it is wiser to use the government's power to tax, rebate, or otherwise marginally subsidize
to achieve a desired result in the public interest than it is for
the government to engage directly in economic activity.

A fourth rule follows from the others: a national planning
group should be backed by the highest political authority; but
it should be small. Again, Jean Monnet makes the best case.
In setting up his planning commission in 1946 he asked de
Gaulle's *chef de cabinet* for a small team and some meeting
rooms, noting that a small staff was least likely to incite bu-
reaucratic jealousy; it would avoid the temptation to do every-
thing by itself; and it would thereby engage others in the
planning process by making them do most of the work. The
professional staff in the planning commission was never more
than thirty, the inner team five or six. They operated in a
baroque town-house close by the Church of St. Clotilde, "a
small island of tranquility in the heart of the great ministries."
The meeting rooms for the commission were on the first floor.
The staff worked in an "absurd" set of small offices, "cut by
corridors and irrational stairways." Meals were taken in common, and their frugality "disconcerted more than one minister
and more than one trade union leader." Monnet concludes

that the absurdity of the setting must have reflected some profound logic. In thirty subsequent years the planning commission stayed in its original quarters: "At least, their awkwardness protected it from the risks of administrative proliferation."[8]

One cannot reproduce, of course, the unique historical setting in which French sectoral planning was launched in the villa at 18 rue de Martignac; and least of all can one reinvent Monnet and his team. Moreover, the American administrative style only rarely expresses itself in small, catalytic, highly motivated, congenial teams. But the scale, method, and setting of the French venture is, nevertheless, worth recalling in the America of the 1970's. It is a reminder that no great new bureaucracy is required in Washington to do what badly needs doing. The raw materials for sectoral and regional planning are scattered all over the town: among others, in the Departments of Agriculture, Interior, Treasury, Commerce, Labor, Energy, Transportation, the Office of Management and Budget, the Council of Economic Advisers. The departments and agencies now contain able men and women thoroughly capable of playing a creative role in the planning process, if its goals and methods are clear and command a consensus, led by the President, backed by the Congress. Equally, there are among business and labor leaders men and women in the private sectors competent and, I believe, willing to enter into the formulation of national economic targets and methods for achieving them by public–private collaboration.

What, then, would American government planners of the 1970's do? Working with business, agricultural, and labor leaders, they would confront, essentially, these five tasks:

—To translate certain agreed national objectives into concrete production or other economic targets, in particular sectors, looking ahead, say, ten years.

—To estimate the orders of magnitude of investment required from the present forward to achieve those sectoral targets.

—To estimate the extent to which the private sector could,

under existing incentives, generate the appropriate levels of investment in each sector; the extent to which alternative forms of indirect government assistance could narrow the investment gap; and the extent to which direct public action would be required.

—To examine the implications of these sectoral targets for other sectors, the economy as a whole, specific regions of the country, the balance of payments, and the conduct of foreign policy.

—In the light of these analyses, to outline the policy choices open to the Executive Branch and the Congress, and to make the recommendations the planners are moved to make.

The key sectors requiring such interconnected planning are now familiar to the reader: energy and energy conservation; agriculture; raw materials; transport; water development and conservation; pollution control; research and development. To these should be added productivity (although, in part, the problem relates to R&D) and the major structural problems of the regions, notably chronic unemployment in the central cities and chronic underemployment in the rural South.

Once set in motion, by presidential decision and congressional action, a plan of this kind would, of course, be regularly modified in the light of unfolding experience.

Where should the planning team be located in the Executive Branch? Obviously, it must be, in the end, the President's instrument. It could be placed in either the Office of Management and Budget or the Council of Economic Advisers. It might even be located in the Treasury. But those bureaucracies and their chiefs are already heavily weighed down; and the planning effort ought to be launched with prestige, visibility, and the momentum of a fresh start. Therefore, I would suggest it should be a separate office, headed by a person of obvious distinction who clearly had direct access to the President. Whether or not a town-house of appropriate modesty on Lafayette Square can be found, the size of the staff should be in the Monnet tradition.

Wherever a planning unit is centered, however, it is essential that the Council of Economic Advisers develop a capability to disaggregate its analyses of the economy by sectors and regions. Its intellectual tradition and the data it mobilizes and presents are understandably in the neo-Keynesian tradition. The creation of the Council in 1946 was, after all, the major institutional acknowledgment that the Keynesian revolution had been accepted in American political life. Its annual reports, for example, do not contain detailed data on the composition of investment; productivity in the various sectors; regional growth or unemployment statistics. Occasionally, a sectoral problem will assert itself strongly enough to be reflected in those reports; for example, energy in the past few years. But if the President and the nation are to be properly served by the Council of Economic Advisers, the Council must become a center for systematic analyses which relate the aggregate course of the economy to the forces at work in the key sectors and regions of the country.

These recommendations concerning planning and revised modes of thought and work in the Council of Economic Advisers all require the collection of statistical data either not now available or not available in appropriate form. This should be no surprise. Governments collect statistical data mainly in response to the problems they confront, occasionally influenced also by the intellectual fashions of the day. There is a time lag at work in these matters. The well-organized data available reflect problems and ideas from the past. Therefore, governments confronted with new and difficult problems usually lack the data needed to analyze those problems satisfactorily. Every domain considered in chapters 3–11 requires that additional data be mobilized for policy makers. A good deal of it will be found already to exist, gathering dust in the far reaches of existing government departments, studied only by quiet professionals never, or rarely, summoned to their Cabinet Secretaries' offices. But some data will have to be freshly collected.

Two other institutional arrangements flow, I believe, from

this view of the imperatives of sectoral economic planning in the fifth Kondratieff upswing. First, as noted towards the close of Chapter 10, we shall require some public development banks, along the lines of the old Reconstruction Finance Corporation. These are needed to permit public and private capital to act in concert in solving certain structural problems in the regions, which the private sector cannot deal with on its own. At the national level, there was wisdom in the proposal of the Ford administration for a national energy bank (Energy Independence Authority) which might accelerate the pace at which new technologies in energy production and conservation moved from laboratory and pilot project to commercial viability. In addition, we need regional development banks, perhaps four: for the Northeast, Middle East, South, and West. They would find it easier than a big bank in Washington to develop intimate public–private collaboration; they would be closer to the problems and possibilities where small- and medium-sized loans could get things moving. A national bank could confine itself to large, critically important projects beyond the resources of the regional banks. As noted often in this book, the nature of the key supply-side tasks of the fifth Kondratieff upswing requires a margin of public responsibility; and public development banks, properly administered, have a good chance of operating free of those short-term political pressures that afflict the process when public development funds are generated, year-by-year in legislative bodies.

The necessarily enlarged public role in resource development and conservation suggests a second innovation. Both federal and state budgets should be split to exhibit separately their investment and more conventional outlays and transfer payments. We are in a time when quite different criteria should be applied to these components so long as the productivity standards for public investment remain high.

The outcome of a successful public–private effort of the kind suggested here would, I believe, be a protracted period of high employment and rapid economic growth in the United States. One cannot predict with certainty the magnitude of the investment levels required to deal with the multiple structural problems in the sectors and regions; but from such estimates as I can derive, they would, if all were implemented together, require a larger working force than our population now provides. Those now trapped in unemployment in the central cities or underemployed in the low-productivity margins of rural life would be increasingly viewed as potential national assets, rather than victims of sad but intractable social settings. There would be strong incentives to retrain them, get them out to jobs, or to bring jobs to them. I would guess, in fact, that priorities would have to be observed in executing a national investment plan if demand-pull inflation were to be avoided.

In historical perspective, this is the outcome to be expected. Kondratieff upswings were normally periods of high effective demand. On top of what might be called the normal demands of the economic system were piled the requirements for enlarging the flow of inputs to sustain the system. In the first Kondratieff upswing, there were the requirements for enlarged agricultural production, notably in Britain; in the second, for opening up the American West; in the third, for exploiting the agricultural and mineral resources of Canada, Argentina, Australia, and the Ukraine; in the fourth, for launching a new, high-productivity capital-intensive phase of agriculture in the advanced industrial nations, as well as opening up the oil resources of the Middle East. The high unemployment rates of the years since 1974 are, in this sense, historically unnatural. They stem from the central fact with which this book tries to grapple: policy towards resources is in the hands of governments, but they have lacked the concepts, tools, and will to act in ways required by the imperatives of the fifth Kondratieff upswing. The kind of national planning outlined in this chapter is designed to break out of that impasse.

13

The United States and the World

THE increasing interdependence of nations and peoples since the Second World War is so large and obvious a phenomenon that it scarcely justifies comment. But the contours of the fifth Kondratieff upswing have intensified the web of interdependence in ways still only partially understood and, even less, reflected in the current policies and attitudes of government.

For example, the virtual exhaustion of world grain reserves at the end of 1972 elevated to a new priority the array of domestic and international tasks set out towards the close of Chapter 4 related to family planning and the world's food supply. The heightened concern for population growth that resulted is forcing developing nations to adopt policies which reach deep into the lives of village families in distant rural areas. The priority for agricultural production has been similarly raised, as has the issue of international grain reserves. On the other hand, the depletion of grain reserves has put the farmers and consumers of the United States (and other countries) at the mercy of each year's global grain harvests, with respect to income and the cost of living, respectively. The quadrupling of oil prices in the autumn of 1973 has altered the economic setting of literally every nation within the world economy, in most cases substantially and for the worse. The fact that this rise rather accurately reflected the true marginal cost of producing additional energy outside the OPEC nations indicated the onset of an era which had been postponed only by price policies of self-deception in the 1960's—in the United States, notably, but elsewhere as well. And down the road in the mid-1980's, a still more severe energy crisis is likely in the world economy, unless extraordinarily vigorous anticipatory policies are launched. This the democracies have found it difficult to do.

By a route I shall try to describe later in this chapter, the success of OPEC in forcing a rise in oil prices has led to a systematic effort at emulation by other developing nations over the whole field of raw materials. A new dimension of North–South diplomacy has crystallized under the ambiguous rubric of A New World Economic Order. Virtually every foreign office in the world contains sections and divisions devoted to the conduct of these negotiations, embracing the law of the seas and the future exploitation of the seabeds, as well as the conventional issues of aid, trade, technology transfer, and raw materials agreements. Meanwhile, in the relatively comfortable 1960's the advanced industrial countries became aware that they, and the world community as a whole, had been dangerously eroding irreplaceable capital in the form of clean air and water. In a reformist mood, sparked by earnest crusaders, they began to act to preserve the environment. But as the straitened circumstances of the fifth Kondratieff upswing closed in, they confronted the difficult calculus of reconciling environmental concerns with the equally pressing imperatives of energy production and the conduct of policies of relatively full employment. The environment has also become an issue of foreign policy. All this interwove with a decelerating tendency in productivity which began to pervade the advanced industrial world in the second half of the 1960's. Even here, in an area of primarily domestic policy, there is a critical international dimension. Despite a post-Bretton Woods regime of floating exchange rates, the state of each nation's balance of payments and its degree of freedom in conducting domestic policy are closely linked to its relative productivity performance. And, as we saw in Chapter 10, the contours of regional change within the United States were strongly affected by the shift in international prices which marked the opening phase of the fifth Kondratieff upswing.

The reality of economic interdependence was, of course, not a new fact in the 1970's. During the fourth Kondratieff downswing (1951–72) important new areas of interdependence were recognized and institutionalized. In the wake of the success of the Marshall Plan, the OECD was created. It developed sophisticated staff work on the common problems of the advanced industrial world, an annual review procedure for each member's economic prospects, and special committees for exchange of views on particular issues. Its committee on financial problems became an important instrument for dealing with monetary and balance of payments crises. Through its Development Assistance Committee, the OECD sought to co-ordinate aid policy towards the developing continents. In addition, the advanced industrial nations sought systematically to liberalize international trade through a series of negotiations conducted within GATT (General Agreement on Tariffs and Trade).

These various instruments of cooperation were constructively related, on the one hand, to the global activities of the World Bank and the International Monetary Fund, and, on the other, to the work of the regional development banks (in Latin America, Asia, and Africa), aid consortia for individual major developing nations (e.g., India, Pakistan, Indonesia), and the programs of particular industrialized nations towards regions of special interest (e.g., France with former colonies in Africa, the U.S. with Latin America). Ad hoc efforts were undertaken to deal with erratic price fluctuations for particular commodities (e.g., coffee, tin), involving both producers and consumers; and there were the beginnings, at least, of regional economic cooperation within the developing continents, in emulation of Western Europe.

Taken altogether, the international economic machinery developed after the Second World War, with all its inadequacies, represented a unique historical achievement. The notion of a global economic community acquired considerable substance, as did the concept of regional and sub-regional interests transcending nationalist impulses. Nevertheless, the central economic processes at work could proceed substantially on a national basis, within the framework set by international cooperation in trade, monetary, and aid matters. This was the case in the advanced industrial countries because their growth was driven forward by the diffusion of the private automobile and durable consumers goods, the migration to suburbia, and the expansion of public and private services facilitated by rapidly rising real incomes. In the developing nations, the heart of the matter lay in national plans: the scale and allocation of the investment resources mobilized; the quality of the private entrepreneurs and public servants that moved into positions of responsibility; the political capacity to generate a sense of national purpose. Of course, the flow of aid from abroad mattered a good deal; but, by and large, the high and regular momentum of the OECD economies provided a setting in which exports could be sold and foreign exchange earned. The fall in relative prices of raw materials in the 1950's was, indeed, a burden to many developing nations; but relative prices tended to level off in the 1960's. And those developing nations which were able and willing to diversify their exports found markets for them.

Now, as we move into the final years of the 1970's, the

scope for national action is still substantial. Governments and peoples can still to a significant degree shape their own destinies. But their field of action has been narrowed. Put another way, the challenges of the fifth Kondratieff upswing require a higher degree of international cooperation than those of the previous two decades.

Consider, first, the dilemmas of the OECD nations in an era of high energy and other raw material prices. The resource endowments among them vary—and their sense of vulnerability varies accordingly. Norway, for example, must weigh its possible contribution to easing the European energy problem by expanding production at a maximum rate against distortions in the composition of its working force and other costs to its national life. Australia and Canada, for example, are so greatly endowed with natural resources they may feel a temptation to join with less-developed raw material producers in OPEC-type organizations in other fields. For example, the three major OECD agricultural food exporters (the U.S., Canada, and Australia) face the conflict between a desire to maximize foreign exchange earnings in a world close to the margin of food scarcity and domestic pressure on the cost of living in societies which are overwhelmingly urban. On the other hand, Japan and Italy, notably, but others as well, live with a heightened sense of vulnerability; and they are tempted to seek secure flows of essential supplies by special bilateral agreements rather than through OECD or global arrangements. These and other inner tensions and differences in endowments and interests complicate the tasks of effective cooperation within the OECD.

But on the whole, the convergence of security and political interests with a mature knowledge of the virtues of economic cooperation and the large costs of economic confrontation tend to pull the OECD countries together. Despite initial uncertainty in the field of energy cooperation, the OECD has moved towards a consensus on appropriate technological, economic, and political lines of action. While useful and stabilizing, this broad consensus has thus far had a mainly negative result, important as it is: it has avoided a mercantilist tearing apart of OECD's political cohesion. Energy, energy conservation, and energy-efficiency programs remain essentially national. The major changes required to increase OECD's bargaining position vis-à-vis OPEC lie substantially in the hands of the United States which, as Chapter 5 described, has not yet decided how to use its rich, high cost, resource potential to constrain effectively its rate of increase in energy utilization, and to cut its level of oil imports. Working cooperation in R&D within OECD has hardly gone beyond the exchange of information. There is, moreover, no coherent OECD agricultural and raw material policy; and anti-pollution policies remain mainly confined to actions within each nation. Above all, there is profound intellectual confusion and, therefore, no effective policy consensus on how the OECD economy as a whole can return to high and stable rates of growth. The best estimate of the CIA is that the growth rate of OECD Europe in the first half of the 1980's will be only 3.5% as opposed to about 5% in the 1960's; for Japan, 6% versus 11% in the earlier decade.

There is, of course, a particular reason for the limited scale of OECD cooperation: the problems before us inherently transcend the OECD world. The global energy problem was, after all, pressed inescapably on the world community by OPEC's quadrupling of oil prices; the dangerous underlying global food–population balance was forced on our attention by the bad harvests of 1972 in Russia, India, China, and Africa; the terms of trade which have struck nations in such disparate ways are the related results of changes in global energy and agricultural prices and the OECD recession. Evidently, it is in North–South relations that the greatest challenges to statesmanship lie. Indeed, the possibilities of serious cooperation within OECD are closely related to progress made in North–South cooperation.

In this respect, 1974, the first year after the rise in energy prices, was not a good year. For many intellectuals and politicians in the developing world, the success of OPEC in asserting its power in the autumn of 1973 was a memorable and heartening event.[1] Here were nations—mostly small, in some cases poor, in all cases not fully modernized—using their control over a basic raw material to shake the foundations of the rich and comfortable societies which had based their prosperity on cheap energy. Hitherto weaker states successfully asserted their capacity to divert more resources to themselves. At last, they could feel that the unfair allocation of the benefits that their raw materials had provided in the past was redressed. Whether that allocation was, in fact, fair or unfair, OPEC's action was a demonstration of power through a disciplined cooperation the developing nations had never before been able to generate.

The historical fact is, of course, that the problems in many parts of the developing world are less the result of prior colonial or quasi-colonial relationships than they are of the lateness with which the developing nations got themselves into sustained industrial growth. That lateness can only be explained in terms of their histories and their cultures which, with all their richness, lacked initially the capacity rapidly to absorb the expanding pool of technology the early-comers were generating. They were not able to do what the Japanese did after the Meiji Restoration of 1868. In fact, despite real inequities and humiliation, the contacts with more advanced nations, even colonial contacts, on balance accelerated the process of modernization rather than forestalled it. From Alexander Hamilton's *Report on Manufactures* to the 1791 Congress to the present, it was the perception within less developed nations that their independence, as well as their prosperity, was involved in industrialization that drove them on. The impulse to industrialization has ultimately been rooted in a reactive nationalism flowing from the intrusion or feared intrusion of more advanced on less advanced nations. I would by no means defend all the relationships that grew up in the eighteenth, nineteenth, and twentieth centuries between the more and less advanced nations and peoples; but moralizing is not the point. The fact is that what we are dealing with is a problem of early-comers and late-comers to modern economic growth, and with the problems and sentiments of vulnerability and dependence which that gap in time generates among the late-comers.

It is, therefore, not difficult to reconstruct the inflamed hopes which led some developing nations to believe that they could emulate OPEC by organizing in ways which would also divert resources from the rich to the poor. And it is not difficult to understand why politicians in the developing world chose in 1974—and still, to a degree, choose—to posture in ways which suggest the desire for a systematic North–South confrontation.

If one reviews the major international conferences of 1974, one might guess that North–South relations had already polarized, and that we faced inevitably a protracted neo-mercantilist struggle. There was the acrimonious United Nations General Assembly debate of April 1974; the population meeting at Bucharest; the food conference at Rome; and the sterile session on the law of the seas at Caracas. In all of them, the air was filled with rhetoric about imperialism; with claims for the unilateral transfer of resources from the rich to the poor; and with the ardent assertion of national sovereignty by the less developed nations, combined with equally ardent demands that the more developed states surrender sovereignty and behave in terms of the requirements of the international community. In the face of this verbal and political onslaught, the more developed nations mainly reacted defensively.

It was not difficult to envisage all this yielding a neo-mercantilist fragmentation of political, economic and military affairs—and disaster for the human race—as men and nations squabbled meanly for scarce resources in a nuclear age.

In fact, the state of North–South diplomacy was not quite as precarious as a superficial view of the rhetoric of 1974 (and press reports of it) would suggest. Beneath the surface these conferences generated considerable mutual understanding. The participants listened to each other even if they did not finally act in concert. More important, North–South bilateral relations, conducted beyond the glare of United Nations gatherings, were marked in many cases by a good deal of continued hard-headed pragmatism based on a recognition of legitimate mutual interests. And, as noted in Chapter 4, the Rome conference on food achieved a consensus of far reaching importance; namely, that the rise in agricultural production in the developing nations had to be the principal instrument for dealing with the expansion of population and food requirements.

The special United Nations session of September 1975 was, in tone and substance, distinctively different and less contentious from those of 1974. Three factors appear to account for the change. First, the United States laid out at length both a doctrine of reconciliation and a working agenda for North–South cooperation. Although the American commitment of resources was limited, the rhetoric, the headings for action, and the assumption of leadership were in the right directions. Second, the OECD recession over the previous year had badly damaged prospects in many parts of the developing world, demonstrating in a rather painful way the reality of North–South interdependence. In 1974, close to the peak of the previous boom, there had been much talk from the South about the North's excessive consumption of raw materials: in 1975 the South was concerned about foreign exchange losses from declining raw material sales and prices. Third, the damage done the developing world by OPEC's oil price increase was better understood and the somewhat artificial 1974 unity of the developing nations was thereby strained despite the formal maintenance of a common front against the industrial North.

The upshot was the package of resolutions agreed upon on September 16, 1975. In substance, it covered, from an international perspective, virtually the full array of problems dealt with in Chapters 4–6, with two exceptions: family planning, which was essentially left in the hands of national governments by the Bucharest resolutions of August 1974, and the problem of the oil price, much on the minds of most delegates but not brought to consensus.

The major directions of apparent agreement were these:

International Trade

—The developing countries should expand and diversify their exports, increase productivity, and thereby improve their foreign exchange position and their real terms of trade.

—Special emphasis should be given to the expansion of manufactured exports and to processing raw materials increasingly within developing countries.

—With respect to raw materials, stable and equitable prices and export earnings should be sought through stockpiling agreements, compensatory financing to cushion price declines, and improved marketing and transport arrangements for such commodities within developing countries. The possibility of linking raw material export prices to the prices of manufactured imports should be explored.

—Developed countries should act to reduce or remove, where feasible, nontariff barriers to imports from developing countries and to extend existing generalized trade preferences.

—Restrictive private business practices limiting exports of developing countries should be eliminated.

Increased Aid

—Aid from developed to developing countries should be expanded and, as a general rule, be untied.

The target of 0.7% of gross national product in official development assistance by 1980 was reaffirmed, with, however, significant reservations by the United States and others.

—The IMF was urged to consider linking special drawing rights (SDRs) to development assistance, by allocating a portion of the proceeds of gold sales and through voluntary donations of a portion of their SDR holdings by developed na-

tions. SDRs should increasingly supplant gold as the central
reserve asset of the international monetary system.

—Contributions to the United Nations Special Fund for assistance to countries hardest hit by the economic crisis should
be expanded.

—The role of developing nations in the IMF and World
Bank should be increased.

Transfer of Science and Technology
—Support by developed countries for the expansion of
science and technology in developing countries should be significantly increased.

—The possibility of an international energy institute should
be explored promptly.

—Work on an international code for the transfer of technology, including revision of conventions on patents and trade-
marks, with special attention to the interests of developing
countries, should be pressed to conclusion by 1977.

Accelerated Industrialization
—The transfer of less competitive industries from developed
to developing countries should be accelerated.

—International cooperation should be intensified to accelerate industrial development, including regional and sub-regional
associations among developing countries.

Food and Agriculture
—The doctrine of the 1974 Rome Conference was reaffirmed:
"The solution to world food problems lies primarily in increas-
ing rapidly food production in the developing countries."

—Developed countries should facilitate agricultural exports
from developing countries.

—Post-harvest losses of food in developing countries should
be improved by better arrangements for marketing and distribution.

—The developed countries should insure a stable and sufficient supply of fertilizers to developing countries at reasonable
prices.

—The International Fund for Agricultural Development
should be brought into being by the end of 1975 by voluntary
contributions of developed countries with initial resources of
one billion SDR.

—Food aid should be built up with a target of 10 million tons for grains for the 1975–76 season; a world food reserve should be created large enough to cover foreseeable major production shortfalls; *ad interim,* stocks or funds of not less than 500,000 tons should be earmarked by developed countries and placed at the disposal of the World Food program.

The United Nations
—The United Nations should support sub-regional and inter-regional cooperation among developing countries and, in general, consider ways to restructure its work in economic and social development so as better to support this array of recommended policies.

By normal standards of international institutional performance, the resolutions of September 16, 1975, represent a considerable achievement. An array of complex problems was identified and courses of action to deal with those problems were agreed upon.

The scene then shifted to Paris, where detailed discussions to implement these resolutions were launched. A new international organization was created: the Conference on International Economic Co-operation and Development, in which eight countries represented the industrialized North, nineteen represented the developing South, including OPEC. After some eighteen months of laborious work in committees and subcommittees, the major issues were brought to negotiation at the level of foreign ministers in May–June, 1977. Included among them was one whose importance had greatly increased over the intervening period, the heavy debt burden contracted by some of the more advanced developing countries, with access to private capital markets, in an effort to sustain their growth rates in the face of high oil import prices and the slowdown of growth in the OECD world. The developing countries had assumed a debt burden of some $180 billion by 1977 with more than 40% owed to private institutions.

The major demands made by the developing nations came to rest on these four points:

—a $6 billion common fund to support commodity prices by
financing buffer strocks;
—a generalized debt moratorium;
—a commitment from the developed countries to double aid
levels (from less than 0.4% to 0.7% of GNP);
—a commitment by the developed countries to link raw material export prices to the rise of import prices paid by developing
nations caused by inflation.

The outcome was a limited success for the developing
nations: a promise to raise a special $1 billion fund to aid
the most hard-pressed poorer nations; a commitment to consider at a later time the creation and financing of buffer
stocks and commodity price stabilization; a commitment to
consider debt roll-overs on a case-by-case basis; the offer of
long-term support for transport and communication development in Africa. Evidently, sufficient progress had been made
to justify continuation of the dialogue. A New Realism, to
use the phrase of Maurice Williams, had emerged since 1974
and begun to assert itself.[2]

Behind the failure to make more far-reaching progress lay
three unresolved problems, interwoven in complex ways.
First, the failure of the conference to bring under common
examination and negotiation the questions of OPEC oil pricing
and OPEC aid. Both technically and ideologically, the impetus
for the new North–South dialogue had arisen from OPEC's
action in 1973. Technically, it was that action which had
thrown the advanced industrial countries into a phase of
reduced growth and exacerbated inflation. At the same time
the new oil price bore down heavily on the economies of the
oil-importing developing nations both directly and through its
impact on the North. In a world governed by simple, direct
economic interests, the oil importers, developed and developing, would have united to press OPEC to moderate its prices
and to make large compensatory contributions to aid the other
developing nations. For reasons outlined above, that was not

what happened. Psychologically, the sympathy of the governments of the developing nations lay with OPEC. That instinct was, no doubt, strengthened by certain oblique economic considerations: the hope that the OPEC example could be extended to other commodities or that the threat of its extension could force the industrialized North to make concessions with respect to the stabilization of other commodity prices; OPEC's use of selective development aid as an instrument for holding the developing nations together; the belief that the overall bargaining position of the developing nations would be enhanced by having OPEC representatives among them; the lack of effective bargaining position versus OPEC of either the industrialized or developing nations. Whatever the rationale, the fact is that the North–South dialogue is significantly diminished and lacking in reality so long as energy prices and policy are excluded.

Second, the document of September 1975 and subsequent negotiations were too one-sided for the good of the developing nations themselves. Liberalized trade agreements and measures of price and/or income stabilization for raw material exporters are thoroughly legitimate objectives, of potential mutual advantage to all parties, as Chapter 6 emphasized. The North can benefit from cheaper and more abundant imports and from less volatile incomes in (and thus exports to) the relevant nations of the South. But to be effective, the South must commit itself to maintain a regular flow of supplies, uninterrupted by political or quasi-OPEC considerations. The agreement negotiated in February 1975 between the European Common Market and forty-six developing nations (The Lomé Treaty) is a potential model for such arrangements. It includes: a fund to compensate exporters in case their prices fall below a stated percentage of the average for the three previous years; duty-free access to the Common Market for all manufactured products and most farm exports. It is significant that the participants in the Lomé Treaty were African and a few other nations, most of which were former colonies that had maintained aid and other amicable political ties with the former metropolitan powers. There was a reasonable basis for mutual confidence. That political element was useful, perhaps essential for a pioneering effort; but a more solid political base, embracing a wider group of nations, will be required if such methods are to be expanded in trade and other fields. That political base must, moreover, include understandings about the role of private as well as public capital in expanding raw material production in developing areas. As noted in Chapter 6, the attenuation of such capital flows is likely not only to raise raw materials prices but also to force developed nations to expand higher cost raw materials production in their own or politically hospitable territories. It is a sign of immaturity and evasiveness that this real and serious issue cannot yet be temperately addressed in global gatherings and is left to more pragmatic bilateral negotiations.

Similarly, there is an aura of unreality about much of the debate over the transfer of technology. There are, of course, types of external assistance which can increase a developing nation's scientific and technological base; for example, through the education abroad of individuals, the strengthening of local educational institutions, the setting up of specialized research institutions. And there is legitimate scope for re-examining the potentialities for transferring technologies controlled by governments as well as in reviewing private patent arrangements for elements of monopoly and other inequities. But the central fact is that the bulk of new technologies has been absorbed in developing nations by the creation of business firms which incorporate them in their production. Local, foreign, or joint entrepreneurship capable of putting the technology to work efficiently in the production process has been the critical factor rather than the transfer of the technology itself. This has been true since, say, Francis Cabot Lowell in 1814 set up his mill in Massachusetts on the basis of pirated

British technology. Some developing nations, like the United States in its early days, have generated cadres of domestic entrepreneurs capable of bringing into effective use new technologies drawn from abroad. In other cases, foreign firms and entrepreneurs are initially required. And there is a wide spectrum of local capacities and external needs in between, including the possibility of management contracts. Thus, for the flow of technology to be accelerated, what is required in many cases is a stable resolution within developing countries of the criteria for accepting foreign firms or managers and stable rules of the game for their profitable survival on terms economically and politically acceptable to host governments. This is extremely important, for example, if chemical fertilizer capacity is to be expanded rapidly in many developing countries which now lack management and technological skills on a requisite scale. One can explain psychologically and politically why this issue periodically becomes inflamed within developing countries; but one can explain equally why such reactive nationalism produces, in turn, grave responses in the parliaments, congresses, and board rooms of developed countries. These responses, in turn, limit the possibilities of generating political support for increased aid and liberalized trade. By discouraging private investment from abroad, they also reduce the flow of new technology and the building of badly needed industrial capacity.

This is a tough and complex set of issues; but it is capable of rational resolution. No North–South partnership will be truly serious until it is faced and resolved. This judgment is not only a recognition that any partnership must be a two-way street; it is also rooted in the narrower circumstance that the most efficient arrangements for the progress of developing nations must be based on the realities of economic interdependence, including the absorptive capacity of developing nations with respect to new technologies.

The third unresolved problem which has limited the possibilities of North–South negotiations is the failure of the

OECD world to deal with the changed contours of the fifth Kondratieff upswing and to recapture the momentum of the 1960's. That failure has direct economic and political consequences of major significance.

Economically, the deceleration of growth in the OECD reduces the capacity of developing nations to export, to import, and to grow. In a useful set of calculations, the World Bank concluded that, assuming the oil price remained constant at the 1974 level, in real terms a resumed OECD growth of 4.9% would permit a 4.9% growth rate in the developing countries as a whole. A 3.5% OECD growth rate, however, would push the developing nations back to a 3.8% rate of advance. Given the rate of population growth in the developing world, average per capita income would grow only 1.2%. For the poorest developing nations the outcome would be virtual stagnation in per capita real income. The rather disturbing fact is that present prospects for the OECD growth rate in the decade ahead are for a figure of about 4%.

The large role of the OECD growth rate in determining the pace of progress in the developing nations is illuminated in Table 10 by comparison with other international forces that might affect the outcome.

Clearly, the maintenance of a high OECD growth rate is as powerful or more powerful an instrument for sustaining progress in the developing world than either a 25% cut in the OPEC oil price or a radical liberalization of trade permitting an accelerated flow of manufactured exports from developing nations. To these abstract but illuminating calculations should be added a fourth World Bank estimate; namely, that an expansion of aid to a level of 0.7% of OECD income would permit an average growth rate of 6% in the developing world, perhaps 3.5% per capita—a somewhat better aggregate performance than that achieved in the 1960's (say, 5.64% and 2.15%, respectively).

The point of these abstract numerical exercises is to underline an important fact: clearly, there is some combination of

Table 10. Growth Rates in Developing Nations:
Alternative Assumptions
(*GDP per capita, per annum*)

OECD Growth Rate 3.5%[1]	1.2%
OECD Growth Rate 4.9%[1]	2.3%
OPEC Oil Price $9.40 (1974 dollars)[2]	1.8
OPEC Oil Price $7.50 (1974 dollars)[2]	2.1
Manufactured Export Annual Growth, Developing Countries at 15%[1&2]	1.8
Manufactured Export Annual Growth, Developing Countries at 20%[1&2]	2.3

[1] Assumes OPEC oil price remains fixed at $9.40 (1974 dollars).
[2] Assumes 4.2% average annual OECD growth rate.
SOURCE: World Bank.

high OECD growth, easement by OPEC, liberalized trade, and expanded aid that could permit the developing nations to move forward more rapidly in the 1970's and 1980's than they did in the 1960's.

But when one moves from the realm of economic calculation to politics, all these possibilities come to rest on an acceleration of OECD growth rates. This is the case because it is simply beyond the capacity of democratic legislative bodies to liberalize trade in manufactures and radically to expand aid unless their economies are experiencing low levels of unemployment and rapid growth. And, if the analysis developed in this book is by and large correct, this will not happen unless the United States, notably, and the OECD, in general, pursue much more vigorous policies of energy production as well as conservation. Such policies, in turn, offer the only likely route to a serious OECD–OPEC negotiation, which should include an enlarged OPEC contribution to the developing nations either through special reduced prices or much enlarged, long-term compensatory aid.

But in the end a true North–South partnership, rather than endless diplomatic fencing with the language of resolutions, requires more, even, than renewed, rapid OECD growth and the more generous policies which might then commend themselves to the several electorates. A stable and effective partnership must be based on a fresh, shared vision of the common task. The common task is to transit successfully this next, rather precarious quarter-century; to preserve industrial civilization as a whole by bringing forward to full modernization the late-comers of the South, while permitting the early-comers of the North to continue to grow and to evolve societies of higher quality and equity. This requires, in turn, that both parties address themselves jointly to the generation of the additional resources, to the measures of resource conservation, and to the creation and diffusion of the new technologies required to make that vision viable. That vision also embraces a special concern for the least advantaged nations, just as wise, unifying national policies include measures to bring forward less advantaged groups within societies. Moreover, the OECD nations must view the kind of measures outlined in September 1975, and carried a small step forward at Paris in the Spring of 1977, not as a tactical exercise in multilateral diplomacy but as very serious business indeed, on which the well-being of the advanced industrial societies as well as the developing nations will increasingly depend.

The articulation of that vision of a common task and a common destiny will probably not soon supplant the rhetoric of aggrieved dependency and the waving of the imperialist bloody shirt in United Nations councils and defensive reactions to such talk. But all parties ought to take this matter seriously; for language and rhetoric are important. What government representatives say in public, in response to domestic constituencies, can be costly or helpful to working diplomacy. Soon or late the full exploitation of the potentialities of interdependence requires a mature and explicit acceptance of the extent to which the progress and fate of each nation, North and South, is bound up with the fate of all. Without the spread of this technically accurate as well as healing doctrine, down from the pronouncements of politicians and diplomats to the grass-roots of societies, the political foundations for North–South partnership will remain uncertain.

In dealing with the heightened international interdependencies of the fifth Kondratieff upswing, the United States has a somewhat larger role to play than in the 1950's and 1960's. There has been a limited but real reversal of a powerful trend. Since 1948, when the Congress passed the Marshall Plan legislation and Tito split with Stalin, the central underlying trend in the world arena has been a diffusion of power away from both Washington and Moscow. The primacy of the United States in the immediate post-1945 years was the product of inherently transient circumstances: the war-induced weaknesses of Western Europe and Japan; and the full recovery of the United States during the Second World War from the depression of the 1930's. Putting aside strategic matters, there is every reason to believe that the diffusion of economic power will continue over the long term.

But the special character of the economic issues that have emerged on the world agenda since the end of 1972 has increased, for a time at least, both the responsibilities of the United States within the world arena and its capacity to influence how well and promptly those issues are dealt with. The United States cannot, of course, dictate international policy; but in a time of structural change, when the inputs to sustain industrial civilization must be expanded, its role is necessarily more important than during a generation when the absorption of the fruits of high mass-consumption dominated the life of Western Europe and Japan, and the world appeared to enjoy cheap energy and surplus food supplies.

The American role, as the critical margin in carrying forward the common agenda, emerges from five circumstances.

First, the United States alone commands sufficient alternative energy resources (and, perhaps, special possibilities for economy in consumption) to reduce sharply OECD dependence on OPEC oil and, thereby, set the stage for well-balanced agreements between oil producers and consumers, including special provisons for the hardest-hit developing nations.

Second, the United States, if it continues to nurture its agricultural base, is and should remain the dominant source of food exports, including exports required by certain developing nations until their own production can be expanded at a higher pace. The U.S. agricultural export capacity is also a significant cushioning factor in its balance of payments, strengthening the relative position of the dollar among the major currencies.

Third, the energy and energy-related investment requirements in the United States are so large that it should be easier for the United States to return quickly to full employment and thereby help lead the OECD world in that direction. Changed patterns of investment will be required in all OECD countries in the next phase of growth. They cannot rely wholly either on the further diffusion of the energy-intensive paraphernalia of high mass-consumption or on a prior American revival permitting a return to full employment based on expanded exports to the United States. But the scale of additional investment required in the United States in the expansion of energy output, the diffusion of methods for energy conservation, mass-transport facilities, insulated housing, and energy R&D are such as to make it somewhat easier for the U.S. than for others to return to full employment on such foundations and to help, at least, to lead the OECD world back to sustained full employment.

Fourth, the U.S. evidently has special advantages and responsibilities in the R&D sector as a whole. These stem from the absolute scale of American R&D resources and the potentialities for orchestrating them efficiently within a single national community. As noted in Chapter 9, the proportion of U.S. GNP spent on R&D has fallen; but its absolute level still towers over that of the other major industrial nations. If organized around the appropriate priority tasks, R&D is an asset of universal value; and it places on the United States a special responsibility for bringing about effective international cooperation in this domain.

Finally, the United States has a special responsibility for political leadership. This is not a matter of higher virtue. It is the case because, if the United States fails to lead, there is, as yet, no one to fill the gap: Western Europe is insufficiently unified; Japan too vulnerable; the Soviet Union too constricted by its ideological commitments to lead comfortably a heterogeneous mixture of polities; China similarly constricted and at a stage of development when its inner problems and border anxieties dominate its energies. American leadership in this context in no way implies dominance. It requires a mixture of three elements: a national capacity to act significantly with respect to the major issues; a capacity to define common objectives in ways that are not excessively self-serving; and, then, the capacity to help translate those objectives into a working agenda, and to help move it forward with dogged stubbornness. These are assets the United States potentially commands.

Whether the United States will fully use its potentiality for leadership remains to be seen. It depends on an altered view within American political life of the world and the American relationship to it—a change in perspective which, in the end, will be required of all nations, big and small, north and south, east and west. But it will also require the change in domestic economic doctrine and policy which this book advocates. Without that change, our economy will stagger along uncomfortably, with excessive unemployment, excessive inflation, excessive oil imports. It is most unlikely that the United States can look after its interests abroad and fulfill its responsibilities to the world community unless these problems are solved. Never since the 1930's have the fate of American diplomacy and the nation's security been so closely related to the success or failure of our domestic economic policy.

14

Epilogue:
Can Democracy Survive?

T HE agenda outlined in this book poses three challenges to the democratic process. It requires that government concern itself to a significantly greater degree than it normally did in the past with the *composition* of output as opposed to merely the *level* of output and employment and the balance of payments; it requires that public policy accept the reality of long lags between action and results and address itself to the solution of problems many years before those problems become acute; and it requires the generation at home and in the international community of a sense of common purpose.

Challenges of these kinds are not new to the democratic experience. In times of war, democracies have been systematically tested in all three respects: production had to be geared to the precise requirements of the conflict; future requirements had to be anticipated; a domestic political consensus and alliances had to be built and sustained capable of holding up under the multiple strains of war. Governments in nations at early stages of development must, if they are to be successful, act consciously to achieve sectoral goals as well as high GNP growth rates; they must act currently to achieve results which will be apparent five to twenty years in the future; and they must develop among their peoples a sense of national commitment to and participation in the whole development process. These requirements help account for the difficulty of sustaining the democratic process in the early stages of a nation's modernization. But the advanced industrial democracies have also known times of peace when one or more of these challenges were faced; for example, in the severely depressed years after 1929 and in years of reconstruction after the Second World War.

The reader will recall the rather long list of public interventions in the economy, sanctioned by democratic electorates, under Adam Smith's criteria for the imperatives of "the great society" (see above, pp. 213–214). They have yielded a situation where total government expenditures in the United States (federal, state, and local) approximate a third of GNP. Some public expenditures do have consequences for the composition of output; for example, outlays for military hardware, schools, roads, public housing, medical services. But excepting the rise in the past generation of the public role in housing and the provision or financing of medical services, these are classic, Smithian headings. Other public expenditures merely transfer income to individuals in certain groups, leaving to those individuals the choice of what they will purchase. (Food stamps are, of course, an exception.) As for the government role in the economy, it aims either to assure that the economy approximates competitive behavior or that certain results are achieved which a competitive economy will not yield; e.g., relatively full employment, clean air and water, equal treatment for minorities.

Having admitted, through the political process, these massive exceptions to pure competitive market behavior, it nevertheless remains true that the capacity of political democracy to reconcile individual freedom of choice with the economic viability of society depends significantly on the creation of policies which permit competitive markets, to the maximum degree possible, to solve the problems now on the nation's agenda. With the exception of certain public services, including national defense and a reasonable environment, democratic governments have not been greatly concerned with the composition of output; they have counted predominantly on the markets to signal in what sectors investment should take place and productive capacity be enlarged; and they have regarded the exercise of private consumers' choice and the pursuit of private profit within the law not merely as tolerable but as major expressions of the human freedom democratic societies are committed to nurture.

The ultimate questions posed in this book are then: to what extent will political democracies have to change to deal successfully with the agenda of the fifth Kondratieff upswing; to what extent will a mastery of that agenda require further restrictions on human freedom and private enterprise?

I believe the short answer is this: the sooner effective public action is taken to come to grips with the array of problems posed by the fifth Kondratieff upswing, the fewer the restrictions on freedom government will have to impose. Put another way, drastic and inhibiting measures may, indeed, be required if we drift along, hoping that somehow the circumstances of the 1950's and 1960's will automatically be restored and the deeply grooved habits of mind and action of that period will suffice.

The energy situation presents this danger in an acute and lucid way. If the United States, Western Europe, and Japan do not urgently mount all-out efforts to expand production and economize energy use, they will generate oil import requirements in the 1980's beyond OPEC's productive capacity. They will confront further increases in energy prices but this time, unlike 1973–74, under circumstances where there is no excess OPEC productive capacity available. And they will confront the OPEC production ceiling under a further constraint; that is, the long lead times between the decison to invest in energy production and the time new mines, nuclear power plants, oil wells, etc. come on stream. Trapped by these realities, governments are likely, then, to introduce energy rationing and direct controls over a wide front while, at last, they undertake intensive measures to expand energy supplies under central direction. That kind of crisis could, indeed, alter significantly the basic structure of democracy as we have known it.

On the other hand, if energy production and conservation measures are undertaken vigorously and promptly, the price system can be used to a substantial degree, while public and private enterprise combine in various more or less conventional ways to assure that the OECD world can operate in a reasonably congenial setting within OPEC's capacity to produce and export.

Although their time dimensions are less clear, we could face similar problems in food, water, and the supply of certain raw materials, as well as conceivably, the control of air or water pollution.

Obviously, one basic way to avoid excessive direct control over the economy is for public policy to permit the price system to reflect accurately the real degree of scarcity of basic commodities both to constrain consumption and to provide incentives for the expansion of supply. This has proved a difficult political task in the field of energy. The problem of accurate pricing could arise in other fields; e.g., water supply. The ultimate alternative to the price system, even if prices are unpleasantly high, is rationing and the direct intrusion of bureaucracy into the markets—an outcome most Americans would regard as less desirable.

But in the areas we have surveyed, something more than accurate pricing is evidently necessary. There are aspects of energy, agriculture, raw materials, the environment, and R&D where more direct government involvement is inescapable. But even here, as Chapter 12 argued, the intrusions of government need not be massive or corrosive of the private institutions of the society. Similarly, I argued in Chapter II the need to bring inflation under control through a long-sustained voluntary wage–price agreement, monitored by the Executive Branch of the federal government. Without question, this would involve changes in the way both the labor unions and the private business sector conduct their affairs. But it is not wholly evident that the quasi-monopolistic negotiations which now take place to settle wage levels are inherently more democratic than those which would take place within agreed national wage–price guideposts. The required monitoring of prices, productivity, and profits would constitute an additional dimension of government policy and of limitation on the private sector. But it certainly proved a tolerable limitation in the period 1961–66. I can only say that, if it brought wage-push inflation under control, it would be well worth the price.

In short, if we are forehanded, generate a lucid and generally accepted view of the nation's problems, and a spirit of public–private collaboration in dealing with them, there is no reason to fear that the policies required to transit with reasonable success the next quarter-century would seriously compromise democratic practice and institutions as we have known them. But a failure to meet these conditions could endanger democratic life in the United States and throughout the Western world.

NOTES

Chapter 1:

1. Donella Meadows, Dennis L. Meadows, Jørgen Randers, William W. Behrens III, *The Limits to Growth,* New York: Universe Books, 1972, p. 23.

Chapter 2:

1. For those who may be interested, I have analyzed these long cycles in *Essays on the British Economy of the Nineteenth Century* (1948), Chapter 1; in *The Process of Economic Growth* (1953, 1960), Chapter 6; and in "Kondratieff, Schumpeter, and Kuznets: Trend Periods Revisited," *Journal of Economic History,* December 1975, Vol. XXXV, No. 4, pp. 719–793. They are fully described in Part Three of my *The World Economy: History and Prospect,* Austin, Texas: University of Texas Press, 1978.

Chapter 3:

1. The best account of the debate is that of D. E. Moggridge, *The Return to Gold, 1925,* Cambridge: at the University Press, 1969.

2. For an illuminating debate on this subject, see W. W. Rostow, "The Bankruptcy of Neo-Keynesian Economics," *Intermountain Economic Review,* Spring 1976, Vol. VII, No. 1; Abba P. Lerner, "A Reluctant Keynesian" and my "Rejoinder" in *Intermountain Economic Review,* Fall 1976, Vol. VII, No. 2.

3. John H. Williams, "The Theory of International Trade Reconsidered," *Economic Journal,* June 1929, Vol. 154, No. 39, p. 196.

Chapter 4:

1. Philip H. Trezise, *Rebuilding Grain Reserves,* Washington, D. C.: The Brookings Institution, 1976.

Chapter 5:

1. Joel Darmstadter, Joy Tankerley, Jack Alterman, *How Industrial Societies Use Energy: A Comparative Analysis* (Preliminary Report), Washington, D. C.: Resources for the Future, 1977, especially. pp. 13–22.

Chapter 6:

1. H. E. Goeller and A. M. Weinberg, "The Age of Substitutability," *Science,* 6 February 1976, Vol. 191, No. 4226, p. 683.

2. See, notably, Stephen H. Spurr, *American Forest Policy in Development,* Seattle: University of Washington Press, 1976.

3. Goeller and Weinberg, *op. cit.,* p. 689.

Chapter 7:

1. Gerald Garvey, *Energy, Ecology, Economy,* New York: W. W. Norton, 1972, p. 206.

2. A useful review of costs for containing pollution and other generalized effects on the economy is in *Environmental Quality,* The Seventh Annual Report of the Council on Environmental Quality, Washington, D. C.: G.P.O., pp. 144–167.

Chapter 8:

1. John Kendrick, "Productivity Trends and Prospects," in *U.S. Economic Growth from 1976 to 1986: Prospects, Problems, and*

Patterns, Vol. 1—*Productivity,* Studies prepared for the use of the Joint Economic Committee, Washington, D. C.: G.P.O., October 1, 1976, p. 1.

2. *Ibid.,* p. 12.

3. Edward F. Renshaw, "Productivity," in *U.S. Economic Growth from 1976 to 1986: Prospects, Problems, and Patterns,* p. 56.

Chapter 9:

1. Workshop on Alternative Energy Strategies, *Energy: Global Prospects 1985–2000,* Carroll L. Wilson, Project Director, New York: McGraw-Hill, 1977, p. 5.

2. T. S. Ashton, *The Industrial Revolution 1760–1830,* Oxford: Oxford University Press, 1947, p. 16. See also W. W. Rostow, *How It All Began,* New York: McGraw-Hill, 1975, Chapter 4, "Science, Invention, and Innovation."

3. Quoted in Donald Fleming, "Latent Heat and the Invention of the Watt Engine," *ISIS,* April 1952, Vol. 43, Part 1, No. 131, p. 5.

4. Jacob Schmookler, *Invention and Economic Growth,* Cambridge, Mass.: Harvard University Press, 1966, p. 200.

5. J. M. Clark, *Economics of Overhead Costs,* Chicago: University of Chicago Press, 1923, p. 120.

6. From the anonymous author of *A Treatise on Taxes and Contributions,* 1679, p. 53, deposited in the British Museum, quoted in Alfred P. Wadsworth and Julia De Lacy Mann, *The Cotton Trade and Industrial Lancashire, 1600–1780,* Manchester University Press, 1931, pp. 113–14.

7. *The Bank Credit Analyst,* February 1976, p. 33.

Chapter 10:

1. J. G. Williamson, "Regional Inequality and the Process of National Development: A Description of Patterns," *Economic Development and Cultural Change,* 1965, Vol. 13, No. 4, p. 44.

2. W. W. Rostow, "Growth Rates at Different Levels of Income and Stage of Growth: Reflections on Why the Poor Get Richer and the Rich Slow Down," *Research in Economic History,* January 1978. Vol. 3.

3. R. R. Widner, "The Future of the Industrial Midwest: A Time for Action," Columbus, Ohio: The Academy for Contemporary Problems, 1976, pp. i–ii.

4. National Science Foundation, "Research and Development in Industry 1974," (NSF 76-322), Washington, D.C.: G.P.O., September 1976, pp. 40–41. (It was wholesome, but not conclusive, to note a substantial article in *The Boston Herald American,* of June 12, 1977, headed: "Solar Energy . . . The wherewithal's right there in Cambridge, just waiting; New England plunges into new technology.")

5. Jean Monnet, *Mémoires,* Paris: Fayard, 1976, p. 306.

Chapter 11:

1. F. W. Paish, "Inflation, Personal Incomes and Taxation," *Lloyds Bank Review,* April 1975, No. 116, pp. 2–3.

2. From introductory essay by D. H. Robertson in Erik Lundberg (ed.), *The Business Cycle in the Post-War World,* London: Macmillan, 1955, p. 9.

3. For an account of this exchange and its setting, see W. W. Rostow, *The Diffusion of Power,* New York: Macmillan, 1972, pp. 138–142. Also, Craufurd D. Goodwin (ed.), *Exhortation and Controls,* Washington, D. C.: The Brookings Institution, 1975, pp. 154–175.

4. Their retrospective views, as well as recommendations for the future, are recorded in Craufurd D. Goodwin (ed.), *op. cit.,* pp. 385–98.

5. Mark W. Leiserson, *A Brief Interpretative Survey of Wage-Price Problems in Europe,* Study Paper No. 11 for Consideration of the Joint Economic Committee, 86th Congress, 1st Session (Washington, D.C.: G.P.O., 1959), p. 55.

6. Craufurd D. Goodwin (ed.), *op. cit.,* p. 378.

Chapter 12:

1. Professor Friedman's attack on this passage from Adam Smith appears in a generally laudatory essay, *Adam Smith's Relevance for 1976,* Los Angeles: International Institute for Economic Research, Original Paper 5, December 1976, pp. 11–15.

2. Adam Smith, *The Wealth of Nations,* London: George Routledge, 1890, p. 540.

3. W. W. Rostow, "The Case for Sectoral Planning," a chapter in *National Economic Planning,* Washington, D. C.: The Chamber of Commerce of the United States, 1976, p. 43.

4. Winston S. Churchill, *The Gathering Storm*, Boston: Houghton Mifflin, 1948, p. 210.

5. J. M. Keynes, "National Self-Sufficiency," *Yale Review*, June 1933, Vol. XXII, No. 4, p. 755.

6. E. R. Black, *The Diplomacy of Economic Development*, Cambridge, Mass., Harvard University Press, 1960, p. 32.

7. Jean Monnet, *op. cit.*, p. 278.

8. *Op. cit.*, pp. 285–6.

Chapter 13:

1. Richard N. Cooper ("A New International Order for Mutual Gain," *Foreign Policy*, Spring 1977, No. 26, pp. 65–120) analyzes well the origins of the thrust in 1974 for a New Economic Order and the specific issues which emerged for negotiation in the three subsequent years.

2. Maurice J. Williams, chairman of OECD's Development Assistance Committee, in the *OECD Observer*, November–December 1976, No. 84, pp. 3–7. In this article, entitled "The Emerging New Realism in North–South Cooperation," Williams usefully identifies seven areas of consensus in the protracted dialogue.

Index

259